REMIXING
WONG KAR-WAI

ASIA-PACIFIC: CULTURE,
POLITICS, AND SOCIETY

EDITED BY REY CHOW, MICHAEL
DUTTON, HARRY HAROOTUNIAN,
AND ROSALIND C. MORRIS

Giorgio
Biancorosso

REMIXING WONG KAR-WAI

*Music, Bricolage,
and the Aesthetics
of Oblivion*

DUKE UNIVERSITY
PRESS / DURHAM AND
LONDON / 2025

© 2025 DUKE UNIVERSITY PRESS
All rights reserved
Project Editor: Ihsan Taylor
Designed by Matthew Tauch
Typeset in Portrait Text and IBM Plex Sans
by Westchester Publishing Services

Library of Congress Cataloging-in-Publication Data
Names: Biancorosso, Giorgio, [date] author.
Title: Remixing Wong Kar-wai : music, bricolage, and the aesthetics of
oblivion / Giorgio Biancorosso.
Other titles: Asia-Pacific.
Description: Durham : Duke University Press, 2025. | Series: Asia-pacific |
Includes bibliographical references and index.
Identifiers: LCCN 2024015520 (print)
LCCN 2024015521 (ebook)
ISBN 9781478031178 (paperback)
ISBN 9781478026945 (hardcover)
ISBN 9781478060161 (ebook)
Subjects: LCSH: Wong, Kar-wai, 1958-—Criticism and interpretation. |
Motion picture music—Philosophy and aesthetics. | Motion picture
authorship. | Quotation in music. | Motion picture industry—China—
Hong Kong. | BISAC: SOCIAL SCIENCE / Ethnic Studies / Asian Studies |
MUSIC / General
Classification: LCC PN1998.3.W65 b53 2025 (print) | LCC PN1998.3.W65
(ebook) | DDC 791.4302/33092—dc23/eng/20240729
LC record available at https://lccn.loc.gov/2024015520
LC ebook record available at https://lccn.loc.gov/2024015521

Cover art: Djohan Hanapi / Knuckles & Notch, *Flowery Years*, 2021.
Six-color Risograph, 16.5 × 11.7 in. Artwork inspired by Asian Film
Archive's 2021 program, *Retrospective: Wong Kar Wai*. Courtesy of
Knuckles & Notch and Asian Film Archive.

TO AIKO /

"OCEAN BLUE" /

PIGMENT OF THE IMAGINATION

/ CONTENTS

/ ACKNOWLEDGMENTS

My biggest thanks to Rey Chow for prompting me to embark on this project and sharing her wit and vision when they were most needed. David Clarke, Kal Ng, and Timmy Chih-ting Chen have responded with enthusiasm to my queries and ideas, and for that I am deeply grateful. I would also like to thank my colleagues in the Music Department at the University of Hong Kong (HKU) for their exacting work, open-mindedness, and collegiality. The university's Society of Fellows in the Humanities provided a much-needed forum for cross-disciplinary exchange. I am also indebted to Phil Hayward's work on island cultures.

My deep appreciation goes to the following colleagues, for giving me the opportunity to read my work in progress as a guest speaker at their institutions: Chika Kinoshita (Kyoto University), Michele Corbella (Università di Milano), Ken Ueno (University of California, Berkeley), Lee Tong Soon (Lehigh University), Michael Beckerman (New York University), Paul Anderer (Columbia University), Paize Keulemans (Princeton University), Shih Shumei (University of California, Los Angeles), and Stephen Chu (HKU).

At Duke, Senior Executive Editor Ken Wissoker's support and intellectual acumen have been a blessing and a joy. The three anonymous reviews secured by the press were instrumental in helping me bring the book into its current shape, and the work of the editorial team at Duke has been nothing short of extraordinary. This book grew out of a long essay written in the summer of 2014 for *A Companion to Wong Kar-wai*, edited by Martha Nochimson. Martha's dedication to the project and expert editorial hand were much appreciated then and are fondly remembered now, as is Michael Ingham's enthusiastic support throughout.

For inspiration and the gift of their friendship, a heartfelt thanks to Anandi Bhattacharya, Eugene Birman, Nigel Bruce, Martha Feldman, Lau Siu-yin, Agnes Lin, Jacopo Pellegrini, Gianpaolo Peloso, Lorenzo Restagno, Emilio Sala, Gigi Tarallo, Eno Tsin, and Judith Zeitlin.

I dedicate this book to my daughter, Aiko, living proof of the dynamic possibilities of bricolage.

[Robert] Rauschenberg: Also, being a good artist is like committing the perfect crime—you don't get caught.

[William] Seitz: I'm talking about crimes you get caught for.

Rauschenberg: That's not art.

UNPUBLISHED TRANSCRIPT, CITED IN KATZ,
"'COMMITTING THE PERFECT CRIME'"
/ INTRODUCTION

You should go in for a blending of the two elements, no?
Memory and oblivion, and we call that imagination.

JORGE LUIS BORGES

It's said that memory is the root of Man's troubles
That year, I started to lose my memory

HUANG YAOSHI, *ASHES OF TIME*

MUSICAL

BORROWING

REDUX

Cinema's most famous depiction of bricolage is itself the work of bricolage. In Stanley Kubrick's *2001: A Space Odyssey* (1968), under a gloomy sky, Moon Watcher is squatting leisurely in a semi-open area not far from a shelter (see fig. I.1). Behind him, in the distance and slightly out of focus, is the unforgiving African desert. In front, laid out rather like the dishes of a macabre banquet or ensemble of discarded toys, are the remains of an animal. Did it die a natural death, or is Moon Watcher contemplating the remains of someone else's meal? A bass drone appears in perfect sync with the image. Initially, the sonic intrusion barely registers as sound (let alone as music). Yet we'd do well to honor its appearance. For the sync point marks both the beginning of the episode and a shift in attitude on Moon Watcher's part: from boredom to hunger, frustration, and then curiosity and even playfulness. By the

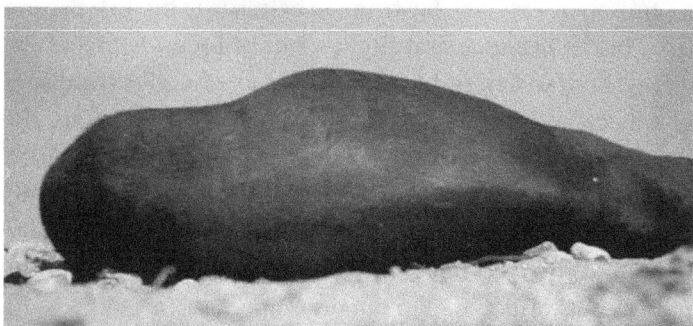

I.1–I.4   A bone turned into a weapon: *2001: A Space Odyssey*.

time the trumpets intone the famous C major triad that opens Richard Strauss's "Also Sprach Zarathustra," we realize we've heard this music already (over the beginning titles). The awareness of a repetition matters more than the title or programmatic tenor of the piece. Given its triumphant quality, a quality broadly accessible irrespective of any prior knowledge, the recurrence tells us that something pivotal is about to happen. What would otherwise pass as just another day in the life of a hungry ape man, the music seems to be implying, is of vital importance to no less than the emergence of a new species.

The remainder of the sequence bears this out. At first, the actions performed by Moon Watcher belie the grandiosity of the music. Having quickly surveyed the scene with what (anthropomorphically) looks like a bored look, the ape appears to lack anything resembling a plan of action until the crucial moment in which he moves closer to the bones lying on the ground. He seizes a femur, inspects it, then smells it. Unimpressed, he drops it and then picks it up, only to drop it again. The gesture causes a long, arched rib bone to pirouette before his eyes. Aimless tinkering gives way to a more deliberate chain of actions as Moon Watcher realizes he can break bone with bone. The found object has morphed into a tool—indeed, a weapon—a crucial passage that Kubrick marks with a striking change of tempo and camera setup.[1]

A new image shows the cloudy sky as seen at an angle (fig. I.2). Kubrick's ulterior aim is to capture to best advantage Moon Watcher's charging arm ripping through the frame—in slow motion (fig. I.3). As if possessed, Moon Watcher continues to crash the remaining bones, including the large skull that lay prominently to his left, largely intact. It is a striking reversal. Images of a plump tapir collapsing on the ground as the result of being bludgeoned to death—the very same animal whose skeleton he is now breaking into fragments—flash through Moon Watcher's mind (fig. I.4). They prefigure his future status as predator. At last, the solemnity of the music is commensurate with the significance of the passage. No longer merely simultaneous to the images of Moon Watcher, Strauss's "Also Sprach Zarathustra" is now *synchronized* to them, moving at the same tempo as they do, its own majestic tempo contributing to the monumentalization of Moon Watcher's triumph. The music also determines the length of the episode (which is cut to its strains). As the sound of a distant organ ceases to prolong the sound of the final, glorious C major chord, Moon Watcher fades from view.

Like the bone turned into a weapon, Strauss's music has been found, tinkered with, and retooled.[2] The fanfare matches the narrative segment of *2001* that Kubrick had in mind: the way the bone fit in Moon Watcher's hand, setting into motion a process that altered not only the direction of the narrative but the very mode of existence of the music. The exhilaration that accompanies Moon Watcher's epiphany (femur = weapon) may be said to also apply, self-reflexively on the director's part, to the realization that Strauss's symphonic poem functions brilliantly as the film's recurrent theme. Along with Jean-Luc Godard's abrasive use of the classics and Pier Paolo Pasolini's montages of high and low, Kubrick's reinventions of Strauss and Beethoven (among others) have since resonated across the world of film with the force of a manifesto. This lesson was not lost on the filmmakers of the Hong Kong new wave and, through them, on Wong Kar-wai, the filmmaker who more than anyone else embodied the resurgence of the spirit of the 1960s in Hong Kong.[3] Wong's films are lauded for their striking visuals, poetic dialogues, and sensuous re-creations of 1960s Hong Kong. Seemingly incapable of going down a well-trodden path, Wong has injected new life into such genres as Chinese melodrama, the road movie, and the action film. Central to this effort is the wide range of preexisting music that has found its way into the soundtracks of his films. The musical nexus at the heart of Wong's cinema has been shaped by the circumstances of his films' production and reception, the history of Chinese-language cinema, and the involved relationship, in his oeuvre, of cinephilia and musicophilia. Consider the use of Laurie Anderson's "Speak My Language" in *Fallen Angels* (1995). The song is of a piece with an elaborate feat of self-presentation on the part of the hitman's female partner. Styled after MTV and gesturing toward New York's rarefied downtown scene, the episode is nonetheless informed by a bluntly melodramatic premise: the music fills a void left behind by an absent lover (the hitman, who seems blissfully unaware that the "partner" is in love with him). Played by the improbably glamorous Michelle Reis, the "partner" sets the song into motion by dropping a coin into a beaming, impressively built retro jukebox bathed in pitch black. The machine doubles as an impassible partner, the music choreographing a series of frustrated sexual innuendos. The presciently digital vibe of the locale, barren arrangement, and breathy, closely miked voice make Anderson sound like a crooner from cyberspace. Wong's enshrining of Anderson's voice stands in stark contrast with the treatment the same song underwent in the likely source, Wim Wenders's *Faraway, So Close* (1993). The retooling betrays a debt to an admired filmmaker but is also a lesson in musical curation and a "perfect crime" in Rauschenberg's sense (see the first epigraph). In Wenders's film the same song is hardly audible. It is only on looking up the history of Anderson's song and subsequently the items listed on the CD of the soundtrack that I became aware that Wenders had used the song in the first place.

Remixing Wong Kar-wai charts the emergence of a unique modus operandi, which I interpret as a way of channeling creatively the habit of chancing on, collecting, and listening to music in the commercial and artistic entrepôt of Hong Kong. Directing films, I argue, turns Wong Kar-wai the music lover and end user into a bona fide composer or, better, re-composer of the very repertoires he explores—the listener as bricoleur. Bricoleur seems an intuitive description of Wong the urban dweller and media consumer conjuring worlds from the detritus of the mediascape. Correspondingly, I use *bricolage* to refer to a mode of creating film soundtracks characterized by the choice and assemblage of already-existing music. This modus operandi stands in contrast to the creation, ex nihilo, of new sound structures tailor-made for the final edit of the film (as in the traditional notion of film scoring). But in one important sense it is symptomatic of filmmaking, tout court. Bricolage pervades set design, costuming, and makeup and is built into the postproduction process as a matter of course across all other meaning-making elements of film.[4] By the time the director begins to edit a film, for example, the footage shot in production has, too, become preexisting. What becomes fixed in the final edit is the work of a collective, which produces a single entity in the director-as-bricoleur. While directors can justifiably lay claim to bringing all the material produced by their collaborators under a single, unifying vision, the result, to adapt a statement by Claude Lévi-Strauss, will always be a compromise between the structure of the instrumental set and that of the project. After it materializes, the project will therefore be inevitably at a remove from the initial aim (which was moreover a mere sketch), a phenomenon that the surrealists have felicitously called "objective hazard."[5] Hence the propensity of bricolage, despite its apparently constrained means, to produce "brilliant unforeseen results."[6] For this reason, in this book "Wong Kar-wai" refers to the flesh-and-blood director but is also a placeholder for collaborative work with materials—visual, sonic, plastic—the affordances of which do not emerge until one begins to combine them.[7]

BRICOLAGE: A REAPPRAISAL

The term *bricolage* requires if not an endorsement then at least a qualification. Famously introduced by Lévi-Strauss to capture a dimension of mythical thought, the metaphor of bricolage initially gave a new impetus to the study of style in fashion and the emergence of subcultural movements such as punk.[8] It has since languished at the margins of the academic discourse on the arts. This was initially due to its association with structural anthropology—a branch of the social sciences then thought to have been superseded, if not altogether discredited—and deconstructive critiques by the likes of Jacques Derrida and Gilles Deleuze and Félix Guattari.[9] Derrida's critique is worth revisiting if only to correct what I see as his misperception or strategic misappropriation—which comes to the same thing—of Lévi-Strauss's thinking (not to mention that it is in part responsible for our lingering unwillingness to build on it). In a philosophical vein, Derrida questions not so much the applicability or heuristic value of Lévi-Strauss's metaphor but rather its logical validity. In particular, he questions the key dialectic that underpins Lévi-Strauss's introduction of the term, that between the bricoleur proper, who creates by imaginatively combining ready-to-hand things, and the figure of the engineer, who has a precise goal in mind and builds out of raw materials or components made or sourced.[10] Swiftly moving to considering the engineer the counterpart to a writer or thinker, as per Lévi-Strauss's metaphor, Derrida makes the point that it is both practically and logically impossible for anyone to be "the absolute origin of his own discourse."[11] To the extent that there is borrowing involved, as must be the case, every kind of discourse is a kind of bricolage. The figure of the engineer, concludes Derrida, is itself a "myth" created by the bricoleur.[12]

Derrida is correct in questioning the absolute difference between the bricoleur and the engineer and indeed denying that the existence of the latter is at all plausible (he calls the engineer a "theological figure"). Speaking a language, to make an example, always involves borrowing of one sort or another.[13] The counterpart of the engineer in the realm of speech would be the etymologist or, worse still, the "neologist" (not-withstanding the fact that neologisms are in fact the result of bricolage: the combination of two or more already-existing words). This is a patently absurd scenario and would fly in the face of our knowledge of how language works. Yet it is not to say that differences do not remain and, what is just as important, that they are not observable in our everyday commerce with the world. Derrida exercises a kind of logical purism, which robs the bricolage/engineer distinction, however imprecise or blunt, of its considerable—and continuing—descriptive and explanatory power. In subjecting Lévi-Strauss's argument to such stringent logical analysis, moreover, he betrays the spirit of the text he critiques. The very figure of the bricoleur is introduced precisely to demonstrate the value, to the bricoleur, of pragmatic compromises (such as, for example, classifications based on sensible properties). In so quickly moving from the vehicle (bricolage) to the tenor (myth) of the metaphor, finally, Derrida underplays the (admittedly unresolved) status of the metaphor itself. For Lévi-Strauss is as interested in bricolage and engineering as practices as much as metaphorical counterparts to mythological and scientific discourse. Not coincidentally he follows with a cogent exploration of the artist (his example is a painting by Camille Claudel).[14]

For all its strengths, however, I am less indebted to Lévi-Strauss's discussion of art-making than his elucidation of the operations of bricolage. By the same token, I do not draw on Lévi-Strauss's analogy, suggested in various forms in *The Raw and the Cooked*, between music and myth. The analogy depends on a belletristic and unduly narrow view of music as a self-standing art form as exemplified by sonatas, quartets, symphonies—and Richard Wagner's operas. It is a decidedly Eurocentric view from a man who in his ethnography surely noticed that music is inseparable from work, sociality, and ritual. Or did he? Be that as it may, Lévi-Strauss understood music as an almost perfect equivalent of mythic structure: recursive, unified, and transcendent. It is the kind of formal reductionism that gave structuralism a bad name.[15]

Royal S. Brown has revived Lévi-Strauss's analogy between music and myth to argue that film music affords the spectator a "mythic mode of perception."[16] A mythic or paradigmatic, as Brown also calls it, passage transcends the determinations of the here-and-now of a narrative. A leitmotif associated with a place or a character, for example, transports us intratextually beyond the immediate present to call up prior or subsequent moments in the narrative. The use of a waltz in a scene of courtship is, on the other hand, an example of extratextual relation. As a widely recognizable topos, the waltz helps convey the gist of the action by tapping into a vast pool of shared memories.[17] Brown's application of the notion of paradigm to film music is fertile. But to account for the power of film music to afford a mythic mode of perception on the basis of Lévi-Strauss's analogy between music and myth is a non sequitur. It is a characteristic of all narratives, whether they feature music or not, that they resonate with our experience, irrespective of their specific features. To the extent that film music supports Lévi-Strauss's understanding of myth and its underlying cognitive principle, the paradigmatic, this has little to do with his view of music as a formal homology of myth. It is bricolage—plundering the musical archive for the purposes of telling a story—that accounts for the successful retooling of a specific piece of music in order to serve the paradigmatic ambitions of a narrative.

There is another reason why Lévi-Strauss's notion of bricolage is more germane to the study of film music than his belief in the homology between myth and music. This is the feedback loop between chancing on recordings and creating film soundtracks. We must appeal to bricolage if we wish to grasp the mutual implication that binds, in the artistic sphere, aesthetics and poetics. Consider Pablo Picasso's well-known sculpture *Bull's Head* (fig. I.5). The work is the record of a moment of looking, of seeing-as to be precise: the saddle and handlebars change aspect. By combining them, Picasso gives material form to this perception, preserving it for posterity as in a time capsule. Seeing is one with making. The gesture of combining two found objects sanctions not merely a new union but a newborn identity in something like the way synchronization helps congeal a moment of listening or brings to light a new facet of a familiar sound through a new, expanded form of musical composition.

Bull's Head is unique in Picasso's oeuvre in its invitation to recognize the bicycle parts as such. This brings me to another aspect of Lévi-Strauss's discussion of bricolage that is central to my undertaking, and elided in Derrida's critique: the ability of the bricoleur to repurpose the borrowed or discovered material in ways that make its past use or identity difficult to detect or, even when flaunted, simply immaterial. In *2001: A Space Odyssey*, the ape man's bricolage is akin to film music in that, in the words of Pasolini, "film music can be conceived before a film is made . . . but it is only at the very moment it is cut to the images, that is

1.5 Pablo Picasso, *Bull's Head* (1942).

born as film music. Why? Because the encounter and subsequent amalgam between music and the moving image is fundamentally poetic, that is empirical."[18] By the same token, a bone is born as weapon only in the act of manipulating it.[19] The bone-as-weapon is neither a found object nor a readymade. For it to be an example of the former, its novel use value would have to be discovered *before* one can say it has been found (a patently absurd scenario). As to the latter, "The feature of the 'readymade,'" as Claude Lévi-Strauss stated in a little publicized yet enlightening 1959 interview with Georges Charbonnier, examined afresh by Julia Kelly, "was very rarely reducible to a single object: in order to make a 'ready-made,' there must be at least two objects."[20] Kelly continues:

> Charbonnier posited Duchamp's *Bottlerack* as a counterexample of a single-object readymade, to which Lévi-Strauss responded that to remove the bottle rack from its original context was to bring about a semantic "fission" separating the signifier and the signified and, by separating them, creating "an unexpected fusion between another signifier and another signified." For Lévi-Strauss, then, all uses of found objects are a kind of assemblage, involving the collision of meanings: "It is the 'sentences' made with objects which have a meaning not the objects themselves."[21]

Lévi-Strauss's analogy between ready-mades and the sentence in language is needlessly reductionist. Even so, his basic point is well taken: despite manipulating one and only object (albeit in multiples), Moon Watcher reinvents the bone by removing it from its original context and mentally placing it in another. The outcome is contingent on the object being subsumed under the novel situation—what Lévi-Strauss calls a "sentence"—brought into being by Moon Watcher's tinkering with it. Kubrick, too, has a "second object" at his disposal: the moving image. He reinvents Strauss's music not merely by assembling or fusing it with the image but also by tinkering with it in the process of editing the film and hearing it under a dual aspect: as integral to a dramatic *situation*, itself the target of the attention of a situated listener, namely the film spectator.[22]

Before retooling the idea of bricolage to buttress the impossibility of a "discourse breaking with a received historical discourse," Derrida refers to the borrowing of concepts as carrying with it a formidable baggage: "Since these concepts are not elements or atoms and since they are taken from a syntax and a system, every particular borrowing drags along with it the whole of metaphysics."[23] Again, Derrida extrapolates from philosophical discourse and privileges logic over experience.[24] His truism tells us precious little about the extraordinarily wide range of outcomes produced by borrowing in the arts and their impact and significance at a particular time in a particular place under particular circumstances. A successful retooling, pace Derrida, sheds baggage as much as drags it. Forgetting is of the essence to the creative reinvention of the received tradition. To unleash its full potential, Lévi-Strauss's notion of bricolage must be lifted from the rarefied time-space of philosophical commentary and reclaimed by the very "human sciences"—anthropology, history, and art criticism—whose value Derrida's intrusion sought to question.

My interest in bricolage has been spurred by Derrida's deconstructive critique of Lévi-Strauss—and my wish to counter it. As a critical category, however, bricolage did not fade into the margins only because of Derrida's attack on structural anthropology. Its loss of potency can also be attributed to its dilution in a cultural field dominated by adjacent and to an extent also overlapping notions of intertextuality, appropriation, and allusion, and such practices as hyperreferentiality, sampling, remix, and nowadays also content generated by artificial intelligence. Yet it would be a mistake to subsume bricolage under, not to mention confuse it with, these adjacent, if undoubtedly significant, practices. Consider, for example, Véronique Altglas's work. Drawing on Roger Bastide's scholarship on religious syncretism in the Americas, Altglas has revived the idea of "bricolage as a response to the holes of 'collective memory.' It is thus about replacing something missing. As such, bricolage can be seen as a quest for coherence rather than a celebration of eclecticism."[25] Altglas's timely rediscovery of Bastide reminds us that if Wong's cinema would be unthinkable without access to a plethora of cultural resources, it is also a symptom of a quest for a lost tradition.[26] If I revive bricolage as a metaphor and an analytical tool, then, this is also in the attempt to liberate what we might call its literary resonances. Bricolage captures the expedient nature of borrowing in a saturated marketplace. It makes palpable the gestural quality of stitching together found music and the moving image.[27] Indelibly tied to mythology and myth-making, as per Lévi-Strauss's seminal formulation, bricolage also evokes end-of-history scenarios and the exhaustion of genres and ideas that underpin the use of all manner of preexisting materials by such artists as Andy Warhol, Godard, Cindy Sherman, and, more recently, Christian Marclay.[28] Such preoccupations are central to the reflections on contemporary pop culture by the likes of Simon Reynolds.[29] As a filmmaker but also pop artist in the broad sense of the term, Wong may be said to partake of the "addiction to the past" that, as Reynolds rightly observes, informs so much popular music of the past twenty or so years. Yet his winning bricolage of music and the moving image is not reproductive but transformative. Wong's films exemplify the very changes—stylistic, formal, of sensibility—that Reynolds finds to be lacking in the trajectory of pop itself.[30] Lévi-Strauss, too, was haunted by the end of history but in a literal, material sense: nuclear Armageddon.[31] It is therefore only too fitting that the artwork that perhaps best captures the climate of fear that defined the postwar period would be Bruce Conner's *Crossroads* (1976), itself a montage of preexisting footage of the July 25, 1946, Operation Crossroads Baker underwater nuclear test at Bikini Atoll. Through the recursive use of disturbingly beautiful images, complete with a compilation soundtrack, Connor's bricolage brings to life a world bent on destroying itself.

Bricolage and *remix* are like the recto and verso of cultural production. As used in arts criticism, bricolage is product-oriented.[32] In keeping with this understanding of the term, I understand a film as a finished product, a closed system. This is a crucial heuristic, for without positing the film, albeit temporarily, as a complete, self-contained entity, it would be impossible to contemplate the new identity the borrowed music has assumed in it. But, of course, a film is but one link—a station—in an open-ended, and potentially infinite, process of transformations. This is the domain of remix, which is process-oriented. Bricolage goes to the heart of the ontological change that, from the music as a self-standing object, forces us to consider it as an integral element of a dynamic combinatoire of elements. Remix stresses the open-endedness of the history of the musical borrowing viewed as an independent, recognizable entity with a history apart—both prior and subsequent to—the film in which it is embedded.

Remix also describes the concrete steps the director takes in splicing the music to the image and the sound mix: the material conditions under which a soundtrack is put together. Like turntablists and DJs, many filmmakers work with mediated audio objects and transform them in the studio via recording and mixing technology. In *2001: A Space Odyssey*, to return to my initial example, Kubrick used a specific performance of "The Blue Danube" as found on a commercial release. The singular qualities of the recording may or may not impinge on the impact of the episode. I personally believe it does but suffice to say here that on using preexisting music, directors do not cite musical works but rather remix recordings, a fact that is self-evident when the music in question is a pop track: for a case can be made that in pop the recording is the work.[33] It isn't just that the music arrives on a filmmaker's desk in the form of commodity. It is also that it has already been mixed or, indeed, is itself the product of remix and a chain of rewritings and transformative performances at the hands of multiple agents. It follows that the filmic use of a given piece or repertoire is but one step in a potentially infinite chain of materializations that stretches back into the past but also forward into the future. Insofar as the physical output remains the same, each materialization is a repetition. Yet the music evolves and sheds the traces of the past as it breathes new life into a new configuration. This is the space of the imagination, as per Borges's epigraph quoted earlier. Borges's definition of the imagination as a mix of memory and oblivion is not only consistent with the psychology of creativity: it also makes Harold Bloom's theory of the anxiety of influence moot.

Interpretation and criticism partake of the remixing process. In viewing Wong's films as an exemplary site for the study of musical borrowing, I am myself remixing his cinematic oeuvre—hence the title of this book. My own remix entails that certain aspects of Wong's films are emphasized at the expense of others. The emergence of the book's main argument will, I hope, provide a rationale for the exclusion from the discussion of such films as *Fallen Angels* (1995), *Eros* (2005), or *My Blueberry Nights* (2006) and such memorable moments in the Wong canon as, to give two examples, the use of Astor Piazzolla in *Happy Together* or the radio broadcast of Chinese regional operas and especially "Hua Yang de Nian Hua" in *In the Mood for Love*. Having covered this territory in previous publications of mine in terms that I find are no longer consistent with my current interests and methodological orientation, I dare say that in this book I am also remixing my own work.

THE GLOBAL VERNACULAR

With virtuoso camera work, a proneness to punning, and the unabashed exploitation of their leads' star power, Wong Kar-wai's films are deeply indebted to the values and practices that have jelled in and around the most representative genres of the Hong Kong film industry.[34] At the same time, they represent a signal departure in that they trade in those very genres in a decidedly reflexive, indeed predatory, mode. As with Godard, Wong's almost excessive love of cinema, and exuberant, unselfconscious penchant for borrowing, has resulted in films that are at once viscerally derivative and utterly different from the mainstream fare feeding it. To the knowing cinephile, his films come across as a kaleidoscope of citations, chunks of borrowed materials reshaped into a fractured yet strangely compelling original surface (for a visual analogy, see Mimmo Rotella's "décollage" in fig. I.6). Conversely, they may be described as a finely textured collage or mosaic exhibiting what initially appears to be a novel design yet consisting, upon closer scrutiny, of tiles borrowed from preexisting representations in now-fluid, now-jarring combinations (fig. I.7). Wong's borrowings range from narrative tropes to title songs, from costumes to the casting of old actors. While the extent of his plundering may seem perplexing, one cannot help but admire the brilliance and clarity of the retooling.

The reference to photomosaic or, say, collage paintings is not meant to suggest a deliberate convergence, let alone a genealogy.[35] But it is representative of my attempt, throughout this book, of aligning Wong's oeuvre with explicit bricolage practices, such as appropriative photography, mixed media arts, DJ-ing, and mashups.[36] The analogy with

1.6   Mimmo Rotella, *Cinemascope / Marylin* (décollage, 1963).

1.7   Photomosaic.

photomosaic is also specific in that, like a photomosaic, Wong's films are complete, self-sustaining representations. Their appeal does not depend on the deciphering of the borrowed materials that constitute their material substratum (though they may invite one to ponder them). Consider, for a revealing contrast, Japanese portraitist Yasumasa Morimura (fig. I.8). Having chosen photographs of exceedingly well-known artworks (e.g., Édouard Manet's *Olympia*) or icons (a celebrated close-up of Che Guevara), Morimura craftily inserts his own image in place of the putative subject. In so doing he makes the recognition of what he borrows not only easy to achieve but also of the essence to the uncanny effect of the insertion. An equally instructive counterpart to Wong's modus operandi is the installation pieces of the acclaimed Vietnamese-Danish artist Dahn Vo (fig. I.9). Many of Vo's works consist of ingenious combinations of what at first blush appear to be found objects from disparate sources (the raw materials, that is, of the bricoleur). Whether they come across as carefully executed assemblages, provocative juxtapositions, or lumps of objects casually put together, the stark setting of the contemporary art gallery or museum provides them with a striking frame that enhances their ritualistic power. Paratextual materials add to the ponderousness of their presentation, aiding us to view the installations as powerful statements about the life of objects, colonization, and displacement. At this juncture, however, one realizes that Vo is no bricoleur at all. The repurposed objects are not chanced on but, to the contrary, hounded, indeed scouted with the relentlessness of a prodigal son retracing the path to one's lost home (the Vietnam of his forgotten childhood). They may be said to be "lost and found." They evoke a highly personal, even esoteric trajectory. Their selection and presentation are studied in the extreme. It follows that without knowledge of what they are and what they stand for, Vo's works are all but opaque. Viewers have no choice but to excavate meanings and associations for their encounter with them to be meaningful. In prosaic terms, access to the aboriginal meaning of the objects, and hence the key to Vo's works, is possible only through a careful reading of the captions. The caption inverts the literal or surface meaning of the object (be it a chandelier, washing machine, or piece of fabric). In this way, the objective remnants of the colonizers' world are turned on their heads, as it were, to tell a story their very production and deployment were in fact once upon a time meant to conceal. It is a powerful reversal of mimicry, to be sure. But it comes at a cost: the return or, better, retreat to what I would call the "aesthetics

1.8   Yasumasa Morimura, *Portrait (Futago)* (color photograph, 1988).

1.9
Dahn Vo, *Oma Totem*
(mixed media, 2009).

of the gloss." As Claire Bishop has suggested, "For many of Vo's fans, the idea of research and the lure of history still lend a certain assurance of critical substance to his art."[37] Worse still, such a retreat into "research" is forced down our throat. Given the moral turpitude of the narratives alluded to—colonization, the Vietnam wars, the "boat people" crisis of the late 1970s—any attempt to escape or evade the programs implicit in his works would make us complicit in the moral failures that precipitated the crises they allegorize. So, we reach for the gallery walls.

If I dwell at some length on Vo, this is because he typifies the successful postcolonial artist crafting an original language out of the remnants of the colonial past. Wong Kar-wai, too, is a postcolonial subject coming to terms with a colonial past (most explicitly in his 1960s trilogy). Yet the configurations that emerge in the here and now of the film experience take precedence over the provenance of the borrowed materials that form their inspiration. This is first and foremost because of the apparent polish and sensuality of the finished product. Wong's borrowings do not come across as fragments but are seamlessly integrated into a new and internally coherent gestalt. Such a process of seamless integration is facilitated by the fact that film is a time-based medium that encourages the stringing together of disparate elements to create a coherent narrative (compare, in this respect, film spectatorship to the leisurely and contemplative nature of art viewing). But to insist on medium specificity begs the question of why Wong borrows so copiously in the first place. Wong seems blissfully unpreoccupied with the adaptation of Western classics (as, say, Akira Kurosawa was). This is not to say he is not privy to the reasons behind his own preference toward recurring motifs, texts, sounds, or images. Homages to older Chinese films and divas, for example, are often delivered in poignant tones. Outside this first circle of references, however, whether the source is Louis Cha or Julio Cortázar, Michelangelo Antonioni or Seijun Suzuki, Brian Ferry or Piazzolla, one detects a joyful and not infrequently expedient indiscriminateness as to what Wong borrows, as if combining the catholic taste of a true cosmopolitan with the expediency of an artist on the run.

Several concomitant factors account for Wong's seemingly cavalier attitude toward borrowing and repurposing. First, he inherits a long-standing Chinese tradition of allusionism in both prose and especially poetry, the tendency to draw as a matter of course on a deep well of shared texts and motifs.[38] Given the opening of this tradition in republican-era Shanghai and subsequently colonial Hong Kong to the sounds, texts, and images of global media—especially Anglophone and Japanese—this tendency has naturally resulted in a frenzy of borrowings whose range is beyond the pale of most filmmakers working in other film industries. Hong Kong has been as much a cosmopolitan free-trade zone as a colony. As such, it presents us with the compelling case of a distinctive culture emerging to the beat of the pulse of alternating cosmopolitan and vernacular tendencies (rather than the friction between colonizer and colonized or the struggle for emancipation from venerable local traditions or Western models).[39] Of this culture, and despite their distinctiveness vis-à-vis mainstream Hong Kong cinema, Wong's films are an exceptionally representative example. He came of age in a film and television industry bent on plagiarizing and delivering knock-offs that winked at a knowing audience while simultaneously minimizing production costs. For all the arty pretensions of his work, Wong's break from the ethos of Hong Kong's "copycat" culture has in my opinion never been clean.[40] He would fit the mold of the quintessential *shanzhai* artist except that he seems incapable of not remodeling, sometimes to the point of making the materials he borrows unrecognizable.[41] One could almost say he is an original despite himself. The personal nature of Wong's trajectory in the Hong Kong (and subsequently global) film industry, his hard-earned status of auteur, vindicates the right of the postcolonial artist to carve a unique space as shaped by one's own proclivities and choice of collaborators as much as impersonal sociohistorical processes. For this reason, this book is also a study in the irreducible individuality of the creative process. But if I focus on Wong's musical borrowings, this is not only for their range, scope, and intrinsic interest; it is also because I intend to draw attention to the emergence of a new and important form of music-making. Folded in my argument about Wong Kar-wai as artistically emancipated postcolonial artist is a reflection on borrowing and repurposing in film as central to musical culture.

RELINQUISHING AUTHORSHIP?

Exploring the use of preexisting music through the lens of bricolage brings to light several ambiguities that are central to the significance—and continuing appeal—of Wong's films. Consider, first, the extent to which music shapes our understanding of Wong as a film auteur. Compilation soundtracks have given new impetus to auteur cinema and added a new dimension to our understanding of it.[42] In the wake of the invention of the cassette, the MIDI and portable devices, and even virtual music archives, directors have reverted to their collections more and more, their musical taste and sensibility imbuing their work with the unmistakable veneer of personal style.[43] My interest, however, lies less in authorship per se than in the ambiguities nested in the sourcing of preexisting music and its subsequent utilization in a film. Wong's oeuvre is a choice example of such ambivalence. For the more marked the music, and distinctive its deployment, the greater not only a director's ability to project its appearance as a function of his taste and proclivities but also the risk that he will come across as having abdicated the role of creator. Put bluntly, by using already-constituted materials a director is relinquishing responsibility as much as exercising it. The music originates with someone other than the director or, at best, the hired composer working under his supervision. It is not just that the director does not literally craft the material. After all, that is precisely the difference between the bricoleur and what Lévi-Strauss called the engineer (namely, someone who works with component pieces that are conceived and procured specifically for the project at hand). It is also that the borrowed or found musical material is itself used as music. In contrast, the bricoleur recycles, say, gingerbread to make a house or an emptied-out watermelon as a cup, thereby masking the natural function or point of origin of the found object. Not so with preexisting music, whose baggage of associations may in fact overwhelm the image and indeed defeat the very purpose of its borrowing.[44] Second, the film director deals with elements—footage, recorded dialogue, music tracks—that are singularly cumbersome, unmalleable, and ultimately intractable due to the high degree of technological mediation involved in their creation and/or combination. Alfred Hitchcock was speaking on behalf of many a director when he complained about and agonized over the lack of control over the composition of the soundtrack (and by implication, aware as he was of its significance, the film in its entirety). The choice to work with preexisting music is a partial remedy to this predicament. But it does not return full control to the filmmaker. The sole window of intervention lies in the right to exercise one's taste and cunning in the selection of a track and the display of skill in combining the chosen music with a given shot or sequence. The end result of this combinatory art is by its very nature emergent, which is not to say unpredictable or, worse, arbitrary but nevertheless constantly subject to negotiations and thus to some extent endemically outside the remit of the director. Lévi-Strauss's model of the bricoleur working in blissful isolation and in full control of the process of retooling is an idealization inspired, one presumes, by the likes of Duchamp or Picasso.[45] Preexisting music speaks through the director as much as the director speaks through it. It is a significant instance of the diffusion of agency. This is not to say that authorship is made irrelevant—to the contrary—but rather that its affirmation is of a piece with the appearance of relinquishing it: hence the paradoxical role of preexisting music in both diffusing and fostering the director's identity as auteur.[46]

THE (AMATEUR) MUSICIAN AS (PROFESSIONAL) FILMMAKER

Through their compilation soundtracks, directors such as Wong, Quentin Tarantino, or Sofia Coppola channel their own history as listeners in an intensely mediatized, DIY world. Only they do it on a world stage, that of global film distribution. Substituting for the piano and the actual engagement with music-making, the mass media have fostered the emergence of listeners who cultivate an art whose rules of composition and performance they are not acquainted with.[47] Such listeners purchase music as produced, curated, and distributed by agents and commercial entities beyond their control and listen to it mediated through technologies outside their remit. For all this, the exercise of a certain musical taste and sensibility remains an active pursuit, one that is not confined to musically literate individuals (let alone professional musicians). Music lovers, and filmmakers among them, build collections, develop a set of preferences, and form listening and social habits that are at once expressive and constitutive of their identity.[48] To cultivate one's love for music is not only to perform the self; it is also to re-compose the music by playing it under circumstances that cast it in a novel or even unique perspective. This occurs whether one searches, collects, and listens to music privately for one's own sake or whether one adapts it for the purposes of making a film. The outcomes are vastly different, however. The soundtracks or song lists of a famous filmmaker are distributed, publicly observable manifestations of the productive nature of any such performance of agency.[49] Films are vehicles of a director's musicality, thanks to their imaginatively mixed, technically polished, and often also lucrative soundtrack releases. The inclusion of a certain piece of music, even more so when skillfully executed, is an oblique endorsement that endows it with a new lease on life.[50] It is against this context that Wong passes as a musical "taste-maker" on a par with famous performers, DJs, and critics.

Wong's use of preexisting music points to the world of amateur filmmaking as well. As with the Coen Brothers, Tarantino, and, further back in film history, George Lucas, Kubrick, and Pasolini—to name but three—the roots of Wong's soundtracks lie in the rudimentary synchronizing practices that have sustained the work of photographers, cinephiles, and amateur filmmakers since the advent of recorded sound. Professional film releases have historically provided models of how music and the moving image might be combined in the context of an 8mm family film or a slide show. The use of preexisting music by noted filmmakers in the 1960s marked a new phase of this development in that it not only legitimized but emboldened countless image makers to make unabashed use of their recordings. This applies to amateur filmmakers, lecturers, DJs, photographers, video artists and makers, as well as, more recently, mashup artists, social media mavericks, and YouTubers.[51] Compilation soundtracks consisting wholly or at least in part of preexisting music have galvanized the process by which listening has become an aspect of making: the premise for an audiovisual poetics. The use of one's favorite music as the soundtrack to a film brings the amateur and professional image maker closer together in the name of a shared practice, and their shared status of musical amateurs and record collectors. Wong wears his love of music on his sleeve, so to speak, all the while inviting us to join in the game. In this respect, too, and not only in respect to the quality of the musical selections themselves, he employs music to reach out to a hip, urban, global audience. The underlying methods of selecting, compiling, and editing preexisting music are to some extent the same for professional and amateur filmmakers alike. Access to relatively inexpensive technological equipment has made filmmaking and compiling one's own soundtracks a distinct possibility for practically everyone. The high degree of professionalization of studio filmmaking entails unbridgeable differences, however. Wong the amateur musician is nested within Wong the professional—and celebrated—filmmaker. The full realization of his musical vision depends on the support of considerable logistical, technological, and financial instruments. Like any director working with a budget, he has access to technology, labor, and a huge archive. These conditions underpin the emergence of new skills and ultimately new forms of musical creativity, which remain out of reach for the amateur. It is a set of circumstances that has set the stage not merely for the assumption of authorship over the music in the form of mechanical and especially recording rights but also for the remediation of whole repertoires in keeping with a wholly original audiovisual language.[52] Wong has transfigured the basics of film scoring—spotting, selecting, and synchronizing—into a wholly new musical practice, one the amateur or occasional filmmaker can only dream of.

RECASTING "CASTA DIVA"

There is no denying Wong's uncanny ability to reinvent, as opposed to merely cite or reference, a repertoire. The term *uncanny* applies literally here, as his films make the familiar sound new (if not altogether strange). Like a consummate DJ, Wong has turned the tools of musical reproduction—cassette and CD players, turntables, iPods, and so forth—into means for music-making. Where the DJ reframes a piece by breaking it or mixing with other pieces, Wong places it in the context of a dramatic situation or setting, with striking imagery, thereby creating a metaphorical loop between output (the playback system) and input (the film). Like a microphone, the latter picks up the musical signal but repurposes it to fit its own specifications. The resulting feedback amounts to a new and unfamiliar performance of even the best-known musical work.

Arved Ashby has called the use of preexisting music by filmmakers a new "form of music-making."[53] Wong's practices tempt one to take a step further and call such activities of choosing, compiling, and synchronizing music to a given scene a new form of image-driven composition. Historical musicologists call the repurposing of preexisting music via the fusion of old and new "parody."[54] Wong's repurposing of well-known pieces is sometimes so radical and whimsical that it divests preexisting music of all but its most familiar associations. Like a medieval scribe composing a new text for an old melody, thereby turning, say, a secular piece into a sacred one—a practice sometimes referred to as *contrafactum*—Wong creates dramatic situations that transform the music's acknowledged identity by shifting the terms of its reception. Far from being citations, allusions, or appropriations, many of his borrowings are deployed in such a way that the provenance of the music either is rendered irrelevant or remains unknown.[55] This is due to several, sometimes concomitant, factors: the audacity of the retooling, the sheer obscurity of the source, the tendency of a given musical selection to camouflage itself in a new context, Bloomean "misprision" or self-citation. Mikhail Iampolski refers to this process as "source repression" and views it as the seed out of which new figures of cinematic language germinate.[56]

The idea of bricolage throws much-needed light onto Wong's multi-media combinatorial art, paving the way for a new understanding of the dynamics put in place by preexisting materials both in his cinema and the history of film music, and filmmaking, more generally. Like any product that involves craftsmanship, music-making may seem inaccessible to those who are not themselves well versed in the craft itself. Wong is not in the position of forging the musical materials from scratch but can only manipulate them (by altering the balance of the parts, manipulating the acoustics, or pushing volume to the threshold of inaudibility). This limitation is to some extent convenient for, insofar as he seeks to retain the identity of the music he has borrowed, he is unwilling to change its outward appearance. As heard in *2046* (2004), for instance, "Casta Diva," from Vincenzo Bellini's opera *Norma*, is a well-known token of the operatic repertoire. Its very recognizability depends on the integrity of its musical parameters (rhythm, melodic contour, range, and so forth). Wong leaves these parameters untouched, but the filmic context eats into the historical associations accrued around the piece by operating on the conditions of its reception. Unlike the operagoer or record collector, the film spectator will not lavish much attention on Bellini's music. In fact, the film makes a point of its incidental status by introducing it as a distracting sound through which a protective father and former opera singer seek—in vain, as it turns out—to drown out his and his daughter's voices amid a heated argument.[57] The episode neatly allegorizes the true raison d'être of the musical bricolage practiced by Wong: expediency. It is expediency rather than allusion—or homage—that underpins the musical borrowings in Wong's oeuvre.

The same example also clarifies the process by which his films invest music with new meanings. Wong shows little concern with the opera's historical background or the associations it has acquired over its long reception history. Deploying characters as vectors, he invites us to listen to the operatic excerpts the way they do. When Bellini's music reappears later in *2046*, it choreographs the slow-motion ballet of the

I.10 The attendant (Faye Wong) moving to the sounds of "Casta Diva" in *2046*.

attendant on the train heading toward *2046* (see fig. I.10). The attendant is played by Faye Wong, who also impersonates the young woman involved in the altercation that is responsible for the aria's appearance near the beginning of the film. We could not be further away from the world of Bellini's opera, even in its most radical stage incarnations. Repetition and recasting tie the music to a new set of concerns, characters, and a wholly new iconography.

THE ANXIETY OF REPRESENTATION

As indicated above, I understand Wong's soundtracks as simultaneously affirming and relinquishing his responsibility as author. My stance is at least partially spurred by the same desire to demystify the idea of the author as the sole source of an artwork that also informed the emergence of intertextuality in literary studies.[58] Stressing that Wong re-composes the music he borrows, as distinct from merely citing it, is compatible with the questioning of authorship I pursue in this book. For to re-compose, in the model adopted here, is not to be the author of a musical work in the traditional sense but rather to create a participatory space in which preexisting music, as reconfigured in a film, is heard anew (or made unrecognizable). To be sure, Wong is deeply aware of the unique qualities of the materials he is manipulating (if only to clear rights). In fact, he often chooses a track precisely because of its origins and history. Yet in the end he uses it in ways that render the significance of provenance irrelevant or moot. Why a track is chosen and the work it ends up doing in its new "host body" are very different things, a point that is well worth rehearsing because a director will often describe his musical choices in terms of the former (rather than the latter).[59] We heed a director's statements about his sources or rehearse the place of a borrowing in the culture at large—its received meanings—at our own risk. At bottom, such statements are casual reminiscences or rationalizations. As basis for interpretation, they are a function of that old chestnut: genetic criticism and the intentional fallacy that is its foil.

Let us look at the same issue from the other end of the analytical spectrum instead—that of the spectator. Provenance, even when obvious, can and very often will be glossed over. The spectator may ignore where the music comes from or they may exercise the right to ignore the intertextual resonances of what for a director is an explicit citation or allusion, wallowing instead in the new dimensions it takes in a richly nuanced dramatic situation.[60] It would take a very pedantic or, worse, patronizing neighbor or filmgoing companion to interrupt the show halfway to point out that a track was lifted from such and such record or film. Yet that is precisely what we scholars often do when, with undisguised pride, we point to the source or provenance of any given musical selection (especially when it turns out to be esoteric). For it to work, preexisting music must perform some kind of function (whether thematically or in terms of tone). Consequently, and unsurprisingly, it will invariably be found to be "meaningful," "enriching," "appropriate," or alluding to a symbol, theme, or other artwork. Thus, the judicious work of glossers and philologists transforms a *contrafactum* into a buried or hidden, esoteric intertextual reference (a reference that, because it is buried or concealed, requires the work of an interpreter, in a seemingly endless, self-reinforcing cycle). Glossing of this kind is a welcome exercise insofar as it makes us more informed spectators. All too often, however, it has the unfortunate effect of surgically removing the music from the context in which it is embedded. Insisting on provenance frames it apart from the film, turning it into a historical, musealized construct rather than as an unstable field of potential, and unforeseeable, meanings temporarily activated by a new configuration. The entirety of its sustained, moment-to-moment impact is reduced to its having a role in a static intertextual system, the recognition of an ostensible reference or association (one that, moreover, takes place almost by definition after the fact in the form of a footnote or commentary). In glossing borrowed music through one's received wisdom, in other words, we overlook its unfolding in time in a multimedia construct that may or may not honor the associations by which the music is known or remembered. We create an "origin myth," according to which a piece of music must be judged on its own prior to being used in a film, without realizing that what we believe to be the music's aboriginal manifestation may itself have been the result of a recontextualization, or even a chain of recontextualizations, planned or accidental, reaching all the way back to its historical birth. We do expect a horn to evoke a hunting scene, but can we apply the same kind of expectation to a musical work and even a whole repertoire? Doesn't the appeal of a form like opera lie precisely in its capacity for renewal at the hands of, among others, singers, set designers, stage directors—and filmmakers? Instead of glossing Wong's films as if they were exercises in musical citationism, or poems riddled by now-obscure, now-platitudinous musical references, I propose that we focus on the sensuous dimensions and dramatic values of the music, irrespective of its identity and reception history (no matter how conveniently pertinent they may seem in revisiting the films).[61] This is not to engage in a patronizing or disingenuous parroting of the "average" spectator. The researcher is in a unique, delicate, and ultimately ironic position when it comes to borrowing. Knowledge of Wong's sources, when possible, is not merely desirable but must be pursued, only not so much as evidence that Wong is quoting earlier models but rather as a background against which to appreciate music's remarkable capacity for self-renewal.

As far as Wong's soundtracks are concerned, no anxiety of influence applies. It is a matter, rather, of the anxiety to represent.[62] Wong the bricoleur is not, or at any rate not only, referencing his sources; he is engaging in (expedient) parody like the medieval musician or troping his sources, in the manner of a Shakespeare, with the goal of creating a new world all along. Intertextuality posits the work as an open, dynamic field that both reconfigures and prefigures other works. The cases in which borrowings from other works are not recognizable as such—even by the author—are perhaps the most revealing, for they would seem to prove that language speaks through authors as much as they through it. Equally pertinent to a theory of intertextuality is the work of readers whose readerly past affects the way in which the present text is interpreted (again, through the filter of texts that may all be unknown to the author). What this means is that the workings of shared practices at both the production and reception point are as important as the singular, flesh-and-blood author in determining the meaning and impact of a work. This much is unproblematic. Intertextual readings, however, have the unfortunate result of privileging textuality over representation.[63] We can preserve a sense of the openness of the work, and the shared, inherently social and historical nature of artistic processes, by reference to the real world in which artworks exist, the circumstances—personal, social, political—that frame both their production and reception, and the situations they depict. Hence my appeal to worldmaking or, to paraphrase André Malraux's famous dictum, the move from pastiche to full-blown representation.[64] Like figure and ground, worldmaking and intertextuality are not merely alternatives: they exist on different orders of reality—hence, ironically, their ability to coexist in our encounter with an artwork (whether literary or cinematic). Which path we choose is not just a matter of preference, let alone the intrinsic nature of the texts we interpret, but a point of view. My own take on Wong's work is that for all their mashing and mixing of an extraordinarily wide range of preexisting materials—musical and otherwise—his films are first and foremost an attempt to conjure a world. The foundational role of music in conjuring such a world deserves a second hearing. It is the job of this book to argue for the boundedness of this vision to Hong Kong as both a subject and sociocultural space but also to account for its global resonance.

ONE

SPLICING

"The world's first Wong Kar-wai moment," as one internet fan dubbed it, is shot in slow motion and involves two budding stars, a phone booth—and the cover of a famous movie song.[1] To the sound of "Take My Breath Away" of *Top Gun* fame, sung (in Cantonese) by Sandy Lam, Wah (Andy Lau) and Ah-ngor (Maggie Cheung) kiss passionately in a washed-out, brightly lit phone booth redolent of what would soon be Chris Doyle's signature shooting style (fig. 1.1). More the drawn-out resolution of a characteristically convoluted sequence than a "moment" in the strict sense of the word, the episode is the climax of Wong's debut feature, *As Tears Go By* (1988).

By a significant coincidence, the same episode returns in inverted form in Wong's next film, *Days of Being Wild* (1990). Maggie Cheung plays Su Li-zhen and Andy Lau, Tide. Once again, a phone booth is their meeting place. A major prop displaying the requisite adornments of a classic colonial-era artifact—the film is set in the early 1960s—the booth holds a commanding presence. Tide has fallen for Li-zhen but she cannot reciprocate as she is embroiled in an unhappy affair

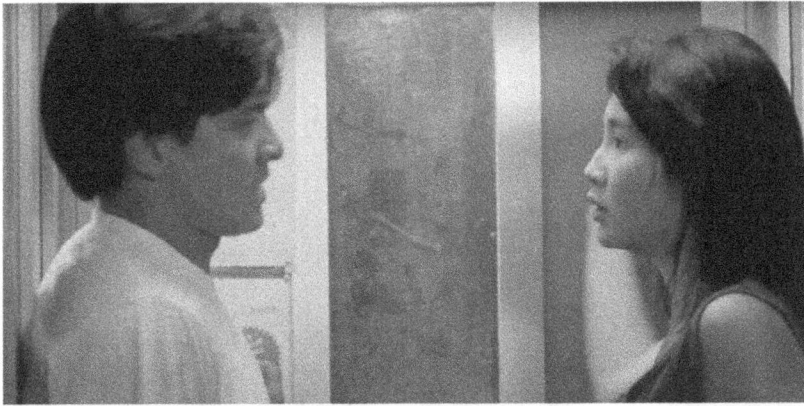

1.1 The world's first Wong Kar-wai moment? Frame from *As Tears Go By*.

with Yuddy (himself involved with Fung-ying [Carina Lau]). Li-zhen and Tide never step inside the booth, nor will the phone ever ring. The booth remains a deactivated place. Not yet a name in the industry, Wong is already borrowing from himself. The reenactment of the phone-booth scene remixes the same ingredients. But the context is richer and the resolution starkly different in (musical) tone. The leads have multiplied in *Days of Being Wild*. We can count as many as six, if one includes Yuddy's foster mother, Rebecca, and his pal Zeb (himself hopelessly in love with Fung-ying). This web of relationships accounts for the extraordinary resonance of the musical intervention that marks Tide's seemingly final, yet, as it will turn out, only temporary, withdrawal from the film. His exit takes the form of a characteristically ambiguous ensemble of shots (figs. 1.2–1.4). Their status as a montage sequence emerges only gradually.[2] We begin with a conversation between Tide and Li-zhen in which she is only seen from behind, frame left. As she walks past him, there is a cut to a close-up of Tide looking at her as she moves up the slope. Cut to a long shot of the street flanked by colonial-era walls and graced, in typical Hong Kong fashion, by protruding tropical foliage.[3] In keeping with continuity editing, this is ostensibly a point-of-view shot. But Li-zhen is nowhere to be seen. What we get instead is an image of her absence.

The nocturnal, atmospheric shot is infused with the melancholy of an aborted encounter. Just as we begin to contemplate the empty slope, the appearance of Xavier Cugat's 1959 orchestral version of "Perfidia"

1.2–1.4 Aborted romance in *Days of Being Wild*.

1.5 Frame of Tide's voice-over from *Days of Being Wild*.

suggests an even more radical dislocation. The sync point marks a threshold. An image that at first blush seemed to bring the episode to an end turns out to be the beginning of an extended coda. As if cued by the music, Tide begins to talk in voice-over. The action zooms off into the future. Tide's tone is summative, retrospective, and self-deprecating (fig. 1.5). Over images of him waiting under the cone of light emitted by the lone streetlamp, he tells us that, for some time, every time he passed that telephone booth at night he'd just hang on a bit (in case Li-zhen called). In fact, Tide adds, he never seriously hoped that she would take his invitation to call. As so often in Wong's films, the voice-over mono-logue is less the unfiltered record of a character's stream of conscious-ness than a somewhat contrived attempt to own the narrative in order to rationalize the pain of loss, defeat, or, as in this case, unrequited love. Having waited in vain one last time, Tide signs off his duty card, walks up the street, and disappears into its unlit zone. In yet another change of narrative mode, we experience this last image of Tide as the represen-tation of a singular moment, itself the product of a final, irreversible act: his mother has passed away, and he has decided to leave Hong Kong to become a sailor.

Standing on the shoulders of this lengthy and emotionally charged portion of the narrative, the bolero rhythm, delicate downward arpeg-giations, sighing figures of the strings, and, above all, period sensibility of "Perfidia" infuse the episode with the requisite amount of tenderness and longing. But the music also helps propel the narrative swiftly forward and endows Tide's reflections with a resonance that transcends the contingencies of his own predicament. In Cugat's arrangement, the slow-moving tune is carried by the trombone and cuts across the dotted, walking inner part and the brisk accompanying flourishes at the strings. Soaring gradually from the texture, the expansive melody sets the tempo of the sequence and insinuates itself into Andy Lau's voice-over. It is Tide's plaintive, remorseful—and unambiguous—words that set the tone, however. For its part, and simply by virtue of its appearance, the music reassures us that the episode is turning to a close. It has earned this function irrespective of the song's text, pertinent as it may be ("And now, I know my love was not for you / And so I'll take it back with a sigh / Perfidia's one goodbye"). It isn't just that we only hear an instrumental rendition. Timing and the stylistic features of the track suffice to call up instances of similarly scored codas. Wong Kar-wai is exploiting what we might call the metrical value of this juncture of the film, underpinned by the need for closure. The result is a narrative cadence that the music helps herald without, ironically, cadencing itself. To the contrary, "Perfidia" comes to an unceremonious end in midphrase as the action moves to another place and another time, namely, the scene in which Yuddy also decides to leave Hong Kong. As if mirroring Tide's own trajectory, Yuddy, too, will take to the sea to search for his biological mother in the Philippines.

Almost exactly halfway through the film, this is the hinge of the whole narrative. The episode opens up a space where, albeit momentarily, Tide is the protagonist. But the scene also implicates us as omniscient observers of a complex thread of relationships. What begins as a transitional, if skillfully assembled, ensemble of shots of primarily syntactical import then morphs, thanks to the lyrical character and paradigmatic function of the music, into a poetic utterance about the knot that, unbeknownst to them, ties together the lives of as many as six characters. If I were to pick my own candidate for "the world's first Wong Kar-wai moment," this episode of *Days of Being Wild* would unquestionably be my choice. For it encapsulates several recurring, indeed defining characteristics of Wong's oeuvre: his subtle brand of lyricism, the episodic form, and the use of parallel yet subterraneously converging plotlines. The episode is also symptomatic of a fourth and just as crucial aspect of Wong's cinema: the unabashed derivativeness of his films. Wong uses a recognizable iconography of urban loneliness traceable to Edward Hopper and the various articulations of his style in popular culture East and West; a famous recording, itself a cover of a well-known song; and ultrafamiliar faces, Andy Lau and Leslie Cheung already being stars at the time of the film's release. The midpoint of *Days of Being Wild* is grafted on the climax of *As Tears Go By*. The latter film is, in turn, a remake of sorts of Martin Scorsese's *Mean Streets* (1973), while *Days of Being Wild* itself gestures toward *Rebel without a Cause* (1954). In staging Tide and Li-zhen's missed encounter the way he did, Wong is also recycling himself implicitly or, better, backhandedly placing himself in this illustrious genealogy.

While Wong's curiosity, omnivorous taste, and proneness to incorporate borrowings into his own work have duly been noted, the implications of this tendency for both film theory and musical aesthetics remain unexplored. When so much emphasis is placed on the distinctiveness of his cinema, it should perhaps come as no surprise that the extent to which Wong borrows, recycles, and repurposes preexisting materials remains poorly examined or, worse, is brushed aside. Yet the challenge is not to choose between extolling the strong stylistic signature of his cinema and demystifying its allure because of its reliance on precedents (literary, musical, or cinematic as they may be). The challenge, rather, is to rethink Wong's creative process as being channeled by a distinctly bricolage-y manner and devise a language that does justice to the resources that enable him to manipulate preexisting materials in such a way as to morph them into something novel. To do this, as we shall see, entails nothing less than a new theory of borrowing.

WHY CUGAT?

Let me return to the music that underscores the missed rendezvous between Li-zhen and Tide, and the latter's decision to leave Hong Kong. "Perfidia" landed on Wong's metaphorical working desk with a long and varied history of its own. Composed by Mexican composer Alberto Domínguez and released in 1939, the song enjoyed a string of successful adaptations in English, with a text by Milton Leeds, recorded by the likes of Nat King Cole and Abbe Lane. There were instrumental renditions aplenty, too, including perhaps most famously two recordings by Lane's husband, famed Spanish composer and arranger Xavier Cugat (in 1940 and 1959, respectively). To account for why Wong picked the song, one need not go any further than the text. In terms now dreamy, now despondent, "Perfidia" tells of a love found and immediately lost: a nearly perfect parallel of Tide's predicament. An instrumental version will evoke the text to those already familiar with it. We may term this the referential function of the borrowing. But there is more to it than being a conduit for a text. Buttressed by the setting and the dramatic situation, "Perfidia" is sufficiently topical to evoke a time, milieu, and state of mind to most if not all spectators, regardless of any prior acquaintance with it. It does this the way music knows best: as expressive sound patterns and colors. Given the dominant role of Tide's voice-over, Wong uses Cugat's instrumental cover as underscoring to a reenactment of the situation sketched in the original song, the words spoken in the voice-over having replaced the sung text of the original.

Not every instrumental adaptation would have been fit for the purpose, however. The Dave Brubeck Quintet's version is too jazzy; Glenn Miller's, too brassy; Los Panchos', too folksy, too reminiscent of its composer's milieu to blend in a melodrama set in Hong Kong at the onset of the 1960s. The version by Xavier Cugat's Orchestra combines urban sophistication and nostalgia without sacrificing the original's Latin American roots. While undoubtedly captivating, this recording must have also held a special appeal in that its release date (1959) and subsequent circulation coincides with the period in which the film is set (1960 to 1961). Also, at the time, this recording must have been an element of the Hong Kong soundscape, thanks to not only its circulation and renown but also the arrangements thereof played by the bands of Filipino musicians who entertained the clienteles of the city's clubs, restaurants, and hotels. "Perfidia" is therefore a symptom of a conscious effort to reconstruct a given milieu or at least ground a personal mythology of Hong Kong in one's memories, oral history, and historical research. Like the so-called Latin tunes of In the Mood for Love (2000), for which it provides a template, in Days of Being Wild "Perfidia" is both a historical marker and an element of local color.

LOCAL COLOR AND THE NOSTALGIA FILM

The use of music as an element of local color or historical marker is long and varied. Think of the "Turkish" music in Mozart's work, chinoiserie in various nineteenth- and twentieth-century operas, or the Spanish references that pepper and not infrequently provide the main inspiration for

French Impressionist music. Cinema inherited from the theater, opera, and program music a tradition of telescoping a locale or historical period via a musical cliché.[4] Whether grounded in historically and ethnographically rigorous research, adapted or invented, these musical topoi help establish a setting, often to the point of (un)witting parody. All one asks of them is that they dispatch a picture or idea of a time and a place. Their effectiveness does not tap into one's personal acquaintance or depend on the activation of personal memories. They are at best a simplified version of the real thing, and once accepted as common currency, they perpetuate themselves.

Whether in a symphony, play, or opera, the use of historical and geographical clichés is sustained by a mutually reinforcing dichotomy between the locally "marked" and "unmarked" music that contains it.[5] Having "cleared" for the filmgoing public a watered-down version of the Western classical repertoire, in particular late Romantic and early Modernist, and having adopted it as its preferred style of dramatic scoring, commercial cinema has perpetuated and even exacerbated the dichotomy between the marked (that is, local) and the unmarked (the film score as a technical device on a par with other elements of film technique). Filmmakers have had at their disposal a vast, and growing, archive of all the music of the world, enabling them to pit a conventional score against unadulterated recordings of, say, Japanese ritual music or garage rock. While the musical language of film scores has grown and diversified to an extent unimaginable even only a generation ago, their range pales against the sheer vastness of the world's musical archive. No matter how little known or esoteric, almost any kind of music is nowadays accessible to a filmmaker willing to retrieve and deploy it to reconstruct a locale or milieu.

In Alfred Hitchcock's *The Man Who Knew Too Much* (1955), the evening call to prayer marks the beginning of a most difficult night for the McKenna family at their hotel in the Marrakesh city center. The sight of minarets signals that we understand the call as completing the location. The sound stands in stark opposition to Bernard Herrmann's orchestral score. This further strengthens its identity as an element of the local setting. Herrmann's music, for its part, does bear the signs of a personal manner, albeit one that comfortably falls within the parameters of Hollywood-style dramatic scoring. As such, it also provides a sufficiently robust foil to the musical centerpiece of the film, Arthur Benjamin's *Storm Clouds Cantata* performed at the Royal Albert Hall (and conducted, in a cameo that is as egregious as it remains unexamined, by Herrmann himself). The cantata is deeply woven into the fabric of the plot yet it, too, is an element of local color. Buffered once again by a strong sense of place, it projects a recognizable icon of Englishness in the form of a middle-brow symphonic work that straddles the line between modern and traditional.[6]

Typically, local color is shorthand for a musical repertoire or performance style originating from and practiced in a given country or region. But a filmmaker may choose to depict a locale by way of what people dance or listen to, even when the music comes from such far-flung incubators of regional or global hits as the British or US music industries. We grasp the flavor of a locale via the characters' own musical preferences or proclivities but also the dominance of (mostly) Anglo-American pop at the expense of local traditions. In Akira Kurosawa's *High and Low* (1963), for example, the youths in the bars of Yokohama drink, cavort, and drug themselves to a soundtrack of American rhythm and blues and jazz. The presence of US servicemen notwithstanding, the music undoubtedly adds to the meticulous attempt to capture a unique, and uniquely local, setting and its predominantly young and bohemian demographic. Michael Cimino's *Heaven's Gate* (1980) features a compelling variant of this scenario. The setting is New York's Chinatown. Gang leader Joey Tai and an associate are seen entering a characteristic Lower East Side tenement via a steel bridge that connects it to a sweatshop across a narrow street. As Tai walks down the long and narrow corridor leading to the back of the building, we hear rock music. The music continues over the cut to a shot of an apartment where a group of young gang members smoke, chat, and play cards. The music is playing on TV, as it turns out, one member tilting his head in sync with the basic pulse. The choice of repertoire signals these young men's ambivalent relationship to both their country of adoption, which still views them as Chinese, and their own ethnic roots. Broadcast across the ether, the track symbolizes not only a facile yet alluring cosmopolitanism but also a space alternative to the squalid hideout in which they find themselves captive as reluctant criminals.

In *Days of Being Wild*, too, the music qualifies the taste and aspirations of the young protagonists. But it is Federico Fellini's *Amarcord* (1973), and the various articulations of the nostalgia film, that we must turn to if we are to appreciate Wong's adroit revival of musical oldies. The characters in *Amarcord* walk to, dance to, and hum along with the notes of what to them are current hits but in the place of origin—the United States, in this case—evoke the yesteryear already. The film is set in the late 1930s in Rimini, a provincial coastal city of Italy. Only a few films were distributed there, and after a long delay at that, due to the combined effect of a slow distribution network and fascist censorship. The center/periphery dynamic is as crucial to *Amarcord* as it is to *Days of Being Wild*. Like Wong, Fellini was at once repelled and fascinated by the melancholy and oppressiveness of a provincial setting. Instead of using recordings of the original songs, he had Nino Rota adapt and, in some cases, rewrite them. In keeping with the film's explicit intent—*amarcord* means "I remember" in the Rimini dialect—Rota conjures a brilliant representation of remembered music: the tunes of the day as refracted by not only the characters' own delusions but also the intervening decades of reminiscing, suffering, and, eventually, forgetting the fascist era. Be it a change of emphasis, faulty memory, or creative misremembering, the music sounds different from any objective manifestation one may want to claim for it.[7] And it channels Fellini's intention to anchor the film in the filmmaking present of the 1970s. In one brilliant, self-reflexive stroke, *Amarcord* relegates the use of period music to the dustbin of both cinematic and musical history.[8]

For all its stylistic flair, Wong's film is less radical, and with good reason. Despite its seeming simplicity and pellucid textures, Rota's rewriting of well-known oldies requires the kind of consummate mastery in short supply in the Hong Kong film industry.[9] Wong, moreover, conceived his own re-creation in the wake of such powerful models as George Lucas's *American Graffiti* (1973) and Scorsese's *Mean Streets*, as well as the numerous spin-offs thereof, all of which made extensive use of original recordings. Historical recordings add to the seemingly documentarian quality of his period reconstruction (an impulse that reaches the breaking point in *In the Mood for Love*). Yet dramaturgically the music they carry treads a fine line between historical accuracy and nostalgic idealization. Without fully embracing a realist aesthetic, and taking a page from Fellini and Rota, Wong does not employ "Perfidia" as source music. No character is ever seen playing it, listening to it, or dancing to it. Unmoored from a realistic justification in the setting and the comings and goings of the characters, the music loses its most immediate raison d'être to earn another, that of encapsulating a shared experience or sensibility: an imagined zeitgeist. It's as if the entire world captured onscreen were resonating with Cugat's arrangement, above and beyond its historical, concrete—and contingent—instantiations.

THE SAMPLE AS ICON

The ability of music to call up a locale, memory, or cluster of associations has been the subject of countless arguments and speculations as well as literary re-creations. Hip-hop scholar Amanda Sewell has come closest to capturing the underlying mechanism with respect to recordings.[10] On describing the use of borrowed lyrics in hip-hop, Sewell draws a startling yet compelling analogy between sampling and religious icons in that they both *embody* the original. Embodiment differs from reference, allusion, and even representation as the relation between sample and source is one of equivalence. Like an icon, writes Sewell, the sampled passage maintains a connection with the original "as a translation does with the original text."[11] Sewell's analogy warrants elaboration. Like a translation, a sample does not conceal its mediated status relative to the original. Where in the former the original is mediated by a different language, in hip-hop the sample is re-contextualized, often in truncated form, in a new sound structure. By virtue of being framed by a new composition, the sample signals a migration, a movement away from an ancestral home toward a new host body. The skillful rapper or producer, moreover, may manipulate a fragment in such a way as to lend it, to use religious imagery, the patina of a relic bearing the stigmata of the original track.

While they can set an image, text, or sound into motion, neither the icon maker nor the translator enjoys artistic license. This is ironic considering modern copyright law, according to which a license is needed only when the borrowed material remains unchanged (when the reproduction is transformative, no license is needed). As any translator or icon maker, for that matter, will attest, it sometimes takes a great effort not to betray the original—let alone approximate the mechanical precision afforded by reproductive technologies. When it comes to sampling, mechanical and now digital reproduction—pace Walter Benjamin—is the guarantee of genuineness. A freshly made recording or cover of the original track is a poor second to a sample.[12] In hip-hop, moreover, the original is a recording hence, to adapt Nelson Goodman's terminology, allographic.[13] As such it exists in multiple, physically identical copies, each of which is an equally authentic vessel of a representative instance of a track. Running the analogy backward, we can think of icons as proto-allographic or indeed samples of divine imagery, a suggestion that comes full circle in Andy Warhol's iconic silkscreen paintings of everyday images of commercial products and most pointedly in his *Brillo Box* sculptures.[14] Embodiments of this sort operate within a presentational but also participatory aesthetics. Whether in the theater or the cinema, we know what a radio broadcast of *Für Elise* stands for—itself. No suspension of disbelief is needed. In the byzantine tradition, the abeyance to a certain iconography and the method of depiction are neither a matter of dogma nor mimesis for their own sakes; they are a function of their impact on the viewer. The icon of Jesus *is* the Christ and as such it channels the required behavior on the part of the beholder. By the same token, to follow Sewell, sampling in popular music is more than a question of textual or acoustical identity. The presentation of the source recording appeals to the listeners' ability to hear it as an unmediated fragment of their past.[15] When excerpts are sampled, it is in the expectation that listeners will not merely recognize but, in doing so, also animate them on account of their intimacy with them.

Sewell appears to have arrived at religious icons via a curious but, as it turns out, productive bricolage of her own, namely the appropriation of Frank Zappa's use of the term *icon* in his autobiography. In a compelling aside, the late rock maverick describes the coded body language he developed to tell members of the band when to switch arrangement style from, say, "*Jaws* texture" to "Jan Garber-ism."[16] Zappa calls these stock modules "Archetypal American Musical Icons" and notes that they put "a different spin on any lyric in their vicinity."[17] However, what Zappa refers to here is best rendered by analogy not to samples in hip-hop— let alone icons in religious imagery—but rather to specific works or styles retooled as musical topoi or, more to the point, parody. Moreover, as Zappa explains, "Those modules 'suggest' that you interpret those lyrics within parenthesis."[18] The musical parody, in other words, suggests the appropriate disposition toward the lyrics. It is the counterpart to mood music in film.

If I trace the roundabout way the term *icon* entered the language of hip-hop criticism, this is not only to acknowledge the invariably self-reflexive nature of any scholarly investigation of borrowing; it is also to draw attention to the slippages occasioned by linguistic exchanges from across disciplines. To clarify, then, icons subsume the individual work, image, or motif under a prescribed iconography, which the materiality of the object helps spread across time and space. A sample preserves the vestiges of the original via the acoustical (quasi) identity granted by mechanical and now digital reproduction. Besides preserving the vestiges of the original, a sample encapsulates a moment in the history of the listening subject. But a musician may want to use it simply as a reference or allusion to a specific recording or even as the topical expression of a broadly recognizable style or generic formula. It goes without saying that, absent a personal connection or familiarity with the sampled recording on the part of the listener, this is how a sample will be heard.

These may seem like fast and hard distinctions. But they ought to be difficult to overlook if, as Sewell and several other scholars make clear, hip-hop artists sample lyrics for their artist- and work-specific, rather than general, topical affordances. To be sure, recognizing a sample and giving free play to the resulting associations serve the aesthetic goals of the DJ/producer: historical memory, projecting a sense of lineage, peer-to-peer homage, and so forth.[19] Theorizing samples as recognizable and hence singular expressions of a complex web of references places hip-hop scholarship in interesting company within not only musicology but also literary studies. One thinks of Ives or Stravinsky but also Joyce, Dante, and even biblical studies. Common to all these distinguished branches of scholarly endeavor is a tradition of glossing bent on excavating and reinforcing the accepted and indeed canonical understanding of borrowed material as having sprung forth from a singular author. Glossing counters the lack or inevitable decay of the implicit knowledge that underpins the strategic use of citations and studied references on the part of creators. What glossing does miss, however, is that borrowing also invites that which our recuperative scholarly efforts seek to make up for: lack of familiarity with a tradition, indifference, and the work of forgetting, all of which result in transformative processes we remain ill-equipped to describe. It is not just inexorable historical processes and the attendant disappearance of an interpretive community that need to be addressed. Profound transformations also occur in the here and now of the sampling work itself. Hip-hop is a case in point. While sampled lyrics are indeed hard to overlook, there are countless, unsignaled samples of instrumental excerpts that, whether ably camouflaged or flaunted in the texture, remain blissfully unrecognized.[20] They are too short or obscure for their prior identity to emerge, or they are utterly defamiliarized because of the new material that surrounds them. While musicians may not have the willingness or license to modify the outward appearance of what they borrow, their retooling often amounts to a kind of erasure anyway.

To be sure, films sample recordings in the attempt to revive a fragment of a lost sonic past.[21] But for whom does the proverbial bell toll, beyond the filmmaker? Reference depends on knowledge of the borrowed material. Topoi rely on the audience's familiarity with a musical style and a modicum of proficiency in narrative filmmaking. The re-creation of the Hong Kong soundscape of Wong's childhood is contingent on the partaking of his personal history. One can discover and learn to appreciate the appearance of a song as integral to the director's faithful— and heartfelt—reconstruction. This is the kind of interpretive path that Roland Barthes, with reference to photography, calls the *studium*. Conversely, the singular or, to paraphrase Barthes, *punctual* association of a song to Hong Kong, circa 1960, will only be accessible to those who've experienced it in the first person.

ASSIMILATING MUSIC

To signal a shared state of mind or sensibility is part and parcel of the reconstruction of a setting. This is most clearly, indeed demonstratively, shown when the music crosses the diegetic/nondiegetic divide. In *The Big Chill*, the Rolling Stones' "You Can't Always Get What You Want" plays a dual role in the opening funeral sequence. As Karen Bowen (JoBeth Williams) walks toward the organ to play, the pastor simply introduces the music as "one of Alex's favorite songs." The arrangement is confounding enough to leave the audience—both the fictional and the real one—at least initially unsure of what is being played. As the identity of the piece becomes clear to the knowing few, the music segues into the actual recording, used nondiegetically (at which point it begs to be recognized). The music ceases to be a singular, contingent event to take on a more diffuse presence. The shift coincides with the action moving outside the church and heralds a different, faster, and more compressed style of narration. Old friends, relatives, and new faces greet each other and exchange a few words. A motorcade is seen moving toward a cemetery. Alex is buried. Temporarily pushed aside by the odd sound effect or snippet of conversation, the song retreats to the background of the mix without losing its role as the chorus and structuring principle of the episode. In *Days of Being Wild*, the appearance of "Perfidia," too, coincides with a change in narrative speed (the montage sequence at the sound of Tide's voice-over). The coincidence is significant because it suggests that the collective, epic character of the music is not simply the result of the polished, enveloping quality of its sonic presentation. The velocity of the narration endows the track with a kind of temporal capaciousness: the aural equivalent of a summative glance at a large chunk of narrative.

In *The Big Chill*, "You Can't Always Get What You Want" has the additional role of "cordoning off" the protagonists from those outside their tight-knit group. The song folds a subset of characters within the larger community depicted onscreen. This is not a matter of familiarity per se but rather what the song means and to whom. Its continuing over the aftermath of the service all the way to the burial makes manifest Alex's presence but also the reemerging bond between his old friends. The music makes the past palpable. It is suggestive of a pool of memories, the precise tenor of which is for the time being only known to the fictional characters. As David Shumway notes, "The song . . . serves sonically to bind the members of the group together and to encourage our identification with them through the repetition of a record with which we (the baby-boomer audience for which the film was made) are likely to have already identified."[22] This cordoning off extends to a slice of the audience as well. In one respect at least, preexisting music draws a wedge between those "in the know" and everybody else. This need not break down by age or background (as suggested by the quote above). Lawrence Kasdan's film did in fact have cross-generational appeal—as did *Days of Being Wild*. What matters is that, absent familiarity with it, a soundtrack will function only as a topical, rather than specific, reference to a place or time period (if at all). To those for whom "Perfidia" is an oldie with a special appeal, the sampled track will summon not merely images of a certain style or period but also a flash of recognition and a slew of personal memories.[23] To describe the latter effect, Anahid Kassabian coined the expression *affiliating identification*.[24] She reserves the term *assimilating identification* for the opposite effect, namely the cueing of a large audience into a "single subject position" through the composed film score. The latter plays this role because it is accessible to everyone in the same way. Affiliation creates unity in diversity, so to speak. For while we may all recognize the same piece of music, or share the same memory of the event, place, or historical period it evokes, our encounter with it will ultimately be unique. The music will color the film in a highly individualized manner, bringing into play a "web of memory, emotion and identification" unique to each spectator and allowing for "mobile and multiple identifications."[25]

Though Kassabian does not explore this possibility, the mechanism continues for as long as both the film and its soundtrack retain a place in the culture (that is, at least in theory, indefinitely). Any new meanings and associations the music acquires in its "post-filmic life" are fed back into the film itself.[26] The vagaries of reception increase the semiotic instability inherent in borrowed materials above and beyond the idiosyncrasy of each spectator's pool of memories. Think, to give two examples, of the reversal of fortune of a given song or the revival of a performing artist under a new interpretive frame. If a film marks a key point in the reception history of a song, the latter's continuing life above and beyond its filmic use makes a host film susceptible to changes in turn. As the music invites new ways of listening, the reception of the film where it is embedded is also altered.[27] However successful and far-reaching Wong's appropriation of "Perfidia" may have been, it is far from having put an end to the song's ulterior appropriations and peregrinations into new mediascapes. The attention lavished on it by performers and audiences will continue to resonate in Wong's film, too.

What kinds of entities are subsumed under the generic umbrella term *preexisting music*? Does "preexisting" refer to a work, repertoire, or a whole tradition? Should one think of performers or specific recordings as pertinent examples? The mere presence onscreen of a performer like Lata Mangeshkar will provoke a strong reaction in the cued-up audience (no matter what she sings). A rendering of a symphony or sonata may elicit a self-satisfied nod on the part of the knowing spectator (even more so when the piece happens to be unknown or esoteric). Given the right audience, the mere suggestion that the music partakes of a tradition—say, songs of liberation, or orthodox church music—will elicit recognition on the part of those familiar with the idiom (irrespective of its level of generality). Conversely, the cover of a rock 'n' roll classic, no matter how close it may sound to the original, may fail to excite the spectator in the same fashion (rock, pop, and hip-hop are more deeply identified with specific recordings than other repertoires).[28] Granted, these scenarios do not so much challenge as expand the reach of Kassabian's distinction. But while her either/or proposition has considerable heuristic value, it inevitably also simplifies what is a more shaded field of possibilities. A well-known, preexisting song or orchestral work—think of "The Ride of the Valkyries" or "The Blue Danube," as used by Griffith, Coppola, or Kubrick—may be so iconic that its deployment in a film follows a well-established path of shared significations that is comprehensible to many filmgoers. The cue sheets adopted in many exhibition spaces during the so-called silent era featured well-known excerpts from the symphonic and operatic repertoire. Their assiduous deployment as film scores paved the way for their transformation into a kind of cine-musical vernacular that emptied them of specificity as singular musical works and paved the way for original scores that aped their familiar gestures without quite plagiarizing them. Certain kinds of preexisting music, put another way, are used so often that they are hollowed out of what makes them unique (or as such uniquely equipped to affect the viewer in an affiliating, to cite Kassabian, fashion). Conversely, a composed score may feature details of texture, instrumentation, or performance style such that it engenders highly personal responses.

But there is a more fundamental reason why the dichotomy between affiliating and assimilating fails to capture what is unique about Wong's treatment of "Perfidia." Affiliation rests on what we might call an orthodox, canonical, *deferential* understanding of the music that has been borrowed. The affiliating/assimilating model does not account for the cases in which the film-as-temporary-host transforms, defamiliarizes, or mystifies the source material, thereby liberating preexisting music as an expressive act—above and beyond identification—even or, better yet, especially for those spectators for whom it is utterly familiar and hence personal.

To understand how this process unfolds in *Days of Being Wild*, let me compare "Perfidia" to another period track used in the same film, "Maria Elena." The latter is heard near the beginning of a scene in which Yuddy, following a night tryst, lazily rises from bed, plays a recording on his turntable, and starts dancing to it.[29] Like "Perfidia," "Maria Elena" was a club favorite, and it is played here in a Cugat arrangement for big band. The episode sets us up for the later appearance of "Perfidia," whose "sound" we will recognize as being of a given time and place. There are important differences as well. Yuddy's behavior explicitly folds "Maria Elena" within a specific place, moment of the narrative, and set of circumstances. The scene also stresses the status of the recording as a physical artifact. Should "Maria Elena" earn new functions and shades of meaning in subsequent iterations as either source music or in the form of a film score, it would do so without shedding its identity as an element of the Hong Kong soundscape of that era. Its topical qualities—the late 1950s setting, club culture, eroticism, the cult of North American imports, the Latin vibe—are, as it were, sealed in this first appearance. Because "Perfidia" is never plotted into the film the way "Maria Elena" is, we are not keyed into its status as a broadly recognizable hit to the same extent that its counterpart is. To be sure, a modicum of cine-musical competence and the stylistic similarity with "Maria Elena" will signal "Perfidia" as an artifact of the late 1950s and early 1960s. Its inclusion in the soundtrack follows from Wong's attempt to revive a certain sensibility and to show that it pervaded a whole milieu in something like the way, in *American Graffiti*, the music heard via the radio filled the ether in its respective time and place. Yet the similarity stops there, for in revisiting a well-oiled convention Wong also transforms it. First, as I've mentioned, the music skips the obligatory passage in which it is heard or played by a character. The fact that "Perfidia" appears nondiegetically to begin with loosens its ties to the spatiotemporal coordinates of the story, thereby liberating a range of syntactical functions and semantic shadings that would not be so readily available otherwise. The timing of the editing, moreover, gives it the appearance of a tailor-made film score. This is most apparent when the music begins. The calculated sync point between the opening, cascading motifs of the strings and the shot of the empty street without Li-zhen has the distinct flavor of a composed score. Its placement as the musical coda to a significant juncture of the story, moreover, draws "Perfidia" close to the private concerns and entanglements of the main characters. By splicing Cugat's arrangement with Tide's nocturnal ruminations, Wong teases out new qualities and channels them in the service of a lyrical, and strikingly original, meditation on the emotional tangle that holds back Li-zhen. The only hint that the soundtrack is an appropriated recording adapted to a fixed sequence of shots is the abruptness with which it ends.

BEING *CASABLANCA*

Revisiting the long and eventful history that "Perfidia" has enjoyed since its original release in 1939—as many as two hundred and fifty versions, as I write this—deepens one's appreciation of Wong's retooling. The mercurial nature of the song itself has undoubtedly facilitated the process. Despite enjoying greater renown and circulation than "Maria Elena," and being therefore easier to recognize and as such to assign to a specific time and place, "Perfidia" has a more fluid identity than the benefit of hindsight may lead us to believe.[30] Consider the following highlights. After its first 1939 dual release as both an instrumental and vocal track, "Perfidia" was a *Billboard* hit at number 3 in 1940 with Xavier Cugat's first big-band version.[31] It rose again to number 18 in *Billboard* in 1960 with another instrumental version by the rock band the Ventures. The song also enjoyed attention from such jazz luminaries as Benny Goodman, Glenn Miller, and Charlie Parker—to name a few among those who recorded it—and the privilege of a Nat King Cole cover (as well as, more recently, the dubious honor of an Andrea Bocelli recording). Twenty years after the first, Cugat arranged and recorded another famed instrumental version in the early 1960s, released both as part of an LP and in 45 RPM format as well (with "Maria Elena" as a B-side).[32] This version circulated in Hong Kong at the time *Days of Being Wild* is set and is the one used by Wong Kar-wai.

The song's greatest claim to fame, at least until Wong tore through its reception history, lies with cinema. Hot on the wings of the great success of Cugat's 1940 recording, not one but as many as two films attempted in short order to bank on the fact that "Perfidia" was, as the phrase goes, in the air. First, in Jack Hively's *Father Takes a Wife* (1941), starring Gloria Swanson, the song is sung in Spanish; second is what is arguably the song's finest hour, Michael Curtiz's *Casablanca* (1942). In *Father Takes a Wife*, "Perfidia" is the centerpiece of an impromptu performance by opera singer Carlos Valdés (Desi Arnaz, who performed the song routinely as a nightclub number). We are on the deck of a cruise ship where Leslie (Gloria Swanson) and Frederick Sr. (Adolphe Menjou) are spending their honeymoon. Leslie is playing a record of what appears to be the instrumental version of the song. On hearing this, Carlos cannot help but add a vocal line of clear operatic inspiration and as such stylistically unlike the Cugat arrangement that had made the song famous (the words are sung in Spanish). The scene plays on the lingering notoriety of "Perfidia" and association with Mexico but also its dual nature as both vocal and instrumental tracks. Carlos's performance also doubles as an act of seduction with dire consequences for all and as such marks a pivotal moment of the story. The appearance of "Perfidia" in *Casablanca* is in dramaturgical terms a lot less significant, for we hear it as mere incidental music in the famous flashback sequence (the segment in which

Rick and Ilsa dance in a Paris nightclub, to be exact). Yet the emotional impact of the sequence and enormous reputation of the film have cemented its association with nightclub culture, unfulfilled romance, and personal sacrifice at a time of war in the minds of tens of millions.

That Wong thought nothing of deploying "Perfidia" despite such distinguished musical and cinematic history gives us a sense of the scale of his ambition and the brazenness, and perhaps also recklessness, of the gesture. Diligently gathering as much information as possible about "Perfidia" and its background may lead us to form a clearer picture of its genesis, role in the culture at large, and place in the popular canon. And it would sanction in no uncertain terms Cugat's own egregious appropriation.[33] Yet it will not provide us with the key to unlock what makes the music "tick" in the context of Wong's staging of Tide and Li-zhen's aborted romance. Unlike Quentin Tarantino, who uses oldies and film soundtracks to weave a rich canvas of self-conscious cross-references, Wong is not citing or appealing to knowing cinephiles. Rather, he is turning a cliché into an eminently quotable moment that bears the marks of an immediately recognizable style—his own.

In this respect, *Casablanca* is an important precedent. The prototype of the cult film, *Casablanca* plundered from popular culture and was the result of indiscriminate, uncoordinated improvisation. As Umberto Eco persuasively argued, some of its most striking features—think of Ingrid Bergman's acting, for example—are the product of her actual uncertainty about the role (rather than a scripted effect).[34] The mutual implication between the profilmic and the diegetic on the one hand and the vagaries of production and the shape the finished film would take on the other brings to mind *Happy Together* (1997) (whose very shape, including the soundtrack, was in a sense dictated by the shooting schedule and flight itinerary of the crew).[35] Expediency also accounts for the vicissitudes, and blatant inconsistencies, of Wong's 1960s trilogy as a whole, of which *Days of Being Wild* is the first installment. The latter's famous ending exemplifies this. During a long, unedited shot, to the sound of "Jungle Drums," we see a fashion-conscious gambler (Tony Leung), cigarette in hand, readying himself for a night of drinking, gambling, and socializing. The music, once again, is arranged for an orchestra by Xavier Cugat (and can be found on the same 33 1/3 RPM recording that also features "Maria Elena" and "Perfidia"). The camera meticulously follows the various stages of Leung's preparations, down to the precise height at which the immaculately white pocket square should be placed. Conceived with a sequel in mind, the episode makes little sense in relation to what precedes it. Because a proper sequel never materialized, it has since stood in splendid isolation as a matrix of narrative possibilities, none of them fulfilled and more appealing for it.

LIKE A PROVERB

A latter-day urban bricoleur, the gambler fashions himself after images of the leading men of the day. Like Taipei in the 1960s and in something like the way the fictional Rimini of Fellini's films did, Hong Kong partook of global fashions at one remove from the radiating centers of everything that was then appealing and fashionable—Japan, the United Kingdom, and, of course, the United States.[36] In the course of the journey across space and time that took them from their place of origin to Hong Kong, the images and sounds that form the bedrock of the gambler's self-presentation have been hollowed out of their specificity.[37] Analytically, he is a bundle of clichés. His outfit is derivative, the accessories old-fashioned, the overall look disingenuous and not a little aspirational, not to say, for a small-time crook, borderline delusional. Yet the resulting bricolage defies mimicry; to the contrary, it has the force of a definitive performance. Wong goes one better by casting Tony Leung and in one stroke erasing the memory of his past roles while at the same time exploiting his recognizability as a well-known matinee idol. Just as Leung makes an off-the-rack khaki suit seem the ideal vehicle for his figure, so he wears the music Wong splices onto him as an essential element of his apparel. The hypnotic rhythm, recursive motif, and swelling textures of "Jungle Drums" infuse the protracted preparations with a sense of anticipation. The transmutation of musical sounds into elements of an iconography, and the coalescing of the latter back into the former, seals the music to the gambler and with it the film. Far from merely receiving it as a ready-made, self-contained bundle of associations that only needs unwrapping, the film dictates new conditions of reception that dent the received identity of the borrowing. "Jungle Drums" is marked by *Days of Being Wild* the way proverbs, in Michel de Certeau's words, are "marked by uses."[38]

This is the case for "Perfidia," too. Rather like quotation marks, the emphatic sync point between the beginning of the track and the image of the empty street alerts us to the appearance of the song. In quotation, in the phrase of philosopher François Recanati, "the quoted material is displayed or presented . . . , the medium itself is brought to the forefront of the attention: the words are displayed, exhibited."[39] "Perfidia," to cite another philosopher, is "served up for special display."[40] It "sticks out" from its immediate context, to quote David Metzer, because of the sparse use Wong makes of it during the narrative.[41] Recanati calls quotation "a form of ostension."[42] But Wong's gesture of combining a striking image with a classic tune is as *ostentatious* as it is ostensive. Wong is not citing; he is sampling. What the sync point draws attention to, it also immediately transforms. Far from merely drawing attention to the song as such, the splice heralds the brazen, virtuosic appropriation thereof. By combining them, Wong makes a bricolage of two received clichés at once: the failed rendezvous between two lovers, made famous by Antonioni's *The Eclipse* (1962) on the one hand, and "Perfidia" as an emblem of Latin-tinged club culture on the other. He effectively out-*Casablancas Casablanca*!

As we've seen, the first stage in Wong's appropriation is the relocation of "Perfidia" to Hong Kong by way of "Maria Elena." Having retooled the Latin sounds of Cugat's orchestra as an expression of the Hong Kong locale, Wong refits "Perfidia" as film soundtrack by deploying it like the cue of a conventionally styled film score. As Andy Lau's voice-over begins, it behaves like a classic example of underscoring, and as such it supports the meaning of what Tide is saying. This does not make "Perfidia" "subordinate" to the image. The image, what one sees, is itself a composite. Besides, the voice-over is arguably the dominant element. Wong's structuring does nonetheless subsume the music under the drift of the narrative. This is as it were sanctioned by the fact that the length of the cue is determined by the editing and duration of the images (not the other way around). Made common currency by Hollywood studio personnel, a "cue" describes any piece of music of any length in a soundtrack that has a beginning and an end. Whether three seconds or ten minutes long, a cue occupies a specific place in a given film. Its placement in the film is what gives it its musical and dramaturgical identity. A cue's sequence is fixed and is prescribed by the so-called cue sheet (which can function both as a schedule and a primary tool in the distribution of royalties). While the term is commonly reserved for original music (that is, music expressly written for a film), its application to preexisting music has a refreshingly concrete ring to it. *Cue* is precise, true to the technical and material conditions that underpin what one hears:

not "Perfidia" under speciously ideal conditions but rather twenty-eight seconds of this particular recording of "Perfidia" at this particular juncture of *Days of Being Wild*. To paraphrase de Certeau again, "Perfidia" is not an abstract, normative object but a tool manipulated by a user for a specific purpose.[43]

Let me pursue the analogy between Wong's use of preexisting music and de Certeau's idea of everyday bricolage a bit further. Everyday retoolings and ruses are an overdetermined, slippery, opaque object of investigation. This is due to the elusiveness and sheer complexity of the factors at play in determining their outcome, their ephemerality, and what de Certeau calls the "radical non-autonomy of the field of action."[44] Statistically insignificant except in their abstract, generalizable, and hence least identifying features, vanishing the moment they emerge, forgotten, the repurposing of everyday objects "leaves behind no products, texts, representations, only ways of using."[45] The challenge for the scholar is therefore dual: first, to give such fugitive, ephemeral acts a fixable form or weave around them a narrative so as to make them not only relatable but also analyzable; second, to write about them as tokens of a class of examples without losing trace of their status as uniquely situated, and in some respects unrepeatable, events. To convey a sense of this challenge, de Certeau compares everyday retoolings and ruses to speech acts: linguistic utterances, the meaning of which is contingent on a myriad of contextual cues and that elude transcription into recorded form.[46] It is a felicitous analogy. Speech acts rely on a large stock of preexisting materials—a common vocabulary, metaphors, turns of phrases, mannerisms—which users bend and twist to their own advantage or simply to meet the needs of a given situation. To understand a speech act is to move beyond an evaluation of the intrinsic features of the utterance; it is to reconstruct a specific, unique, and in some respects unrepeatable set of circumstances. The value of an utterance, expressed in terms borrowed from economics, is contingent on its extrinsic utility or "value" (in the parlance of moral philosophy). This is perhaps most clearly manifest in the case of failure, as when a metaphor misses its target, a joke falls flat, or a promise rings hollow. Despite being objectively inscribed into Wong's films, the musical borrowings can be similarly construed as acts. They are the *bon mots* of a witty *musiquer*, the loan tracks of a cosmopolitan artist fluent in many genres and international charts.[47] For all their long and varied existence in the mediascape, in his work they yield novel, unique, and sometimes surprising results (as does the use of metaphors, proverbs, or citations as they are deployed in ever-changing circumstances). They call for an interpretation sensitive to their unique structuring in the context of a filmic situation and consequently also their emergent, and uniquely expressive, features.

THE SOUNDTRACK AS CONSUMMATION

Thinking of a soundtrack along similar lines as everyday ruses or speech acts would seem to fly in the face of the fact that it exists as a fixed recording. The allographic nature of cinema, the fact that a film is both fixed and circulates in multiple and largely equivalent instantiations, also mitigates against such a characterization. Where the engineer or product designer is directly engaged in the creation of a prototype, film directors and their teams are responsible for crafting a final edit (as are sound engineers, producers, and, of course, musicians in the crafting of a master recording). But just as the fixed, polished, and standardized form of a piece of machinery or text should not deceive us as to the chain of sometimes unpredictable and tumultuous acts that led to it, so the fixity, polish, and multiplicity of a released film should not blind us to its status as the precipitate of uniquely situated gestures.

In the musical domain, when it is made at all, the analogy to acts is normally reserved for performance, that is, music-making in the sense of Christopher Small's "musicking."[48] It is an unfortunate consequence of Small's insistence on a strict definition of music as social process that anything having a fixed form—scores, scripts, recordings, and so forth—has been viewed as carrying not merely the stigmata of objecthood but also that of a fixed, inert entity. But, *pace* Small, a musical object is the end result of a string of actions, script for a potential act, or the material manifestation of a virtual, intentional object. Compositions, in the sense of finished works, bear witness to actions such as choices, conflicts, and compromises. So do recordings, with their production, curation, selection, and packaging into a sequence of files. Traditions are forged and kept alive or divined, thanks to the power of memory and the imagination, because of the fixed material supports—instruments, texts, recordings—that preserve and distribute their presence across time and space. Such seemingly inert entities such as scores, recordings, and sound files become themselves the springboard for subsequent actions. In short, the matrix of performing and listening may constitute

an ideal in certain quarters but fails to capture the manifold manifestations of music in our intensely mediated and object-oriented culture. It
is better, I contend, to view things and acts as in a dialectical rather than
mutually exclusive relationship.

In what ways can we conceptualize musical borrowing in the cinema
as an act? Insofar as actions entail agency, the bricolage I am describing
calls for some version of what legal scholars call purposivism. It isn't just
that bricolage involves chance encounters, happenstance, and the myriad constraints dictated by the ecosystem one moves within. It is also
that, on borrowing preexisting music, one gives the impression of relinquishing responsibility for the creation of an element of the finished
work while simultaneously assuming agency for the shape of the whole.
Authorship follows not from forging but rather from arranging a certain
assemblage of elements (like a practitioner of *ikebana*). Under this broad
understanding of intention, the chain of events that leads from the encounter with a recording to its deployment as an element of the final
mix is construable as a string of acts driven by a conscious intent. In a
granular account, such acts would include the stumbling or chancing
upon, recalling, and eventually choosing of a track; deciding when and
for how long to use it; licensing it; re-recording it; and materially synchronizing it to the image and calibrating its place in the sound mix. In a
coarse account, all the above amounts to one sustained course of action.
We can reimagine such a course of action as a spontaneous, extemporaneous series of gestures in the manner of the early Jean-Luc Godard; the
protracted, trial-and-error process of a Kubrick; the systematic scaveng-
ing of B- and C-movie soundtracks of a Tarantino; or the guerrilla-style,
cut-and-paste of a Wong Kar-wai. Irrespective, conjuring a soundtrack
from existing recordings is only observable in the here and now of its
unfolding in the production process itself. Yet this remains off limits to
all but the closest collaborators of a filmmaking team (for whom production is a means to an end, the finished film). The outcome of this continuum of actions—not the actions themselves—is publicly observable
but only as their consummation or, at most, trace.[49] Synchronization,
and with it the musical bricolage that underpins it, unveils itself to us
as a fait accompli.[50] The consummated track is transfigured into an inseparable element of the audiovisual ensemble that is the finished film.

Like the operations of ordinary citizens that de Certeau wishes to re-
deem from their status as "obscure background of social activity," filmmakers' use of preexisting music is, too, a kind of "secondary production."[51]

Because listening is functional and goal-oriented, preexisting music becomes a tool. It is tampered with. It is subjected to several "experiments" in tandem with this or that image, this line of dialogue or that sound effect. Yet by the time a film is completed, the analogy breaks down. The result presents us with a scenario that is the opposite of the instances of creative consumption examined by de Certeau. The repurposing of the music does not remain "hidden in the process of utilization."[52] To the contrary, the final, agreed-upon version of a film sees the light as a publicly accessible, indeed widely distributed representation and enters the public sphere as an object of critical scrutiny and purchasable commodity. Where the ruses examined by de Certeau "leave . . . behind no products, texts, representations, only ways of using,"[53] Wong's ruses, and the ruses of any artist working with preexisting materials, for that matter, are manifest in the form of music-image combinations in their work. It is the modus operandi of the artist-bricoleurs that remains hidden. This is not because their actions are unrecorded, but because they have jelled into the finished work. When the trial run of a musical idea has hardened into the finished film, it is difficult to imagine the creation of a soundtrack as a string of unique, transformative acts—hence my attempt throughout this chapter to reverse-engineer the production process.

APPROPRIATING BRICOLAGE

De Certeau's thesis notwithstanding, the ruses of ordinary citizens have occasionally enjoyed the privilege of retelling and memorialization in the form of representations. And what is more, these representations were crafted by those ruses' actors themselves. The Great Cat Massacre, revisited in a famous essay by Robert Darnton, is a telling example of a bricoleur-in-chief doubling as the author of his own deed's memorialization.[54] In 1730, printing-shop workers massacred scores of cats as a symbolic act of rebellion against their employers. Though Darnton stops short of using the term *bricolage*, he describes the event as an instance of skillful appropriation, a punning and ultimately symbolic exchange within a context where the workers made do with what was at hand, thereby creating new, albeit fleeting, symbolic values. Their skillful montage of objects, situations, and, as it turned out, live and subsequently dead animals was driven by their lack of access to the means—legal, social, and linguistic—to stage an official protest. Their critique could only take the form of a work of theatrical bricolage replete with a symbolism that was as gruesome and precisely targeted as it was fleeting. Unlike the direct, one-to-one representation of such sanctioned metaphors as lion = valor, the massacre could only mean what it did under specific circumstances within specific spatiotemporal coordinates. The printing-shop workers bent objects, beings, and situations to mean things they do not normally mean; the emergent meanings, like those of speech acts, were highly context-dependent.

The episode achieved notoriety and was recounted by one of the protagonists, Nicolas Contat. Contat's reconstruction is cast in the context of a (presumably self-serving) memoir, and as such it may or may not be reliable. What matters to my argument is that it is incidental to the event it bears witness to. To capture and fix in writing or some other medium the ways in which people repurpose objects in their everyday may serve an agenda but does not in and of itself constitute the reason why such retoolings occur in the first place. To the contrary, when a filmmaker browses through catalogs and poaches sounds and motifs from a record collection, the use of the objects found is instrumental to a later representation. The representation is not an incidental, de post facto affair; it is the raison d'être of the retooling of preexisting materials to begin with. In Antoine Compagnon's words, the recordings browsed through by the filmmaker are "transitional objects."[55] The tactical scouting and poaching of preexisting tracks is subsumed under a strategy, a totalizing gaze—and ear. Enmeshed yet at the same time floating above the vastness of popular culture on account of a mastering gaze underpinned by capital and the driving force of a goal-oriented project, the filmmaker who borrows already-constituted objects short-circuits the dichotomy between strategy and tactic, which is one of the pillars of de Certeau's theory of the everyday. For in ritualizing the everyday, the artist also transcends it.

As avid consumers of media products, both filmmakers and their audiences are everyday bricoleurs; yet as they face the same fence splitting the public sphere, they also sit on two different sides of it. It is not so much, as de Certeau claims, that the ruses of ordinary citizens leave no trace. It's just that their extemporaneous creations have no venues (however temporary) or audience (however small). They do not enjoy the fruits of the cordoning from the everyday, which is the precondition for spectatorship and subsequently the memorialization and exegesis that are the hallmarks of deeds possessing intrinsic value. Their gestures do not gel into texts and objects that speak to a virtual community across time and space. Social media may turn each of us into agents eager to project our statements and creations into the public sphere. In fact, most participants enjoy the attention of a restricted circle of acquaintances, if at all. Facebook posts do as much to boost one's reputation as an editorialist as karaoke stints for our career as performing artists. The oxymoron of a public platform functioning like a private one goes some way toward explaining the power of social media in reinforcing the divide between the amateur and the professional in something like the way the ease of access to means for movie-making has not narrowed the gap between amateur and professional filmmakers. If ordinary citizens' ruses do find an audience, that is an anonymous one, often not as their own work but someone else's. Photographers capture the reinvention of urban space by children, workers, and passersby. Artists bring everyday objects— whether immaculately preserved, retooled, or hacked—into the gallery space. Filmmakers retool known recordings. And a scholar such as de Certeau turns the everyday into the subject of a sociological tract.

BORROWING AS SCRAP . . .

Whether retooled, reinvented, or parodied, "Perfidia" retains its identity to the extent that a unit of expression—a word, sentence, or proverb— does as a speech act; a pillow as a weapon during a mock fight; or, in a chase, a city street as an escape. The song remains the same not just because it's fixed in grooves and tapes (or a film). Nor is its identity merely the result of a socially sanctioned stipulation (as a legalist or nominalist reading would have it). As is the case with any musical work, the status of "Perfidia" is contingent on collective intentionality: the ability of minds to be jointly directed at objects, matters, or states of affairs. This effort is joint not in the sense of synchronous or unanimous but because it is sustained by the belief that one is listening to the song signaled by the title. Such a belief emerges because of various cues, which predispose one to listen for certain features. It follows from a certain kind of readiness or "bias," as well as such objective features as sound structures or lyrics. The song's various manifestations and circumstances of reception reaffirm the limits of its identity just as they stretch or even temporarily suspend them. Indeed, the longer the performance and interpretive history of a song, the more secure its status as an aesthetic object with a distinct identity. It's truly a case of having a cake and eating it, too.

The instrumental intro to a song, even one as famous as "Perfidia," may not be recognized for what it is, mistaken for something else, or pass as a bit of standard film music fare. Whether because of a failure of attention or memory or of a simple lack of prior acquaintance with it, the borrowed song is no longer recognized as a self-standing entity. It meshes into the background of our experience of the film. This is especially the case when it is buried in the mix. Under these circumstances, the "glee of recognition," in Carolyn Abbate's words, is akin to an epiphany.[56] But it is fleeting and depends on the convergence of many unpredictable circumstances, including the physical circumstances of the film screening. In Abbate's case, the intertextual echo is an allusion to the overture to "The Flying Dutchman," as heard near the beginning of *The Thief of Bagdad* (1939). The seriousness of the allusion seems excessive in the context of a geographically challenged divertissement produced under comically chaotic circumstances.[57] Rather than setting into motion the wheels of hermeneutic interpretation, then, what Abbate calls the "proximity alarm" triggered by the allusion inspires a reflection on the merits of "ludic distance," which she pits against both "critical detachment" as well as its naturalistic nemesis, "absorption."[58]

What makes the bit of Wagner so hard to notice in *The Thief of Bagdad* is that it is short, unexpected and buried in a long cue whose job is to sustain a sequence packed with narrative interest and visual spectacle. The extraordinarily unusual set of circumstances needed for the epiphany to occur is not especially representative. In fact, they are specific to this particular passage of this particular film—and a particular listener. And because scrap is not meant to be recognized, Abbate's epiphany is a classic instance of *déformation professionelle*. It is as if someone were handed a hammer to perform a certain operation and then stopped in her tracks to contemplate the tiny bit of precious metal accidentally cast into the handle. The comedy of catching oneself digressing from the ostensible task at hand leads seamlessly to the contemplation of the comedy (and chaos) of film production. The slightly self-deprecating tone is exquisite and doubles as a mocking allusion to generations of music scholars bent on a self-reinforcing "guess-the-reference" game in which they pat each other's back for spotting dubious "motivic resemblances" and unearthing hard-to-hear "citations" in musical, theatrical, and now also cinematic works to build interpretive castles on them. Abbate's "proximity alarm," in short, is a wonderful parody of standard musicological practice. Yet her real target is opera spectatorship, which the experience of seeing *The Thief of Bagdad* at an old Loew's Movie Palace provides the foil to. The appreciation of the ephemerality and clumsiness of performance, the ease with which high culture is (literally) thrown into the mix, offers the best antidote to what she sees as the "ruinous absorption in sham tragedies."[59] Extrapolating from such light, if admittedly spectacular, fare such as *The Thief of Bagdad* raises the following question: why is an ostensibly incongruous musical allusion in film being used as a linchpin to an argument about aesthetic distance (albeit of the ludic rather than the critical kind)? The incongruity speaks of "fortuitous choices in the moment."[60] But rummaging through a pile of musical references and patching things up as one goes along need not result in work that is ephemeral, let alone unserious: witness the case of *Casablanca* or the films that form the subject of this book. What makes the Wagnerian bit in *The Thief of Bagdad* symptomatic of the comedy and absurdity that is film, and by extension opera production, are the genre of the film and the specifics of its production history, not the fact of being a borrowing per se.

Is the choice of Wagner fortuitous? The specificity of the allusion and the factors enabling the moment of recognition, as recounted by Abbate—the visual field; the humming, male chorus; the live acoustics of the palace, resembling to an extent that of an opera house—indicate that a musical logic, however simplistic or redundant, was in place. Perhaps the allusion is not entirely coincidental. This is not to say it is intentional or "scripted" (to borrow Abbate's term). It is the detritus of a moribund tradition, a tiny bit of Wagnerian texture that has become all but indistinguishable from the main tissue out of which a film score is woven. As such, it is incongruous only to the extent that we pay to it the kind of attention that it does not invite in the first place. The glee of recognition rescues the individual piece from anonymity. What makes it representative is that it is ordinary, not incongruous, and its ordinariness is symptomatic of a system heavily dependent on the scrap metal of music history. As a modus operandi, working with "scrap" is dictated less by the desire to allude to or reference the source material than by the intention to bank on the work of forgetting. If the borrowed music does the proverbial job, it does not matter whether it is recognized or not (in fact, it is much better if it isn't). It is not the use of Wagner in a Hollywood score that is fortuitous, then; its being recognized is.

As seen on a score, Abbate insists, intertextual relations are merely scripted and hence abstract, devoid of physical reality. Only when realized in sound and recognized as such by the listener is their potential fulfilled. At the cinema, making sure a reference is heard during a screening is the only way to ensure the intention is honored (the bulk of the paying audience doesn't explore films by reference to their screenplays, let alone the scores of their soundtracks, assuming they exist). Notwithstanding its renown among a slice of its intended audience, in *Days of Being Wild* Wong did his best to draw attention to "Perfidia" by signaling its appearance via a sync point. Kubrick's repertoire choices, when the case requires it, are also geared toward maximum recognizability. Cinema is a public art, and filmmakers often err on the side of overexplicitness when it comes to the music they borrow. So, what makes a reference hard to hear? Contingencies do matter. But being an outsider matters more.[61] Hearing a reference is like getting a joke. A joke is funny because it is unexpected and touches a nerve. Getting it betrays a certain kind of knowledge and by extension membership in a community. Given the distance that separates us from the milieu that nurtured the creation of the canonical works of the high art tradition, it is not surprising that one must learn to identify intertextual references in them, and through the support of written scores at that. They are like jokes that need explaining. Except that "explaining the joke is like dissecting a frog," E. B. White said famously. "The frog dies in the process."[62]

But for all this, is a reference that one can only learn to hear as impractical or obsolete as all that? I wholeheartedly share Abbate's impatience with a scholarly tradition that is content to identify borrowings and allusions solely in the abstract, as if their realization in sound were epiphenomenal, a mere confirmation of what is enshrined in the score-as-text (or affirmed by the composer/author). But having jumped the Rubicon, so to speak, and factored in concrete listening experiences in her discussion of intertextual echoes, she appears to be endorsing a view of spectatorship as a one-off, make-it-or-break-it experience. Either you hear the allusion or you don't. Either you experience the glee of recognition or you are forever condemned to the purgatory of laboriously reconstructing a context, gaining some sort of insider's status, and then moving back and forth between a script, or score, and its realization. True, where intertextual echoes are heard only because of hard, investigative work, there can be no epiphany. The reference loses its power to surprise and excite the way a punch line packs less of a punch when a joke is explained. The experience of hearing the reference may be mediated by notation, a gloss, and the tip of a friend (or an expensive education in music history). Suspense may replace surprise. But the viability of a reference one learns to hear can hardly be doubted. The appreciation and indeed enjoyment ignited by what one learns to recognize as being borrowed, retooled, or alluded to is not a two-step affair. Far from being exhausted the moment one learns to hear it, it is sustained over time by the ability to use a musical piece as a prop in a game of make-believe in which each time we are either surprised, delighted, or frustrated by the recognition of a reference to prior music: the same ability that informs children's ability, indeed delight, at the endless repetition of certain scenarios—as ludic a disposition, incidentally, as one is likely to encounter. But it isn't just the experience of the recognition that can be imaginatively reconstituted, as per the model of making fictional, outlined, among others, by Kendall Walton.[63] It is also that the intertextual echo can be contemplated as an object of study or reflection, irrespective of its realization in sound, only to inform another encounter with the same music as sound, in an open-ended cycle.

. . . OR MESH?

As retold by Abbate, an intertextual echo is like an anamorphic spot. If the screening circumstances allow one to, the anamorphosis will suddenly unfurl under the correct perspective and appear for what it is. Otherwise, it will be overlooked, only to be spotted the next time around (if at all). To contemplate the intertext-as-anamorphic-spot is to momentarily withhold interest in the narrative. The intertextual echo and absorption in the narrative are mutually exclusive. This is specific to a given film and genre, however. There is a myriad of cases in which the recognition does not detract from absorption in the fiction but rather channels it. For every intertextual echo à la *The Thief of Bagdad* that is too banal, didactic, or simply incommensurate to the narrative situation at hand, there is a counterpart that partakes of the worldmaking that is a film's main—if not the main—business. In the Moon Watcher episode of *2001: A Space Odyssey*, the recognition of Richard Strauss's symphonic poem does not inhibit but enhances absorption. Whether one recognizes the fanfare as a recurrence internal to the film or the famous late Romantic symphonic it actually is—or both—one is more, not less, engrossed by the events unfolding onscreen. "Also Sprach Zarathustra" signals not merely a new beginning but a teleology, imbuing an event taking place at an unidentifiable moment in the distant past with a vertiginous sense of its long-term implications. It is neither an allusion nor a citation but a supreme example of a combinatorial art that is profoundly transformative of the raw elements it manipulates. Call it montage, bricolage, or remix: the precise tenor of the nomenclature matters less than the acknowledgment that the net effect is that there is no separate body—the "music" per se—dispatching learned references into a picture-perfect world. That very world depends on the music to emerge in the first place. And it is the depth of one's absorption in this world that is the best measure of the music's transformation.

Anamorphic listening enables us to contemplate the integrity of the borrowed music as a self-standing object by separating it out of the situation that subtends it. Absorbed or, better, *situated* listening causes the music to mesh into the storyworld. The term *palimpsest* may capture the former but not the latter. In the classic definition by Gérard Genette, the palimpsest metaphor attempts to describe the sense of the fuzziness and tension that results from the juxtaposition of two entities, one old, the other grafted onto it.[64] But no such tension exists when preexisting music is enrolled in the job of choreographing the emergence of a freshly crafted fictional world. The preexisting is absorbed—no pun intended—into the storyworld. Unrecognized, a famous classic will function topically or recede into the background din of our experience; recognized, it will shine as part of a new configuration. Jewel in the crown or not, the resulting mesh cannot be untangled. This helps us understand how a film affects the identity of a well-known piece and changes the course of its reception history. It also resonates with Abbate's idea that music is "sticky": "Words stick to it. . . . [I]mages and corporeal gestures stick as well. . . . [P]hysical grounding and visual symbolism and verbal content change musical sounds by recommending how they are to be understood."[65] Talk of music as "sticky" inhabits a type of discourse in which music figures as the object to be parsed (albeit one that bears the traces or marks of both past and potentially future encounters). In the context of narrative cinema, this is moot. Music is as porous or gregarious as it is sticky and as such ceases to be a self-standing entity. In this connection, and building on Abbate's intuition, David Neumeyer writes that "music that is 'stuck' to organized meaning pays homage to the vococentric nature of cinema. The more music participates in supporting, advancing, or commenting on narrative, the more it loses the integrity of its diachronic flow."[66]

SYNCHRONIZATION AS EMPIRICAL ART

Neumeyer's insistence on the loss of "the integrity of its diachronic flow" draws us closer to an understanding of how recasting a known musical work into a new construct will have altered its basic ontology and attendant phenomenology. After it settles into a new environment, music accrues new meanings and functions. This is a dynamic interaction, not a static combination. As with a metaphor, music and the moving image engage in a "reciprocal transfer of attributes that gives rise to a meaning constructed, not just reproduced, by multimedia."[67] But synchronizing a recording to the moving image does not merely implicate the music in an exchange of attributes. The emergence of new functions and meanings is contingent on music losing its status as a self-standing aesthetic object as it is subsumed under a new gestalt, which admits of no distinction between it and the other worldmaking elements it has been blended into. As one component of a fully-fledged dramatic situation, music is no longer the undivided center of the focal attention.[68] This has significant implications for our understanding of how preexisting music functions in cinema. Some of the meanings and acoustical traits that may have motivated its adoption may no longer be available, or not to the same degree, when it is used as a film soundtrack. New meanings and unforeseeable effects may spring into action. Synchronization is an empirical and unpredictable practice. It is an experiment in the sense of "an act the outcome of which is unknown."[69] This Cagean citation is particularly apt when one thinks of his work with Merce Cunningham and especially their deliberate avoidance of coordinating the choreography and the music. While Cage's and Cunningham's attitudes may be extreme, they effectively underline the predicament of the artist, aware that synchronization is something to be channeled as much as crafted. The desired music-image combination is found as much as created. Under no circumstance is the creative impulse an "internal command on the part of the artist to the effect that the work should have such-and-such a look or that the spectator should have a given reaction to the picture."[70] Such level of control is simply not available. This is not to say that synchronization is wholly aleatoric, either. After all, the director retains control over what music to try out and what trials to reject and which ones to choose.[71] It follows that when filmmakers and scholars speak of preexisting music granting greater control, they mean overseeing the production process and enjoying the freedom not to have to share responsibility for the finished work with another person (that is, the composer or songwriter). When asking for a freshly composed score, the director can demand music that fits a picture to the fraction of a second. But the composer can stray when it comes to genre, style, and even instrumentation. Negotiations can be fraught. And the result can be wholly unsatisfactory. The ability—or presumption—to preempt such a state of affairs must be empowering, and not a little reassuring. In this respect, the analogy between musical borrowings and loanwords is pertinent. The adoption of a loanword masks the acknowledgment of the limits of one's own resources. But it is also the result of exacting standards. Why ask a composer for a paraphrase, parody, or pastiche when one can have the real thing? Yet no matter how large the catalog they tap into may be, directors can only hope that what is at heart an experiment will turn out well. The mechanisms underpinning the amalgam between music and the moving image will always elude a director, even when working with a track that he or she is most familiar with or that seems to be exactly right for a certain scene. The proof is in the proverbial pudding, regardless of what one believes the music brings to the table in its received form. It follows that Wong's habit of borrowing music from other films is sensible. It does away with the intrinsic uncertainty of the outcome, because the borrowed music proved its mettle as a film soundtrack to begin with. I turn to this important aspect of Wong's cinema, and its significance for a theory of music borrowing, in chapter 2.

TWO

POACHING

Through the whole of Wong's career, there are a few working habits whose impact on the final shape of his films is nothing short of decisive. The resilience of these habits is surprising, given the distance that separates the precarious funding structure and working environment of Wong's early films from his recent embrace of big-budget production. Continuity of modus operandi and the consistent stylistic signature that is its tangible manifestation are two sides of the same coin, accounting for the widespread view of Wong Kar-wai as a highly recognizable auteur.

One of the most significant—and overlooked—of Wong's habits is that of "poaching" music from other films, ranging from prerevolutionary Chinese melodramas to Rainer Werner Fassbinder arthouse darlings. The practice is in part symptomatic of the working methods prevalent in both the television and film industries in Hong Kong at the time of the director's apprenticeship. With notoriously tight deadlines and even tighter budgets, pastiche, parody, and playful plagiarism were the order of the day throughout the 1970s and 1980s.[1] Ease of access to global products, including films and music, only made this habit more pronounced. This lesson was not lost on the coterie of writers and assistant directors, Wong Kar-wai among them, who were to emerge in the late 1980s and 1990s as directors in their own right. What distinguishes Wong from his Hong Kong colleagues is that instead of limiting himself to hiring a composer to write a derivative score or grab a recording with a passing resemblance to a model, he has increasingly relied on ready-made music from other films. What could be more convenient, indeed expedient, for a filmmaker than to forge a score simply by watching someone else's films? It is a costly habit, however, and thus a reflection of the comparatively generous budgets that Wong's projects have come to command. Clearing rights, after all, can be expensive—sometimes prohibitively so. Conducting due diligence, Wong has never failed to give full credit to the composers and films whose music he has used. A written credit, however, is unlike a reference in a scholarly work, let alone a citation or homage in a literary one. Although a few people might sometimes linger in the movie theater to review credits in search of a musical attribution, the written credits are at best marginal in the spectator's experience. For the act of borrowing to be understood as such in the course of a film, the borrowed music must be both foregrounded and well known. This, as we shall see, is far from always being the case. One is likely to become aware of the sources of Wong's musical selections only after gaining access to the soundtracks of his films in the form of CDs or playlists. This does not make Wong's borrowings any less worthy of examination. Hearing film music on Spotify or YouTube and reading about it in the liner notes of CDs or in online chat forums are in a sense continuous with the encounter with the film itself. Whether retrospectively or in anticipation of a release, they inform the appreciation of a director's work (whose films, moreover, one may watch repeatedly). To realize that Wong has lifted music from another film does not make the borrowed tracks vehicles of intertextual associations, however. Even after realizing where the music comes from, the distance between the original host and its new home is often such that it renders specific intertextual resonances difficult, if not impossible, to work out in any meaningful, productive way. Wong's reliance on preexisting soundtracks is a transfiguration into artistic practice of a distinctive expression of Hong Kong's famed re-export economy: the repackaging of imported goods as if they were its own.

Wong's career is bookended by two conspicuous, strategically placed excerpts from preexisting soundtracks. While in *As Tears Go By* (1988) the debt to a source film is, as we have seen, openly acknowledged, in *The Grandmaster* (2013) the relationship to a precedent is more difficult to fathom. This is all the more revealing as the borrowed tracks, both composed by Ennio Morricone, are prominently featured near the end of the film.[2] "La donna romantica" (The romantic woman), from *Come imparai ad amare le donne* (How I learned to love women, directed by Luciano Salce [1966]) underscores the last, poignant conversation between Gong Er and Ip Man.[3] Morricone's piece is an andante for solo piano and orchestra, styled after the middle movement of an early Romantic piano concerto. In keeping with the definitive, if heartfelt, farewell bid by Gong Er, the music sounds a distinctly elegiac tone. Affective resonance goes hand in hand with the precisely timed placement of the track, which begins just as Gong Er returns to Ip the button that was the symbol of their liaison. As she goes on to confess to have once loved him, the piano solo is enveloped by sympathetic strings. When it is his turn to speak, the music marks yet another major subdivision (the beginning of a variant of the theme with the full orchestra, minus the piano). Morricone's piece, in short, dictates both the duration of the episode and the rhythm of the conversation (hence the timing of the cuts). In preserving the integrity of the original piece, Wong Kar-wai pays a compliment to the composer but also creates the illusion that the music has been written for *The Grandmaster*. Moving so effortlessly in sync with the action is normally the prerogative of original scores. The illusion is sustained by the fact that the source film is too little known, and therefore so is its soundtrack.

Wong borrows without citing. The recording of Morricone's music from which he most likely lifted the music may have some cult status among the cognoscenti. Although there is no generic or thematic connection between *The Grandmaster* and the Italian comedy for which Morricone wrote "La donna romantica," it is at least conceivable that Salce's film carried a special meaning for the director or a collaborator, which the musical borrowing allegedly signals, and which is the responsibility of the historian to unearth and report (whenever possible). But all this does not make the use of Morricone a citation. To function as such, the track would have to appeal to an audience broader than those privy to the director's private motives, or those of a relatively small network of insiders (no matter how significant or influential). Its prior life notwithstanding, "La donna romantica" serves less as the catalyst for intertextual relations between *The Grandmaster* and *Come imparai ad amare le donne* than as a convenient, ready-to-hand track Wong could control without the intermediary of the composer (or the encumbrance of too strong an association to another director's oeuvre). To the extent that the music partakes of the diffuse intertextuality of film music, this is only insofar as it employs familiar stylistic traits and is used in a manner consistent with countless precedents in the history of the medium.

The second Morricone track in *The Grandmaster*, "Deborah's Theme," appears in the coda of the film, as Ip settles into his new life in Hong Kong (following the closing down of the Chinese border after World War II). It is lifted from nothing less than *Once upon a Time in America* (1984). Sergio Leone's film not only enjoyed significant circulation but was also, along with *Once upon a Time in the West* (1974), the oblique inspiration for Tsui Hark as he conceived and directed the first three installments of the six-part *Once upon a Time in China* series (1991–97). Morricone's rumbling, plaintive theme is scored for solo cello and orchestra in the manner, once again, of a Romantic concerto. Alongside the Leone and Tsui Hark precedents, the music introduces a third, and wholly musical, reference. A similar arrangement can be heard in a widely distributed recording of the same music by Yo-Yo Ma.[4] In an informative—and entertaining— exchange with Martin Scorsese that took place at the Museum of Modern Art in New York, Wong himself has spoken of "homage" to Leone and Morricone.[5] Taking a leaf from the book of a recognized master is a request for an admission ticket into the history of the art, as well as a symptom of the younger director's sense of confidence. But what if, following *The Grandmaster*, the music will remind audiences of Wong instead? In the same interview, Wong also mentions the significance of the fact that Morricone's music comes with "a history." Because of the renown and visibility of *Once upon a Time in America*, the reference to Leone via "Deborah's Theme" engages a quantitatively more significant slice of the virtual community of filmgoers than the borrowing of "La donna romantica" does, feeding on their memory and affection for Leone's work. Morricone's theme functions not only like a synecdoche for its source film but also as a tacit suggestion to contemplate a kinship between *The Grandmaster* and *Once upon a Time in America*.[6] This is supported by the thematic parallels between them and the mediation, for those familiar with it, of the six-part *Once upon a Time in China* series as well.[7] Unpacking the musical reference brings to light their common qualities: the scope and epic character of the historical reconstruction, the nostalgia that infuses the evocation of an earlier time, and the aggrandizing filter of memory.

A musical quotation is like a genie in a bottle in that, given the nonverbal, semantically imprecise nature of music, it can initiate an almost infinite chain of associations. For this reason, one must exercise constraint, too, lest the hermeneutic circle morphs into a self-sustaining spiral, feeding itself to no end. The similarities between Leone's and Wong's works, after all, only go so far. Geographical and historical differences aside, the story of a venerable tradition (*wing chun*) coming to a near extinction in the motherland, only to survive in a foreign-occupied outpost (Hong Kong), differs in both spirit and content from Leone's counterpart. It is not without irony, too, that "Deborah's Theme" was written by Morricone many years before for another film, and rejected.[8] At Morricone's urging, and despite Leone's initial reservations, the cue went on to become indelibly associated with *Once upon a Time in America*. It is a lesson that Wong, without necessarily being privy to the details of the history of Morricone's cue, must understand all too well. For time and again, he has taken full advantage of the ease with which a piece of music, no matter what film it was written for, settles into a new home and becomes its emblem (thereby erasing all traces of its past life). The "nomadic" quality of film music can be tested by using it as a temp track during principal photography.[9] Putting his trust in the fact that the music worked well in Leone's film, Wong not only continued to use it in postproduction but also saved himself the trouble of belaboring over its degree of fit (or lack thereof). "If it's good enough for Leone, surely it will work fine for me!" is the implied heuristic. Convenience is naturally a factor but at work in Wong's case is also his intuitive understanding of what we might call the *genius musicae*, the ineradicable quality that makes music tick with a specific dramatic locus, and which allows it to migrate with ease from one "host" narrative to another with minimum hassle and to great effect. That Wong used many of the themes he borrowed as guide tracks during shooting or temp tracks in the editing— as Stanley Kubrick, Leone himself, and many others did—also goes to strengthen the impression that tempo, synchronization, and affect take precedence over homage or studied intertextual references, however ineliminable they may seem in retrospect.

"THE WORLD'S FIRST WONG KAR-WAI MOMENT" REDUX

The dynamics of musical borrowing in *As Tears Go By* depend on the marketing practices that were dominant in the Hong Kong film industry at the time the film was made. The film openly gestures toward pre-existing music in the English title, inaugurating another habit that will prove to be crucial to Wong's modus operandi (as *Happy Together* [1997] and *In the Mood for Love* [2000], both titled after songs, eloquently prove). The adoption of a song title serves an eminently practical purpose by providing a catchy, memorable identifier; it also enriches the film by opening up a maze of references to musical and cinematic precedents alike, tying it to a live tradition, in the world of Anglophone popular culture, of themes, images, and reminiscences shared by thousands of potential filmgoers. Mick Jagger and Keith Richards's "As Tears Go By" jump-started Marianne Faithfull's career in 1964 and migrated across several versions, including a reappropriation a year later (colored by the global success of the Beatles' "Yesterday" and "You've Got to Hide Your Love Away," and, of course, Bob Dylan) by the Stones themselves. *As Tears Go By* (the film) is said to be a "Hong Kong style" remake of Scorsese's 1973 feature, *Mean Streets*. By a dizzying conjoining of a circular chain of associations, the song is also the focus of an important sequence in *Shine a Light*, the Rolling Stones documentary that Scorsese directed in 2008.

Incorporating into the main body of a film a song, as distinct from an instrumental cue, presents a different kind of challenge. Wong usually designs a sequence in response to the length, affect, and tempo of his musical selection. Examples include, but are by no means limited to, Xavier Cugat's "Jungle Drums" (*Days of Being Wild* [1990]) or the Mamas and the Papas' "California Dreamin'" (*Chungking Express* [1994]). Most representative in his catalog are the songs that either spur the protagonist to action or encourage a state of reverie. When this happens, the visual material seems to follow from what the character is hearing, in which case the sequence is (literally) shot through with the rhythms, melodic innuendos, and imagery proffered by the music and its text. This has predictably led to the charge that at this juncture Wong gives up stylistic control, relying instead on a set of clichés drawn from the language of music videos. Aside from stigmatizing the music video as an inferior medium, this claim does not stand up to scrutiny. Framed by a narrative, and often packed with action through and through, Wong's song sequences are not only arresting in their boldness and inventiveness, but also a significant—and prescient—manifestation of the current vogue for self-representation in both the visual arts and social media.

As Tears Go By makes full, unabashed use of a cover, sung in Cantonese by local budding star Sandy Lam—yet another important precedent for Wong, culminating in the casting of Faye Wong and the use of her own cover of the Cranberries' "Dreams" in *Chungking Express*. Lam, who also plays a supporting role in *As Tears Go By*, lends her voice to a soulful and polished rendition of "Take My Breath Away," originally written for the global box-office hit *Top Gun* (1986).[10] Introduced at the drop of a coin into a jukebox, what would become a recurring prop and the stuff of Wong Kar-wai lore, the song not only wipes away the synthesizer accompanying the visit of a desolate Wah (Andy Lau) to a bar but also jump-starts his attempt to rescue his cousin Ah-ngor (Maggie Cheung). As Wah makes his way to her home on Lantau Island, the music goes "in the air" to underscore the staggered, suspenseful reunion with her. Having dragged Ah-ngor to a no more than metaphorically discreet hideout—a telephone booth—"they kiss hungrily, in the retelling of an internet reviewer, the music swells and the phone booth's fluorescent lights burn brighter and brighter until the entire screen sears white."[11]

For the climax of the film, Wong engaged one of the singers of the moment, complete with her cover of a fresh-off-the-charts hit, itself a title song of a box-office success: nothing would seem more representative of the churning-out, piggy-backing vocation of the Hong Kong film industry. And yet, as the same anonymous reviewer concluded, "it was the world's first Wong Kar-wai moment." To account for this apparent paradox, we need to consider the episode in its entirety. In a twist he was to repeat in subsequent films, and which cements one's impression of the significance of *As Tears Go By* in determining the course of his career, Wong constructed a visually complex sequence in response to his musical selection.[12] While its placement at the climax of the narrative ensures it receives emphatic treatment, as befits a well-known preexisting song, technically the music is used as if it were a score originally written for this film. This hardly amounts to a disavowal of the source film. All the same, due to the elaborate way in which he has woven it into the drawn-out reunion between Wah and Ah-ngor, and his understanding of the coda as the song's true emotional climax, Wong's repurposing makes it difficult to hear specific resonances with the original appearance of "Take My Breath Away" in *Top Gun*.

The muted references to *Top Gun* are also explained, and perhaps encouraged, by the trajectory leading from the appearance of "Take My Breath Away" in the source film to its reincarnation in Wong's. The song was still popular in Hong Kong at the time *As Tears Go By* was being filmed. It was not only the "love theme" of its successful Hollywood vehicle but also a self-standing single topping the charts in the United Kingdom—a market of which Hong Kong was, in the late 1980s, keenly aware. In addition, Lam's own cover, whose release preceded the release of Wong's film by more than a year, had enjoyed significant airtime and promotion in Hong Kong. Even prior to filming, then, there were already two degrees of separation between the song Wong was to use and the film from which it originated. "Take My Breath Away," we may conclude, owes its use to a choice of personnel—the casting of Sandy Lam—as much as its specifically cinematic provenance. Employing Lam enabled Wong to address the audience's music competence and their likes and dislikes, thereby activating a participatory attitude dubbed by Brian Hu as a "KTV aesthetic."[13] In doing so, he enlarged the film's frame of reference by placing Wah and Ah-ngor's story in the context of the city's mediascape. It was a choice that the director was to repeat, with added dividends, in both *Chungking Express* and *Fallen Angels* (1995). While the former, as already mentioned, showcases Faye Wong's cover of "Dreams," the latter makes prominent use, once again via a jukebox, of Shirley Kwan's 1995 flamboyant version of James Wong's "Forget Him" (a song made famous throughout the Chinese-speaking world by the legendary Teresa Teng in the late 1970s). Neither song had appeared in a film before.

GLOBAL CINEMA AS MUSICAL INVENTORY

Film music does not normally enjoy the circulation afforded by either a separate, dedicated release or a progeny of covers. Sourcing it can be difficult. Yet well before *The Grandmaster*, Wong borrowed preexisting music whose main, and sometimes only, vehicle was a film soundtrack (whether as score, source music, or source-scoring).[14] Lifting a track from a colleague's work to use it in one's own naturally encourages the search for cross-references or a special kind of affinity. But the search can turn out to be fruitless or, worse, an exercise in tautology, if only because of the unique repertoire of connotations the genus of the music inevitably carries with it (irrespective of the director's intent). Wong's loan tracks do not point to other films intertextually and they are not an homage to other filmmakers via their composers. Wong, rather, treats global cinema as no more than a musical inventory to be appropriated at will, not infrequently with the intent of surpassing, rather than emulating, his predecessors.[15]

Only thus can one account for the liberal exercise of his catholic musical taste and reliance on a wide range of musical genres deftly "extracted" from an equally wide range of films (running a whole gamut from blockbusters to obscure auteur pieces).[16] The fame of a title theme or a borrowed cue is a function of greater availability, and hence ease of access, not the means to elicit specific cine-musical associations. Insofar as a song embedded in another film catches his attention, Wong will employ it, no matter the circumstances under which he catches wind of it and regardless of its fame and potential as a marketing tool. A case in point is Laurie Anderson's "Speak My Language," featured in Wim Wenders's *Faraway, So Close* (and examined in the introduction). Anderson has at most a "cult" status within the popular music scene in the West, but near-zero cachet in the Chinese-speaking world. In Wenders's film, as mentioned, her song is barely audible in a dialogue scene (truncated at that). Did Wong first hear it there, where it plays such a studiedly subdued, not to say esoteric, role? Or did he encounter it in the CD release of the soundtrack or, bypassing Wenders altogether, on the musician's own album *Bright Red* (1994)? Whatever the answer, it is with the memorable jukebox sequence in *Fallen Angels* that "Speak My Language" is now firmly associated. The loan has become a property transfer.

An even more egregious case of appropriation is that of Shigeru Umebayashi's "Yumeji's Theme." Wong's use of Umebayashi's theme in *In the Mood for Love* brought it global acclaim after its largely overlooked appearance—if not, evidently, by Wong—in Seijun Suzuki's extraordinary, and sadly unknown, film, *Yumeji* (1991). The new host body reinvents the music even more than *Fallen Angels* did for "Speak My Language." Despite retaining the original title, "Yumeji's Theme" has been circulating as a self-standing release in the wake of, and accompanied by all manner of paraphernalia associated with, *In the Mood for Love*. Its fate now seems to be forever sealed by Wong's film, a fact the director underscored somewhat perversely by citing it as a reference to his own film, in an appropriately rearranged version, in *My Blueberry Nights* (2007).[17] The seemingly innocent, if somewhat complacent, gesture is a backhanded affirmation of ownership, one that pushes *Yumeji*, the music's source film, further back into the recesses of cinephilic memory. In something like the way a citation can revive interest in a long-forgotten author, however, *In the Mood for Love* went some way, if perhaps not as much as one had hoped, in rekindling interest in Suzuki's film (if only among those who took the trouble to check the film's credits). To realize just how differently Suzuki treats the same theme in *Yumeji*, and how distant the poetic world of the latter is from that of *In the Mood for Love*, gives one pause, but it also elicits admiration for Wong's musical ear and renewed awareness of how much work, particularly in the editing room, must have gone into repurposing Umebayashi's music for his own film.[18]

Be it Umebayashi's theme or a Laurie Anderson song, then, the effacement of any marks betraying the original "site of provenance" of the music is the product of hard labor as much as the inevitable—and expedient—consequence of the esoteric nature of the source film. The success of Wong's transplants is also a compliment to the ease with which music produces an impression on the spectator above and beyond his or her ability to trace its genealogy. This is because no listening experience is unmediated. All music is, to some extent, preexisting in that it shares some generic features with some prior instantiations of its genre.[19] While the recognition of shared features enhances the narrative significance and emotional impact of what one is hearing, the identification of the source of a citation from an unknown or hard-to-identify precedent is overall a rather more cerebral affair. It depends on highly specialized knowledge acquired with some effort, without which its intended effect is all but lost. That is why stressing the intertextual function of Wong's borrowing is particularly insidious. For if the music's goal is indeed to call attention to the original film as an in-between text— as the etymology of the term *intertextual* indicates—it follows that once the reference is dispatched, the primary role of the music is fulfilled. This may open new interpretive vistas at the risk, however, of demoting the moment-to-moment engagement with the musical dimension of Wong's cinema.[20]

There remains the question "Why lift music from other films?" I have mentioned the practice, common in the Hong Kong film industry, of poaching motives, themes, and characters from global cinema. These are refitted and then sold to the local market, and the global Chinese moviegoing diaspora, as re-exports. If only by way of continuing this long-standing practice, inherited by his peers in the industry, Wong has made this approach undoubtedly his own and has liberally applied it to the music for his films as well. Call it the soundtrack by proxy or the poetics of the inventory. Technically, it presents clear practical advantages for underscoring calls for specific requirements. Among these are a modular structure, which facilitates cutting and pasting, and a certain coarseness of texture as well as paucity of melodic material, both of which ensure the music can be used without overwhelming dialogue or other salient auditory information. The use of preexisting music tracks, such as one hears in *In the Mood for Love* or *2046* (2004), circumvents the problems arising from meeting such specifications, as the latter have been met in the first place (in another film). The practice also allows the director full or at least greater control over the quality of music, which he or she can pick from a theoretically infinite number of available possibilities, and without the anxiety of having to turn a final cut over to a composer who, no matter how attuned to the director's specifications, will necessarily confront him or her with an unknown entity. The goal of Wong's strategy, then, is to bypass a potentially fraught working relationship with a composer while at the same time preempting the difficulty of adapting music not originally intended for a film and therefore not suitable to use as underscoring or impervious to a nuanced editing approach.

While Wong refrains from invoking the associations with the source film in any explicit form, his transplants betray his trust in the fact that insofar as the selection he has made had a prior life in another film, it will fulfill its role just as efficiently in his own. There is more than trust at work; the preference for established brands, to invoke another defining aspect of Hong Kong culture, is also a factor. No matter how divergent the solutions adopted, and how little of the source film transpires in the derivative work, the fact that a music track has already done its job in some highly respected colleague's film acts as a guarantor. Yet the counterintuitive choices of repertoire, along with the magnificence and poignancy of the new combinations Wong conjures with them, not only suggest how much thoughtfulness goes into the selection process and the reworking of the music, but also reveal an aspect of the creative process that is symptomatic of a largely overlooked facet of our mediascape: the cinema as an important locus of musical discoveries. More than the concert hall, radio, or the solitary space of the home, a film is for Wong the background against which a piece reveals its most distinctive qualities, the litmus test of its ultimate appeal, whether bouncing off the crevices of the image, moving in counterpoint with the onscreen action, developing in symbiosis with the mise-en-scène, or resonating with various elements of the frame's design.[21]

"BESPOKE" OR "OFF THE RACK"?

Buying "off the rack" to alter and then use as "bespoke" is something filmmakers have done with increasing frequency, and varying success, ever since Pier Paolo Pasolini, Luchino Visconti, Jean-Luc Godard, and Kubrick made the practice acceptable to both mainstream and non-mainstream audiences in the 1960s. Wong, like Quentin Tarantino, and long after François Truffaut, has not only followed this illustrious tradition but also proceeded to give the term *preexisting music* a new twist in showing a proclivity to use someone else's "bespoke" (i.e., original film score) as his own.[22] In a further development, he has also inverted this by commissioning original music only to end up using it as if it were "off the rack." For *Ashes of Time Redux* (2008), for example, Wong engaged noted Beijing-based musician Wu Tong to coordinate a rewrite, for full orchestra, of Roel C. Garcia and Frankie Chan's original music for the 1994 release. Accordingly, Wu and his collaborator, American composer Eli Marshall, created new arrangements as well as new pieces for what was to be the new score for the restored, and newly edited, 2008 version. Like a Hollywood score, many selections of the music were recorded to fit specific cuts of the film (while others were provided as alternate options). Following this, however, Wong changed the film and with it the editing of some of the selections, using their recordings, for all intents and purposes, as if they were preexisting music. "I should stress," Eli Marshall told me, "that a lot of the music was indeed used as originally intended by Wu Tong and his collaborators (primarily me and Li Xun). However, it's true that some other changes did occur after delivery of the music masters. . . . With *Ashes*, some of the changes were slight; some others were used or cut in completely unexpected ways."[23]

Wong's penchant for constantly revising his work, ironically, makes preexisting music easier to work with than an original score. A bespoke score is predicated on exact, down-to-the-split-second synchronization between the music's pulse and the rhythms of the action or the editing (or both); it falls apart, and must be rewritten, after the director makes a last-minute correction. Better, then, to work with longer "sticks" of pre-existing music to return to—and modify—at will. Hence, too, the choice to work with film tracks from the CD releases of the film soundtracks rather than the cues as heard in the films themselves, for while in the latter the music appears in the form of cues, in the former it consists of self-standing, and usually longer, tracks that are still open to manipulation. I now turn to an example of this practice.

BORROWED MUSIC AS MOOD MUSIC

Wong's proneness to appropriate music from other films is most apparent in 2046. The wide-ranging musical refitting that pervades the film from beginning to end is in keeping with a well-established modus operandi. But this flamboyant display is also an important dimension of the self-reflexive nature of the film and the close, if ultimately unresolved, relationship between the film's fictional protagonist and its flesh-and-blood director. The title betrays a deliberate modeling after, if not the intent to adapt or parody, another film as well. The episodes set in the future are Chow's own "time odyssey," a striking foil to Kubrick's arch-famous epic. The choice of format follows from a long history of immersive, participatory extravaganzas marketed as "travelogues," of which both *2001: A Space Odyssey* (1968) and *2046* are undoubtedly two capacious, highly ambitious specimens.[24] Preexisting music, which is a central feature of both films, is key to the creation of a "contact zone" between the audience and the fictitious characters who depart Earth, or the reassuring shores of the everyday, and in so doing take one for "team humanity."

Casting lust as moved by a desire for knowledge, as much as the pursuit of carnal pleasure, *2046* redefines the Casanova as a post-Romantic chronicler of other people's love woes. Given the tenor—and subject—of most of Wong's films, this is already a hint of the privileged relationship, almost akin to a transfer, that runs between the main character and the director. Played by Tony Leung, Chow is ostensibly the same character as the one seen in *In the Mood for Love*.[25] By the time *2046* begins, the repressed love affair with Su Lizhen and the divorce from his wife have obviously taken their toll.[26] Whether in demeanor or degree of ruthlessness to his female conquests, in *2046* Chow cuts a decidedly different figure. This makes it at times difficult to contemplate the continuities between his incarnation in this film and the more reserved, languidly romantic role of the previous one. In shooting the second and third parts of his saga of the 1960s in Hong Kong, Wong made little attempt to hide the evolution of his personal language and changing views about the people and stories involved therein: hence the apparent inconsistencies in not only tone and texture but also character development. The result is striking in that the shape and content of the three-part cycle are tied to the changing circumstances of the working environment that Wong worked in as well as the vagaries of casting, principal photography, or the editing process. As a result, Chow is Wong's alter ego because the director created him in his image and, more obliquely, the fictional story of Chow is folded within the reality of Wong's career trajectory.

The actors' preferences and schedules determined the course of the writing and directing of the three films. Andy Lau's path diverged from Wong's soon after *Days of Being Wild*, for instance. Leslie Cheung died tragically in 2003. This naturally forced painful adjustments. The presence of Carina Lau, who had a major role in *Days of Being Wild*, is important in casting 2046 against its two prequels (and the 1960s in Hong Kong in general). Maggie Cheung's fleeting appearance in 2046, in a pair of black and white "memory" shots that harken back to *In the Mood for Love*, instills a sense of continuity. The introduction of Gong Li, playing Chow's love interest in Singapore, finally and cleverly extends the gallery of characters while simultaneously filling in a blank left hanging from the previous film (his life in Singapore, following the breakup with Lizhen). The fourteen-year span that intervenes between *Days of Being Wild* and 2046, and the preeminence gained by virtually all the actors who played in at least one of them, ensures that Wong is the tutelary figure and his trilogy is the "ley line" along which the careers of a remarkable group of actors, all of whom went on to dominate the local industry, have come to rest. All these actors' careers, in turn, augment our experience of Wong's trilogy by bringing into play a myriad of other roles and other stories.

Tony Leung is the only actor to feature in all three films, and in 2046 he receives undivided attention. For all its prominence, the role he plays is less that of an agent than an observer or, at most, facilitator. Figure 2.1 shows a symptomatic expression of his predicament of "preserver" of other people's feelings. We see Bai Ling musing on her past and how strange it is to "spend Christmas like this" (that is, alone in Hong Kong). She is with Chow, but for all intents and purposes her assessment may be taken at face value, for he is there merely as a listener. While he figures prominently in the elongated, widescreen frame, he is just as conspicuously out of focus: a dominant presence but one that officiates rather

2.1 Chow as listener in *2046*.

than participates in the proceedings. His perspective is dominant, guiding our own response to her tale as well. The shot collapses a reaction into a point-of-view shot. In taking stock, however fleetingly, of his presence and demeanor, we also look at her with him (if not literally from his optical point of view). Although Chow is out of focus, his facial expression remains readable, betraying a tacit acknowledgment, borne out of respect and sympathy, of Ling's need to pour her heart out. Given the content of what we are hearing, and the tone with which she is saying it, it is the most appropriate attitude, notwithstanding the fact that in adopting it, he also hopes to draw her close to him.

Savvy seducer, sympathetic listener, and knowledge seeker: this manifold perspective informs the film and also finds expression in the elaborate filmic language that Wong deploys to show us not only the comings and goings to and from room 2046 but also Chow's visions of the future, his past, and the string of disappointments that keep happening around him. The film bears this out by deliberately confusing our sense of whether *2046* is an account of events as they occurred in real time and space or the fleshing out of Chow's musings and reflections. This ties Chow to Wong in a manner not dissimilar to Guido and Fellini in *8 1/2* (1963). Two key features keep the film this side of Fellini's radical collapse of different levels of reality, however. One is the intercutting of sequences depicting the science fiction novella *2046* (unambiguously the work of fantasy). The other is the fact that Chow is a writer and therefore an agent necessarily other than the *metteur en scène* of the film we are watching. Even so, there can be no doubt as to the film's alignment, at each and every turn, with Chow's own perspective. While the voice-over sanctions this in the most obvious manner, the suggestion of Chow's disposition toward his friends, lovers, and acquaintances is also subtly conveyed, as in the example just mentioned, through acting, camera work, and image composition.

Chow is as much a voyeur, and unrepentant womanizer, as a docile, sympathetic listener. To gain a sufficiently revealing vantage point, he must sometimes become an (all-too-willing) participant in what to him are love "experiments." At once the cynical instigator and profoundly humane teller, he becomes involved with Ling while at the same time keeping her at bay. In exercising his appeal, and becoming her lover, he is arming himself with the best possible position from which to appreciate not only her beauty but also capacity for love (and the grief caused by its being unrequited). Only a hair of difference separates pity from love; knowing from the start that he is incapable of the latter, he decides to pursue an affair with her anyway. In this way, he sets himself on a journey in which he gives free rein to both his lust and his ability to peel beneath the surface and grasp the deepest recesses of a person's soul. Appreciation of another person's pain is, of course, a quintessentially human trait, but in exercising his own humanity in this fashion, Chow is also simultaneously disavowing it in that he must remain uninvolved with Ling despite leading her on. More important still, he must cynically endure the sight of the very pain that he has caused and seems to understand so well.

To represent this devilishly twisted position, one defined by a beguiling admixture of pathos and detachment, Wong gives a new lease on life to that old chestnut, "mood music." He does this by reviving a practice older not only than the sound film but the cue sheet itself: that of lifting music heard in another film. As the evening comes to an end, we see Ling and Chow going home, in slow motion, inside a taxi that bears a suspicious resemblance to that seen in *In the Mood for Love*. Twice Ling rejects the grip of his hand. Inebriated with alcohol, Chow is collapsing past (Lizhen) and present (Ling, whom he barely knows). His involuntary memory is Wong's self-citation. Yet the music is different: a track written by Georges Delerue for Truffaut's last film, *Confidentially Yours* (1983). It is a clever chain of interlocking visual and auditory memories. While visually the shot delivers us back to Chow's past, and with it to *In the Mood for Love*, the music looks forward instead, setting us up for his future relationship with Ling. Delerue's writing is of recognizably classical lineage and, in keeping with the deliberately nostalgic outlook of the film from which it is drawn, harkens back to the composer's own work of the 1960s and early 1970s (the full, resonant, open-string sonority of the scores for *Contempt* [1963] and *The Soft Skin* [1964] come especially to mind). Yet just as crucial to the understanding of Wong's selection is the fact that, unlike, say, the cover of "Take My Breath Away," it is too obscure to be traced back to a specific composer or film. Delerue's music, in fact, might well be mistaken for a generic cue written specifically for this scene of *2046*.

MOOD MUSIC AS POINT OF VIEW

Film scholars and critics have sometimes been unkind to mood music. They have largely used the term to refer to hastily written scores riddled with stock formulas and clichés. It has not helped that they have sometimes neglected to define the term with sufficient precision. There are exceptions. Following Philip Tagg, I understand the term to indicate first and foremost a genre of music defined by its mode of composition, use, and distribution, namely "prerecorded music, usually on LP or CD, produced in anticipation of film, TV, and radio production needs and systematized according to the music's moods and functions."[27] Attempting to capture what mood music does in the context of a film has proven more difficult, however. Jerrold Levinson's nuanced list of the most common functions of film music comes closest, in my mind, to shedding some light on at least five shades of meaning attributable to the term:

> (6) the projecting of a story-appropriate mood, attributable to the scene as a whole: (7) the imparting to the viewer of a sense that the happenings in the film are more important than those of ordinary life—the emotions magnified, the stakes higher, the significances deeper; (8) the suggesting to the viewer of how the presenter of the story regards or feels about some aspects of the story, for example, sympathetically; (9) the suggesting to the viewer of how he or she is to regard or feel about some aspect of the story, for example, compassionately; . . . (11) the direct inducing in viewers of tension, fear, wariness, relaxation, cheerfulness, or other similar cognitive or affective state.[28]

As readers familiar with writings on film music would readily agree, "mood music" has been taken to refer to one or more of these functions, often simultaneously. Most perplexing, perhaps, is the confusion between the representation of character emotion and the inducing of emotion (in the spectator). But rather than belaboring my case for terminological clarity by suggesting, for instance, a restriction in the use of this evergreen, here I wish to single out the relevant—and most revealing—cluster of descriptors that capture the use Wong makes of mood music in 2046. This is summarized by Levinson's functions numbered 7, 8, and 9 above. Whether borrowed from Truffaut's, Fassbinder's, or Krzysztof Kieślowski's films, the music not only captures the presenter, as well as Chow's deeply sympathetic point of view, but also tells us how to receive what we're seeing and hearing during the various stations that mark his path toward loverly wisdom. After all, there are both good and bad ways of lending one's ears to other people's tales as we take stock of their situations. In clarifying this crucial aspect of Chow's picaresque encounters with his neighbors and various acquaintances' love lives, the music helps outline an elaborate etiquette, encouraging us to align ourselves with him as he adopts the most advantageous, but also proper, respectful, and heartfelt attitude toward his interlocutors. The didactic dimension implicit in this strategy is a matter of musical choices and is not channeled via the explicit representation of a certain type of demeanor, for, if anything, Chow's visible behavior comes across as callous. It is the soundtrack, including his voice-over, that conveys his capacity for sympathy.

Chow's successful attempt to seduce Ling illustrates this with extraordinary, and deeply affecting, clarity. Having been publicly stood up by her before a group of friends, he returns to his room alone late into the night. There and then, the two of them meet. He asks for "reparations" and, after some bickering and laughing, they make love. Defying her expectation that they spend the rest of the night together, Chow dresses up and makes his way back to his room, not without the added insult of paying her (for a dress torn in the proceedings). Pain and anger transpire on her finely chiseled, yet now suddenly hardened, face. She initially refuses and only reluctantly accepts a tiny, symbolic sum, not without adding that she has offered her services, as she herself puts it, at "a discount rate." In turning Chow's patently offensive overture into a playful, touching symbol of her fondness for him, Ling proves a match for her deft lover and also scores a point in her favor. Yet there is no doubt that it is he who has set the terms, for her calamitous, of their relationship. The camera fixed on her, Chow unceremoniously walks past and leaves through the open door. In a representative display of Wong's unpredictable tempos, and willingness to let the actors take their time to attain the desired effect, the camera runs for a lengthy thirty more seconds until a tear flows out of Zhang's right eye. Only at this point is she allowed to shut the door and exit the frame, making way for a cut. As she does this, the suggestion of a smile, possibly the expression of the actress's satisfaction at having finally evinced her long-awaited tear, is promptly substituted by a grin. The sense of having witnessed Zhang perform is palpable. Wong is making a spectacle out of the performers' struggle to convey extreme human emotions. The length of the shot gives us enough time to ponder, too, our own uncomfortable position as sympathetic bystanders on the one hand, and unwelcome eavesdroppers on the other. Wong's choice entails the recognition—indeed, the expectation—that the audience will indulge their taste for the sight of unrequited love. Like Hitchcock, he is a master at making viewers uncomfortable with their own feelings, forcing them into the position of having to acknowledge a more than passing interest in the contemplation of a soul being torn apart.

There follows a shot of the utterly still, empty hotel corridor that fleshes out the distance, emotional as well as physical, between them. Despite its seemingly transitional role, the image provides a striking visual metaphor for the lifelessness of their liaison. Another, and just as insidious, connection exists between Ling and Chow, however. Their rooms share a wall, and a small opening in the glass panel above a separation allows Chow to peer in, spying on Ling (fig. 2.2). A cut takes us to an extreme close-up of him doing just that, the upper edge of his head pointedly lit by the glare coming through the crack that leads into her room. The combined effect of the penumbra hovering over a large part of the image and the use of selective focus drives our attention toward Leung's face. His position at the very edge of the elongated frame builds a tension that provides fresh impetus to his looking across, casting about for the offscreen Ling (whose movements inside the room cause slight changes in the patterns of light on his face). It seems an almost gratuitously excessive expression of Chow's nosiness. Having displayed the coolness of the experienced seducer after leaving her room, he is now eager to assess the impact of having broken her heart. It is a naked soul, not just a body, that such a gaze is preying on.

Nearly exactly synchronized to this new, startling image of callous disregard for Ling's privacy is the appearance of a warm, plaintive,

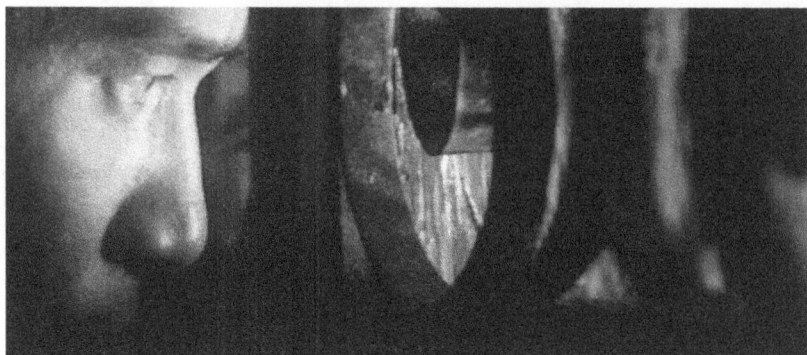

2.2 Chow as voyeur in *2046*.

nondiegetic version of Delerue's music. It is scored for the mellow, full-bodied, dark-toned middle to low register of the upper strings; the angular aspects of their rich, earthy sonority are tempered by the reverberant, large-room acoustics, evoking a time beyond the immediate present and propelling us beyond the here and now of room 2046. The image of Chow spying is held long enough for the music to run through the full antecedent and consequent of the main melody. It is a captivating yet undoubtedly also strange juxtaposition, one that the full volume of the music makes it impossible for us to ignore. The logic underpinning the intervention is musical twice over for, as in earlier Wong films, the cue is not only musical in and of itself but also launches an extended coda to a sequence we thought had ended. The significance of the coda is that Chow's decision to return to his room is pivotal. It is a juncture that calls for an extended aftermath, during which what had seemed the ordinary conclusion to a singular episode—Chow looking through a makeshift peephole—morphs into the premise for a series of repeated events: the filmic equivalent of the frequentative form in language, one that is best rendered, as indeed is the case here, by a montage sequence.

The montage sequence that follows is extremely compressed and consists of just three shots. First, we see images in slow motion of the two lovers, visibly happy, in Chow's favorite restaurant. The camera tracks and pans ever so slightly, as if caressing them, around the large table Chow and Ling are sharing with their friends. We are made to understand that we are seeing one of many such happy rendezvous. Slow-motion cuts against the grain of the joyous whirlwind of activities we see in the frame. Just as the continuous tone of a drone naturally appears to be synchronized with the movement of a camera, picking up the tempo suggested by the resulting visual patterns, so the smooth movement of the camera here appears to move spontaneously in sync with the tempo of the music. Music and slow motion signal a distant, if not detached, look at the scene unfolding before our eyes. Delerue's track, moreover, silences the characters' cries and laughs, its melancholy notes lending the scene a nostalgic tone.

Over the same music, there is a cut to a bird's-eye view of Chow and Ling in bed, making love, the camera rotating gently on an ideal axis at their feet. Despite the audible presence of their moans and sighs, we are made to understand that this, too, is the image of a typical, repeated action. As the music cue ends, an almost imperceptible cut takes us to a closer shot of the same scene. Without the musical envelope, the sound effects bring us back to the here and now of the action: the representation of a singular, precisely located moment in the history of Chow and Ling's relationship. As the camera tilts, first up and then away from their naked bodies, we finally cut to a close-up of Chow, who, turning his head and looking over his right shoulder in the right portion of the frame, whispers, "I am going back to my room." The extreme close-up of the doorknob turning, and the emphatic sound of the shutting door, leaves no doubt as to the fact that his first exit has established a pattern he's still abiding by now. Here, the sequence that began with his seduction comes, at long last, to an end. The musical coda has turned out to be the main argument of an elaborate exposition structured like a chiasmus, sprinkled with recurring visual motifs. Despite its chiasmic form and precious symmetries, the sequence can hardly be called circular, however. As Ling puts yet another ten-dollar banknote in the near-full tin box she keeps under the bed, we come to realize that a lot of water has run under the proverbial bridge.

In complying with the age-old convention of rolling out a montage sequence to the sound of a nondiegetic cue, the music partakes of the dialectic between singularity and typicality that defines this extraordinarily well-wrought episode of the film. As per a long tradition in Hollywood scoring, too, the sustained musical accompaniment smooths over the somewhat fragmentary visual structure of the montage (as well as, on closer inspection, the somewhat less-than-seamless cuts). But as significant as these functions are, the overwhelming impression left by the music is the way in which, to paraphrase Levinson, it indicates that we are to share the compassionate, nostalgic, and slightly regretful attitude of the film's presenter; that is to say, insofar as the film is the fleshing out of his recollections and reflections, the attitude of Chow himself as he looks back to an episode in his past. Whether we construe the presenter as being the character/narrator, an extradiegetic presenter, or the director himself is less important than acknowledging that mood music is a formidable tool for the representation of perspective. Such a representation is no less powerful in shaping our experience of a film for being difficult to attribute with surgical precision to this or that agent.[29] Indeed, to insist on too exact an attribution would be to strip mood music of what differentiates it from its verbal counterparts: the emotional valence of melodic types, colors, rhythm, and textures, and the fluidity with which music attaches itself to, or frees itself from, one or more viewpoints simultaneously, ranging from the expression of a highly individual disposition to the summoning of a shared feeling on the part of a whole community.

In 2046, calling forth a shared attitude of sympathy is key to the insertion of the music whenever Chow casts his seemingly disenchanted gaze on the gallery of fallen characters that surround him. Far from stigmatizing Chow's act as intrusive, let alone immoral, the music cuts against the act's seeming callousness. It complicates the picture of a man furtively looking at a woman caught at her most private by adding a note of genuine concern, even fatherly compassion, to the erotic impulse that underpins his desire to peek into her room. The note of humanity lent by the music to an otherwise disturbing sight may reveal the confusion Chow is experiencing as he spies on her; alternatively, like a voice-over, the music may signal that what we're seeing is the work of memory, the seeming presentness of the image belied by a retrospective soundtrack casting a benevolent, regretful shadow on his own reckless display of voyeurism. Whether we hear it as an aid to the representation of a complex phenomenology or the expression of a retrospective, nostalgic gaze, Delerue's tune is here cast against type. Rarely has a voyeur been accompanied by such euphonious music.

There is yet another way in which the music inflects the paradigmatic image of Chow spying on his unsuspecting lover. As the key element in a nascent montage sequence, it creates ambiguity. Is the close-up of Chow the last shot of a sequence culminating in Ling crying or is it the first shot of the montage sequence? By the same token, is the shot of the corridor between the two lovers' rooms an instance of elliptical editing? Might it be, rather, an image of the corridor captured at any time whatsoever? If so, the close-up of Chow may be presenting us with a moment long before, or after, the episode in which he leaves her room. The implacable temporal and logical sequence of the editing is not perhaps what it seems at first. Spying on Ling he certainly is, but perhaps not with the cruelly dissecting curiosity of someone who has just done something wrong and wishes to observe the impact of an ill-considered deed. The image of Chow transcends not only the singularity of a specific point in time but also the routine nature of his voyeurism, taking on a metaphorical dimension: the exterior manifestation of his sustained interest, in his characteristic role of lustful participant / sympathetic observer, in Ling's beleaguered fate.[30]

REPETITION AS APPROPRIATION

It is now time to redress the significance of the director's choice of Delerue's music. It would be foolish to deny that there exists a chronologically, artistically, and legally prior use of the same tune (as the score to *Confidentially Yours*, that is). But it is in terms of his modus operandi, not the recognition of the borrowing as such on the spectator's part, that Wong's poaching is best understood. Despite the abundant use of preexisting materials, the richness of Wong's peculiar brand of audiovisual language bypasses the seemingly obligatory passage of intertextual references and peer-to-peer homage. Interpreting the music according to broadly recognizable generic features and registers more than suffices in identifying its distinctive role in the characteristically ambiguous blend of past and present tense and first- and third-person narration. Delerue's music absolves its duty perfectly well in its repackaged status. It isn't just that the topical qualities of the track transcend its specific textual origin; it is also that in the source film the music is hardly audible. Truffaut uses it only once as the underscore to Ardant's dramatic journey to Marseille, a journey during which she reminisces about her past in the port city (this is a stage of her life about which we know nothing, as it falls before the time when the story began). It is a poignant aside, to be sure, yet one that Truffaut wisely did not foreground or dwell on, presumably for fear of altering the light, comic tone of the film. Not coincidentally, in *2046* Wong employs a longer version of the cue, one that perhaps Truffaut himself rejected, and that can only be found on the CD release of the soundtrack.[31] Wong endows the borrowing with pride of place by emphasizing its dominant role in the sound mix and by the tried-and-tested method of repeating it at critical junctures. As noted earlier, the theme appears once before, during the otherwise silent shot of Chow and Ling returning home in a taxi after spending Christmas dinner together. Like the several, insisted reprises of "Yumeji's Theme" in *In the Mood for Love*, repetition elicits the spectator's capacity to recognize, as opposed to merely register the appearance of, the music. But short of being familiar with it via Truffaut's film, one does not recognize Delerue's music as such; rather, one notices, leitmotivically, an internal recurrence, bringing the process of appropriation, and with it the refusal to acknowledge the loan as a citation, to its logical conclusion. It's as if *2046* were unseating *Confidentially Yours* as the source of the music's power and raison d'être.[32] Repetition, and the cementing of the tie between the music and its new home, is tantamount to a declaration of ownership.

The ex post facto awareness of the number, range, and provenance of Wong's musical sources in *2046* finally brings to light yet another facet of the process of appropriation. As creators of fiction, both Wong and Chow are worldmakers; they repurpose broken genre pieces or inject new life into long-gone precedents, be they martial arts novels, science fiction novellas, or self-reflexive films. Delerue's music has all the trappings of a temp track freely picked from a tried, ready-to-hand precedent to serve a film that is not so much the documentary account of a lived life but the actual and sole manifestation of a writer's work-in-progress. Yet we can see Chow at work, and his fantasies realized, only in the peculiar brand of audiovisual language universally attributed to Wong Kar-wai. And because we see Chow's work through Wong's film, the latter's choice of music from older films is one important means through which the director's own cine-musical preferences imbue his main character's style as a storyteller. The director liberally takes music from other films, in other words, only to lend what he's just borrowed—subletting it, as it were—to a fictional narrator. It is a sleight of hand that once again enables Wong to affirm ownership or, better, the appearance thereof: for you can only loan out what you own.

THREE

OWNING

The fiction film is a form of forms, the cinema a medium of media. Filmmakers don't work with phonemes, gobs of formless paint, or slabs of stone. Sourced, curated, recorded, and assembled by teams of people, the raw materials of film are often already-constituted objects in the first place: shots of known sites, familiar voices and sounds, the very language used by the actors, not to mention the actors themselves and their personal and professional histories (previous roles, public personas, body types, and so forth). All these elements are difficult to harmonize with one another and bend to the exigencies of a screenplay, which must strike a balance between creating a world that is at once distinctive but also recognizable (or at least comprehensible). For already-constituted objects threaten to puncture absorption by drawing attention to themselves. They evoke other worlds, other stories; imply different trajectories; call up images of other makers. They diffuse and confuse our sense of authorship. The status of the cathedral—multitextured, multiauthored, and perennially unfinished—would seem to be, for a film, a default position.[1]

Hence the job of the director, whose task is at a minimum to reverse the centrifugal tendencies of the material, get the proverbial job done, and lend the composite form a sense of direction and closure.

Preexisting music plays an equivocal role in this struggle for clarity, closure, and direction. Carefully selected tracks can provide continuity across the whole arc of a narrative, more so if the music is to impart a sense of the locale, milieu, and historical time (think of, to make one obvious example, *American Graffiti* [1973]). Similarly, biopics of performers and composers require judicious use of relevant preexisting, and often very well-known, music. This is not only for the sake of creating a plausible character but also grounding the film in a verisimilar historical context. Continuity in modus operandi and musical taste can shape a whole career. To take an oft-discussed example, Stanley Kubrick's selection and bold use of classical and avant-garde recordings remain potent marks of his filmmaking style.[2] These and many other illustrious precedents notwithstanding, preexisting music wears its status of already-constituted object on its—forgive the pun—record sleeve. It threatens to stand out as not merely preexisting but autonomous, all the more so when it clashes stylistically with its surroundings (whether on account of its sonic qualities or incongruity).[3] This is a welcome state of affairs if one uses a musical citation as a modernist device, the locus of stylistic shocks and source of fragmentation, or if, in a postmodern vein, a director wishes to create palimpsest-like narratives that play on the spectator's awareness of cine-musical references.[4] But what of the alternatives, and what does the job of subsuming preexisting music to one's own artistic agenda and commercial imperatives entail?

For all the attention lavished on his meticulously compiled soundtracks, and their afterlife as self-standing works of musical curation, in the films themselves Wong bends preexisting music to the tried and tested recipe of story and character. He is also extremely adept at using carefully sourced recordings to create a sense of locale. The very beginning of *In the Mood for Love* (2000) is in this respect almost programmatic. As Su Li-zhen (Maggie Cheung) inspects her new quarters, Suzhou *Pingtan* resounds in the hallway (a radio broadcast, one presumes). The volume endows the music with presence without the implausible clarity that in period pieces too often mars the re-creation of an environment. The finely calibrated reverberation and slightly grating timbre convey a sense of the hard, polished surfaces of the tiled floors and painted walls that grace the interiors of the tenement buildings (*tong lau*) from that bygone era. It is a strong, exquisitely crafted sonic signature, rich in architectural and historical connotations. The effort to re-create a specific radio signal in a unique living space at a given point in history, it turns out, goes hand in hand with an almost fetishistic reconstruction of a specific event in the musical history of Hong Kong. As Timmy Chihting Chen has shown, the Shanghai Pingtan Group toured in Hong Kong in 1962 and that is most likely why we hear a fragment of one of their performances at the beginning of the film.[5] If that is the case, the broadcast dates the beginning of the story to a specific month and even week (the first week of July 1962).

Wong's investment in the reconstruction of the soundscape of the protagonists' living quarters lends weight to the significance of the historical context as a function of nostalgia. It also offers an insight into the working method that underpins the film. In keeping with his attention to visual detail, Wong appears to have felt the need to also call up a sonic private world during the filmmaking process: the radio broadcast as *punctum*.[6] Perhaps he was convinced or simply hoped that the genuineness of the reconstructed artifacts might rub off on the representation of the emotional drama at the heart of the film. Part auratic object, part talisman, the historically authentic detail does to the creation of a setting what a recalled experience or Stella Adler's "as ifs" do for the method actor trying to capture a given experience onstage. The almost maniacal attention to props, clothing items, or sounds is in excess of what even the most knowledgeable spectator will be able to appreciate. Beginnings are equivocal, moreover. Unaided by a context or explicit allusion, let alone the deliberate excavation of historical trivia, the music comes across as a generic rather than specific instantiation of the soundscape of Mrs. Suen's (Rebecca Pan) household: less the representation of a singular moment in history than the suggestion of a routine action and a habitual state of affairs.

REBRANDING

Wong's use of preexisting music as dramatic scoring entails a similar movement away from the particular toward the general. In a move redolent of an earlier stage of film history, Wong recycles oldies, well-known classics, or esoterica for their generic—rather than specific—qualities. He then makes such distinctive use of these borrowed tracks that they sound as if they had originally been written for his films. Ever the bricoleur, he repurposes them in ways both drastic and persuasive. In so doing, he subtly yet inexorably erases a sense of their original provenance and converts them into elements of the Wong Kar-wai universe. "Instead of selling the music," writes David Bordwell, Wong "makes it part of the expression of the scene."[7] Bordwell's implicit reference to MTV, whose technical vocabulary Wong occasionally employs, is well taken. In a nutshell, Bordwell brings to light the crux of this book: the role of dramatization in the transformation, in postproduction, of already-constituted repertoires. Far from channeling the familiar, the use of music as a dramatic device is transformative. It invests music with a new set of expressive nuances and rhetorical roles. It rewrites its phenomenology but also ontology.

Wong's rebranding of the soundtracks of his films as self-standing recordings is a clear concession to a commercial imperative. He does not just use soundtrack releases to sell his films and remind audiences of them long after their release; he also sells the music itself—only as his own. A shrewd marketer, Wong uses every occasion at his disposal to extend the reach of his work via all manner of mementos and merchandise. For example, a deluxe, limited vinyl edition of the soundtrack of *Chungking Express* was released in 2016 to mark the twenty-fifth anniversary of Jet Tone, Wong's production company (fig. 3.1).[8] The soundtrack features a mixture of original and preexisting music, most famously the Mamas and the Papas' recording of "California Dreamin'." The original recording was released—in CD form—in 1995 and the 2016 anniversary must have seemed a perfect occasion to give the compilation soundtrack for *Chungking Express* a new lease on life. Soundtrack albums are marketing tools, mementos, but also curatorial projects. The remembered film provides the background against which an otherwise disparate selection makes a convincing case of being musically coherent. Think of the soundtrack album like a "concept album" in the manner of *Pet Sounds* or *Sgt. Pepper's* and the film director as the record producer or music curator. Frank Zappa's *Uncle Meat* was conceived and realized as the soundtrack for a film that was not made. The film that never was is the concept, the hinge around which everything revolves.

Hollywood studios began to market their films through their soundtracks as early as the 1950s.[9] Music is nimble. It allows a film to acquire an aural presence in the mediascape with relative ease even prior

3.1 *Chungking Express*, cover of the anniversary vinyl edition of the soundtrack (2016).

to its release (typically on the radio but also via strategically released singles). The sale of a soundtrack album could make millions for the studios, even more so when they own the music rights. Successful soundtrack releases have in some cases outlived the films they served as vehicles for and offered a quick remedy to their oblivion, making sure that they didn't fade from public consciousness. Wong Kar-wai knows all of this but goes a step further. The 2016 vinyl recording for *Chungking Express* marks an important passage in the history not of the music contained therein, but the studio (Jet Tone) that produced the film in which it appears. The recording, moreover, is part of a series that includes all the soundtrack albums inspired by Wong's movies after 1991, as in a virtual *Complete Musical Works of Wong Kar Wai*. The rebranding subsumes the music under Wong's whole cinematic oeuvre. In lifting it from his film and making a recording of it, finally, Wong acts like a tutelary deity of sorts: taking the mantle of the restorer, he returns the more vintage tracks to their original state, a fact pointedly stressed by the choice of vinyl.

Its cleverness and timeliness notwithstanding, such rebranding only works because of the effectiveness and brilliance with which the music is recast in the films themselves. Like any director working with a good budget, Wong has access to technology, labor, and a huge archive. This set of conditions has paved the way not merely for the assumption of authorship over the music in the form of synchronization and mechanical rights but also for the remediation of musical repertoires in keeping with a wholly original audiovisual language. Spotting, selecting, and synchronizing have all been sublimated into the premises of a new musical poetics. Like a consummate DJ, Wong uses the tools of musical reproduction—cassette and CD players, turntables, iPods, and playlists—as the means for music-making.[10] Where the DJ reframes a piece by "breaking" it or mixing with other pieces, Wong places it in the context of a setting and a dramatic situation, itself embedded in a narrative arc, or splices it to a striking image.

Other than "Casta Diva," *2046* (2004) features another Vincenzo Bellini excerpt.[11] Playing to the notes of the "mad scene" of Bellini's *Il pirata*, with Maria Callas singing Imogene, the episode in question takes us from the world conjured by Wong's alter ego Chow to the reality of him sweating it out at his desk (figs. 3.2 and 3.3). While writing, Chow seems to intuitively respond to the register of opera. Only he hears it in terms of generic, inherited schema rather than as a uniquely expressive, individual utterance. Correspondingly, he crafts the episode of the stabbing of a jealous, violent lover in suitably stylized and hyperbolic terms. In a Fellinian swerve, Wong implicates himself in this reflection on artistic creation, and what is more he does so through the music: the opera being played on the gramophone doubles as the soundtrack to Wong's own film. Wong's cinematic fleshing out makes manifest sonic and visual details that Chow's fictional text can only allude to verbally. The artificial reverb would seem to place the music in a resonant space consistent with the somewhat abstract, cavernous interior—not unlike an opera stage—where the two lovers engage in a last, warm embrace. As the episode unfolds, the acoustics retreat into the default position of high volume, minimal spatial signature, and, in keeping with the recording, close-up miking of the voice. The recitative's stop-and-go quality and sparse textures make room for the oc-

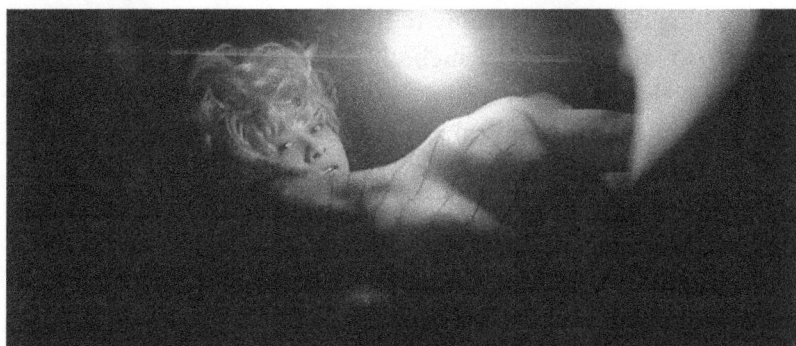

3.2 and 3.3 Chow writes to the sounds of opera in *2046*.

casional sound effect, such as the grating sound of the cage elevator and the murmur of the air-conditioning system of the spaceship as it crosses time and space in its chimerical search for *2046*. Wong cuts the sung portions of the recitative to medium close-ups of Lulu's face and the rousing figure at the strings to the image of her staggering in the corridor leading to a bedroom. The sync point between the climactic "*sepolta!*" (buried) in the music and Lulu's last breath betrays an engagement with the text of the libretto. Yet in the last analysis Bellini's opera has no direct relationship with the onscreen action. The sets and costumes are redolent of the postindustrial aesthetics of cyberpunk on the one hand and cosplay on the other. The psychedelic palette of colors, sharp light contrasts, and insistent play between long shots and extreme close-ups bespeak the unmistakable influence of Japanese manga.[12] The episode neatly allegorizes the impetus behind musical bricolage. Chow openly tells us how in crafting his novella *2046* he liberally borrows from real life. In this episode, he borrows what is ready-to-hand or, better, "ready-to-hear." Not content with demystifying the writing process by anchoring it in the temporal and spatial contingencies of Chow's routine, in this sequence Wong also deflates the significance of the musical selection by segueing from the glory of Callas's voice into the utterly mundane sound of Chow's bed squeaking and creaking as he makes love to the girlfriend du jour. A more precipitous fall from grace would be hard to imagine.

To be sure, Wong is fully aware of the artistic and historical background to the materials he is manipulating. And he invests a significant portion of the budget to clear rights. He is as interested in specific recordings as the repertoire they contain. The recorded performance, not the musical work, is what prompts him to call on certain celebrated releases: interperformativity in lieu of intertextuality. Callas's voice looms very large in the branding of 2046 and I suspect that Wong intended to use her version of "Casta Diva" as well but failed to secure the mechanical rights ("Casta Diva" is used four times in the film, with Angela Gheorghiu singing the part of Norma). The booklet of the EMI soundtrack release prompts us to tie the oblique celebration of Callas's voice, and recording culture more generally, to the film's ruminations about the yearning for permanence against the inevitability of change and senescence.[13] But we heed such statements at our own risk. At best, they rehearse tired hermeneutic plots; at worst, they are casual reminiscences or rationalizations of marketing ploys. The sheer fame of Callas, and the somewhat opportunistic reframing she suffers at the hands of the director, makes one think of advertising and the mixed blessing of a celebrity endorsement instead.

TAKING OWNERSHIP

Wong's most audacious appropriation is the use of "Yumeji's Theme" in *In the Mood for Love*. The music consists of two interlocking elements: a languid violin solo and a steady waltz rhythm, which also carries the harmony, played pizzicato by a small string orchestra. It is famously heard as many as nine times, functioning throughout as a musical interlude marking the different stations of the two main characters' inner—indeed, clandestine—drama. The harbinger of a space other than the sphere of the everyday, "Yumeji's Theme" is the soundtrack to an alternate, slow-motion film as it were concealed in the folds or interstices of the narrative proper. It is paradoxically both a break from, and an intensification of, the main story line.

The music is so intimately tied to *In the Mood for Love* that the realization that Wong poached it from another film is invariably met with astonishment, followed by disbelief. *Yumeji*, the source film, is a wonderfully surreal dramatization of the life of the eponymous Taisho-era painter. Directed by Seijun Suzuki, it enjoyed a limited release in 1991 and was scored by Shigeru Umebayashi.[14] It is impossible to deny that there exists a chronologically, artistically, and legally prior manifestation of the same music (as part of Suzuki's 1991 film, that is). Wong, moreover, took a thematic cue from Suzuki's film. In *Yumeji*, the music underscores a stylized rendering of the main character's seduction of the soon-to-be Mrs. Wakija. Following the latter's involuntary memory, precipitated by the sound of the rain, the music teases out the melancholy of her reminiscing a younger self embroiled in an affair with Yumeji just as she was getting married. The reference could hardly be more pertinent to Wong's own story (as in a compressed foreshadowing, which Wong would go on to flesh out and amplify). But given the obscurity of the film, it is not likely to be grasped as such by the clear majority of Wong's audience. It is at most an esoteric allusion.

Mindful of its history prior to *In the Mood for Love*, Timmy Chih-ting Chen has rightly observed that "as pre-existing film music, the very first emergence of 'Yumeji's Theme' is always already a repetition."[15] But the statement describes the filmmaker's experience more than that of the spectator. Wong uses the theme at critical junctures nine times. This penchant for repeating is itself an appropriation of the modus operandi of *Contempt* (1963) (where Jean-Luc Godard uses Georges Delerue's main theme a staggering sixteen times). Repetition elicits the spectator's capacity to recognize and eventually also habituate themselves to, as opposed to merely register the appearance of, the music. Yet short of being familiar with it via Suzuki's film, one does not recognize Umebayashi's music as such; rather, one notices a recurrence indigenous to *In the Mood for Love*, bringing the process of appropriation, and with it the refusal to acknowledge the loan as a citation, to a perfect conclusion. The force of Wong's reworking bypasses the seemingly obligatory passage of intertextual reference or peer-to-peer homage. Interpreting the music according to broadly recognizable generic features—genre, instrumentation, editing style, acoustics—more than suffices in identifying its distinctive role. In the context of *In the Mood for Love*, "Yumeji's Theme" absolves its duties perfectly well in its rebranded status. The topical qualities of the track transcend its specific textual origin. In the source film, moreover, the music sounds very different. The theme was rerecorded. Through close miking, the new version makes palpable the work of the bow on the strings and bridge of the violin. There is a profuse use of glissandi and plenty of reverberation. The marked waltz rhythm appears to choreograph the movement of the figures onscreen. By a telling inversion, moreover, the music channels the perspective of the spouses that have been cheated on—a fact that becomes clear on hearing it the fourth time around. This causes a readjustment of its expressive values. The violin solo assumes the unequivocal tone of a lament. Most important, perhaps, Wong endows the theme with pride of place by emphasizing in no uncertain terms its dominant role in the sound mix. The music is introduced unceremoniously via a straight cut, as if to call attention to itself (the opposite, in sound editing terms, of Suzuki's discreet fades). The volume is high and the reverberation strengthens the impression that the two protagonists inhabit an alternate space.

In a widely circulated interview with Tony Rayns, Wong says that "daily life is always routine—the same corridor, the same staircase, the same office, even the same background music—but we can see these two people changing against this unchanging background."[16] The structural dimension of the soundtrack, which in the same interview Wong likens to architectural elements of the space inhabited by the characters, is also elaborated on in an equally revealing interview conducted by Chen with sound designer Tu Duu-chih.[17] Tu describes "Yumeji's Theme" as a "block" (*yi zheng kuai*). The metaphor conveys a sense of the rigid contours of the cues. The music is never faded in but rather bursts into the soundtrack at full volume. The metaphor also points to the role of "Yumeji's Theme" in the film's architecture, evoking a pattern of supporting beams or, to return to Wong's definition, an unchanging background against which action and hence change becomes conspicuous. Taking a cue from Gilles Deleuze and Félix Guattari, Chen doubles down on Tu's notion of a block and recasts it as a "compound of sensation . . . that does not close without also unclenching, splitting, and opening." It's a suggestive characterization that paves the way, in a Bloomean vein, to the interpretation of the film via the "repressed" yet simultaneously "purloined" debt to Suzuki's *Yumeji*.[18]

Inspired by the material and technical alignment between sound editing in film and the cutting and remix of records in popular music, I prefer to think of "Yumeji's Theme" as akin to a "break." In popular music parlance, a break is a rhythmic interpolation between two sections of a song in which only the percussions are heard. In both break-beat and hip-hop, breaks are lifted from a preexisting recording to create a new entity. Multiple turntables and subsequently samples made it possible to repeat them ad libitum for the benefit of dancers. The break is foreshadowed in music history by the so-called stop-time in ragtime and jazz, a rhythmic formula that interrupts the line and gives the impression of a change in tempo. While in jazz the stop-time signals improvisation, in hip-hop the break opens up a recursive space for dancers to fill out with moves in additive, theme, and variation-like patterns. In *In the Mood for Love*, "Yumeji's Theme" transports us to a space where time flows differently and the slow-motion choreography of bodies in a subtly shifting setting forges an alternate movie that both interrupts and deepens the main story line. Wong and Tu take that which was in the background and place it in the foreground. In Suzuki's film, "Yumeji's Theme" plays as faint underscoring for a surreal, highly theatrical reenactment of an episode in the painter's life. In *In the Mood for Love*, the same theme receives star treatment as the only element of the mix. Yet the relentless repeating desensitizes us to the force of the music in something like the way repetition of the same break in a live DJ performance does. The dancing unfolding on the floor eventually holds the onlookers' attention captive. By the same token, the subtle yet inexorable bonding of Li-zhen and Mo-wan draws our attention in Wong's film. Exact, seemingly unstoppable repetition does not so much showcase as empty "Yumeji's Theme" of its expressive qualities, as when words seem to lose their meaning when repeated over and over again.[19] This coercive form of habituation is consistent with Wong's statement about the representation of routine. While its bouncing rhythm and melancholy theme permeate the slow-motion sequences of Li-zhen and Mo-wan's clandestine rendezvous, soon enough "Yumeji's Theme" grows into a neutral litmus test for change rather than a focal point per se. For this reason, I think it somewhat futile to search for sync points between this phrase and that facial expression, rhythmic motif and editing pattern, instrumental color and lighting effect (and so forth). While I do not deny that instances of synchronicity may be deliberate and provide pleasure, I believe they are inessential.[20] As used in *In the Mood for Love*, "Yumeji's Theme" is less dramatic scoring than scopitone or, reaching even further back, scoring for the silents: long stretches of (the same) music engulfing the moving image to impart a dominant affect and signal the start of a new segment of the drama.

To the extent that Wong's retooling brought renewed attention to Suzuki's idiosyncratic, poorly distributed film, *In the Mood for Love* is the precursor to *Yumeji*. The realities of film distribution and dynamics of commercial success rewrite genealogies and alter the order of the history of the art form, much like the proverbial "individual talents," which T. S. Eliot championed as the movers and shakers of the literary canon. This reordering applies to a whole range of characters and motifs, not just the music, and across Wong's entire oeuvre at that. My own retelling of Mrs. Wakija's episode against its ostensible counterpart in *In the Mood for Love* endows Suzuki's work with a clarity it may not have originally possessed, and it demonstrates the inevitable reshuffling of narrative values that follows from any new work claiming its rightful place in a tradition. It also rhymes with Chen's contention that the music transports Li-zhen and Mo-wan "back to the future of Suzuki's 1991 film."[21] But Eliot's argument reminds us, too, of the circularity implicit in any interpretation that implicates the work one borrows from in our understanding of the work that does the borrowing. Because the latter effectively rewrites the former, resonances and points of contact are bound to be found aplenty.

SELF-CITATION

Suppose that you know Suzuki's films by heart for having written about them and what is more you are struck by the appearance of "Yumeji's Theme" as an obvious, patent borrowing.[22] Recognizing the cue in the context of *In the Mood for Love*, I want to argue, is akin to realizing that, say, the beginning of *The Thief of Bagdad* (1939) has lifted four bars from Richard Wagner's "The Flying Dutchman" (this experience, which I considered in chapter 1, is recounted with undisguised irony by another self-described, if unwitting, expert, Carolyn Abbate). In both cases, *déformation professionelle* triggers a recognition that is, it is fair to assume, not scripted because it would necessitate esoteric knowledge on the audience's part that the directors did not count on when making their films.[23] The interpretive outcomes could not be more different, however. On recognizing the "Flying Dutchman" excerpt in *The Thief of Bagdad*, one is bemused, not to say puzzled. One does not quite know what to do with that knowledge except to use it to deconstruct the modus operandi it offers an unhoped-for peek into. The quoted fragment hardly enhances one's grasp of the narrative at hand, nor does it deepen one's absorption in it. In fact, in Abbate's recounting, its triviality punctures one out of it in the manner, precisely, of Roland Barthes's *punctum*. By contrast, recognizing "Yumeji's Theme" in *In the Mood for Love* aligns with what Barthes calls the *studium*, namely an attitude toward the artwork informed by historical and documentary evidence and sensibly oriented toward the ostensible subject of the film (or at a minimum, one that the directors would recognize as being consistent with their intentions). The presence of Umebayashi's music is decidedly not coincidental, let alone trivial. This is, first, because of its frequency and obvious significance. While the Wagner citation is most likely the work, possibly unconscious, of the composer, the use of Umebayashi's music follows from a deliberate choice of the director (albeit one that the audience has to sit patiently through the end credits or do some research to find out about). As the work of Chen and other critics indicates, moreover, exegesis of "Yumeji's Theme" can be used productively to add layers of meaning to the narrative of Mo-wan and Li-zhen's repressed romance. Criticism and media commentary allow the lay person to catch up with the expert, turning an esoteric, artfully concealed borrowing into a reference that the audience can talk about. This is possible because of certain more or less apparent parallels between Wong's film and *Yumeji*, which the music draws attention to. The effort at recovering that which is buried or repressed under the surface of the moment-to-moment film experience, albeit only via a tenuous musical link, allows certain objective facts about the film to become manifest (the Freudian language is, of course, hardly coincidental). This is not to say, however, that such a recuperative form of film criticism isn't, too, a manifestation of a certain *déformation professionelle*. To the contrary, it rewards, perhaps to a fault, the work needed to hunt down esoterica and showcase one's mastery of the relevant body of work (and the language needed to make that work come alive in one's own writing). My reservations about this mode of criticism have less to do with signaling a potential conflict of interest, however, than the methodological spin-off it entails. For insisting on a film's predecessors, and the web of intertextual relations that underpin its texture, all too often comes at the expense of the ostensible subject, the fictional world that is a film's main item of business (which is relegated to epiphenomenal status or dismissed as the subject of popular criticism). Focus on intertextual relations, moreover, encourages walking down the well-trodden path of seeking out continuities across the various reincarnations of a borrowed tune or work at the expense of the study of the transformations it undergoes as it becomes embedded in a new work.

Halfway through this book, it will by now be clear that extrapolating from the admittedly special case of Wong Kar-wai's cinema has a heuristic value. Artists can do little to control the impact of what they borrow. Nor can film critics and scholars dictate rules as to what counts as a citation or allusion and what does not. After all, the relative degree of obscurity, familiarity, or topicality of preexisting materials will depend on the audience (down to the individual spectator, in fact). The Pandora's box of associations, personal memories, or semiotic short-circuits precipitated by the encounter with an artwork is utterly dependent on one's cine-musical literacy, cultural background, and personal history. Whether we should consider a spectator uninformed, typical, or ideal is a moot point. Just as it is theoretically possible that some gallery dwellers may not recognize Mao in the eponymous silkscreens by Andy Warhol, conversely a Japanese film specialist may recognize "Yumeji's Theme" as used in *In the Mood for Love* at its very first appearance (and despite its subdued appearance in Suzuki's *Yumeji* in the first place). We need to restore a sense of just how shaky the foundations of what Barthes calls *studium* actually are (or ought to be). Just who recognizes a borrowing and what such a recognition brings with it is impossible to map; we must rest content with proposing hypothetical, albeit plausible, scenarios, without the benefit of a formula that churns out the exact coordinates of a given experience. We can't know how things will pan out and constantly run the risk of selling the spectator short. Which is also why the *punctum* looks to be too easy an escape from this intrinsically unstable field as does seeking cover under attested meanings (be they overt or esoteric, as corroborated by authorial intentions).

Herein lies the deepest significance for this study of Michael Galasso's musical pastiche for the ending of *In the Mood for Love*. Galasso's new composition ("Angkor Wat Finale") is the most definitive concealment of the status of "Yumeji's Theme" as a track lifted surreptitiously from another film. The music reprises the triple meter of the original, though subjecting it to a faster tempo. The color is similar as the new piece is also written for a string-only ensemble. The dominant sonority is that of the cellos, however. Over a faster version of Umebayashi's waltz rhythm, also in pizzicato, jerky cello lines struggle to sketch a definite melodic contour around two main motifs. The faster tempo lends Galasso's track a rushed, recapitulating character, which is apposite, given its placement at the film's epilogue. This stands in contrast to the suppleness and rev-erie of Umebayashi's drawn-out melody. Yet the newly composed track retains an undeniable relation with its model, rather like its diminution or leitmotivic elaboration.[24] Because of where it is emplaced, "Angkor Wat Finale" plays out not merely as imitation but rather as a transfor-mation of "Yumeji's Theme." While exact repetition of the same musical idea numbs the senses, its development rekindles them. The differences between Galasso's music and "Yumeji's Theme" are commensurate with the temporal, spatial, and psychological distance covered by Mo-wan in the intervening years. Leitmotivic elaboration does not merely reflect the changed circumstances of a narrative through subtle yet perceptible changes: it is itself an active agent that embodies those very changes. As the compositional similarities seal a link between Galasso's freshly composed track and the one borrowed from *Yumeji*, the status of the for-mer as original (i.e., freshly written) score rubs off onto the latter. The extratextual origin of "Yumeji's Theme" takes a back seat to the infra-textual process that takes us from it to Galasso's elaboration thereof. It's a backhanded declaration of ownership that puts a nail in the coffin of Umebayashi's music's prior existence as a soundtrack to Suzuki's film.

Leitmotivic treatment limits room for maneuvering. It forecloses the possibility of free associations. Parading "Yumeji's Theme" as the model for Galasso's own riff on it draws the attention to a generative process indigenous to the film instead. It places all spectators in the same boat, so to speak, "assimilating" their responses, in Anahid Kassabian's terms, as they weigh the new track's indebtedness to its putative model. Miscon-struing a borrowing as if it were the source of a self-citation magnifies the impact of this move. The use of a new arrangement of "Yumeji's Theme" in *My Blueberry Nights* (2007) is a case in point. It is the supreme form of appropriation in that it completely clears preexisting music of its association to a prior text, corpus, or author. That I myself slip into calling it a self-citation is an indication of just how underhanded, and effective, Wong's modus operandi is. In sanctioning *In the Mood for Love* as the primal source of "Yumeji's Theme," the latter's status as the product of borrowing is concealed. Wong engulfs the borrowed track within a closed system—his own oeuvre. Repurposing verges on the cusp of fully-fledged counterfeiting.

Wong's use of the Cuban classic "Siboney" is another symptomatic example of a takeover sanctioned by a self-citation. Much better known than "Yumeji's Theme," and just like "Perfidia," "Siboney" has a long history both in and outside the cinema, most notably as part of the soundtrack to Federico Fellini's *Amarcord* (1973) in Nino Rota's subtly defamiliarizing arrangement. Despite such illustrious history, Wong thought nothing of employing it not only to mark a specific setting but also to be an internal refrain in his cycle about the 1960s in Hong Kong.[25] A paean to Cuba by reference to the indigenous population who lived there prior to the Europeans' landing on the island, the song is the expression of homesickness in the form of an open declaration of love. Written by Ernesto Lecuona for a *revista* (theater revue) in 1927, it was recorded soon thereafter by Cuban star Rita Montaner (1928) and went on to enjoy a historic run of recordings by the likes of Bing Crosby (1946) and Connie Francis, whose 1960 cover is also used by Wong Kar-wai in *2046* (more on this below).[26]

Conceived as a theatrical number, "Siboney" lent itself supremely well to not only remediation but also adaptations to a wide range of dramatic situations and modes of cinematic presentation. This was further facilitated by the fact that its celebration of Cuba's indigenous legacy, as distinct from the European influence and Afro-Cuban styles that also mark its style, is masked. Were it not for the title, few if any would recognize the actual referent of the lyrics (let alone the connotation that the term "Siboney" carries to a native Cuban). Such masking of the indigenous roots of the original was in no small part also due to the swift—and equivocal—embrace by Hollywood and repurposing for the North American and subsequently European audience. It was in the 1930s that "Siboney" became an international hit—hence Fellini and Rota's choice to include it in their evocation of that decade in *Amarcord*. As early as 1931, however, Lecuona himself described Hollywood's appropriations of

Cuban tunes in disparaging terms.[27] Cuban writer Alejandro Carpentier was similarly negative in his assessment of adaptations of Cuban songs. Hollywood films exoticized Cuban motifs and turned them into clichés or, worse, *plumas prestadas*: borrowed feathers.[28]

Plumas prestadas is the opposite of bricolage. The borrowing is flaunted with the intent of capitalizing on its notoriety rather than as the opportunity to produce a creative reworking. It is reduced to a token, a cliché whose main job is drawing attention while simultaneously concealing the ordinariness and dearth of ideas of the new (con)text. Something akin to character motivation must exist for a borrowing to transcend the gratuitousness and exploitative logic that characterize such kinds of musical appropriation. In *Amarcord*, for example, "Siboney" is a plausible element of the soundscape re-created by Fellini on account of its being in the air in the Rimini of the 1930s (thanks to the cinema and especially the radio). Fellini, a Rimini native, was the ultimate insider—or mythmaker—when it came to the reconstruction, no matter how nostalgic, of its soundscape. But the reconstruction of the setting was not Fellini's sole concern. In keeping with the main theme of the film, the very presence of the song was transfigured as collective memory.[29] The notoriety of the music is not exploited as a facile form of appeal but is itself woven into the narrative. The work of memory itself, moreover, takes musical form. As with "Perfidia," Rota's arrangement of "Siboney" is a representation of the act of remembering as much as a reproduction of the song itself (in one of its many releases).[30] Fellini and his collaborators, in short, add value as they borrow. In James Young's terms, they engage in a form of "innovative appropriation" that continues and, in a sense, completes the process by which "Siboney" morphed from being a symptom of cultural colonization (from the United States to Italy) into the expression of local culture.[31] Having successfully evaded the charge of appropriation, however, Fellini may be said to have attempted a takeover. And that is precisely the trouble with a successful redeployment of a famous tune: having paid his legal and artistic dues, the director-as-master-of-ceremony threatens to unseat the original author, the composer, or the latest in a long line of appropriating artists. The imagery, characters, and general tenor of *Amarcord* mark "Siboney" indelibly with an element of the "Fellini-esque"; its bittersweet lyrics, major-minor ambiguity, and marchlike rhythm are attributable retrospectively to Fellini and Rota (rather than the Hollywood films that functioned as vehicles, Lecuona himself, or the Cuban tradition he emerged from). Timing, too, conspired to mask the intended connotations of the original. The young slice of the audience who flocked to see *Amarcord* in the early 1970s likely heard "Siboney" for the first time in Fellini's film.

On deploying a resonant version of "Siboney" as the acoustical envelope to the climax of *Days of Being Wild* (1990), Wong exploits a similar advantage. The song was well known in Hong Kong in the late 1950s and early 1960s, thanks to two highly successful covers by Cugat and Connie Francis, respectively.[32] In the context of *Days of Being Wild*, therefore, "Siboney" sounds entirely plausible as an element of the setting. To the young cross-section of its admittedly scant 1990 audience, however, it must have come across as fresh, exotic even. The years intervening between the 1960s and the film's release saw the explosion of Cantonese covers, followed, in short order, by the coming of age of Cantopop.[33] Such a vastly different musicscape cast a Latin tune in sharp relief. Like the proverbial cat, moreover, *Days of Being Wild* appears to have had nine lives, the pool of potential spectators growing as Wong narrowly escaped financial ruin and his reputation grew. As his audience expanded regionally and internationally, and yet more releases cemented Wong's reputation as a cult artist, *Days of Being Wild* came to be seen in light of his later releases. Viewers familiar with *2046*, having caught the film fresh off its wide international release, would have heard the appearance of "Siboney" in *Days of Being Wild* as a recurrence as much as a precedent (in *2046*, as we shall see, the song plays an even more prominent role). Whether one interprets the trajectory of the reception of Wong's films as a self-fulfilling prophecy or an instance of a late work morphing into the precursor of an earlier one, the net result is that the soundtrack of *Days of Being Wild*, and with it "Siboney," has come to be an artifact of his poetics: a show of artistic "thievery" as trenchant and definitive as that of Fellini, whom Wong has now unseated in the minds of many as owning the song.

That Wong's retooling of "Siboney" is shot through with the sensibility of yet another film makes it an even more remarkable feat of appropriation. The unmissable appearance of the rhythmic pattern that opens Cugat's big-band arrangement of "Siboney" kick-starts a long, unedited Steadicam shot that captures a street scene just outside Manila's old train station. We see a horse-drawn carriage skidding along the street dirt, another one waiting seemingly in vain for a client, and a policeman berating a homeless person and asking him to clear out. In one long, continuous motion, the camera moves past these vignettes to climb a dark, dilapidated staircase that leads to an informal, makeshift bar cum dance hall sitting atop the station. There we see Yuddy leaning on a jukebox, having just inserted a coin to play the very music we're hearing (fig. 3.4). "Siboney" is a textbook example of "ambi-diegetic" music.[34] It never pretends to be anchored in the fabric of the character's here and now the way in which, in the same film, "Maria Elena" is. It is too flamboyant for that. This is apposite, for the seeming ordinariness of the moment belies the sense of a menacing presence. The length of the shot and extreme fluidity of the camera work are not coincidental. As in the celebrated title sequence of Orson Welles's *Touch of Evil* (1958), the joyful anarchy of the scene and boisterousness of the music conceal a teleology.[35] The incessant rhythm cuts across what we eventually come to hear as a stopwatch, the music filling out the time it will take before the bloody denouement.

"Siboney" initially overwhelms the backgrounded sound effects. In retrospect, this can be construed as a reflection of Yuddy's proximity to the jukebox. Even at the start of the scene, outside the station, we hear with him. In keeping with the stylistic model of *Touch of Evil*, however, the unrealistic volume is an expressionistic effect that turns up the heat on what would otherwise appear to be an ordinary day in an ordinary locale. Syntactically, the appearance of the music creates a jolt that swiftly moves us from the intimate, indoor setting of the previous scene to the chaotic scene we are about to witness. The camera continues its long journey through the large space by shadowing Yuddy as he takes a seat near Tide. The music is perceptibly softer in the expectation of a conversation between the two of them, which promptly follows suit. Yuddy explains that he is there not to take a train but to finalize a deal. Following a visual cue, he follows a shady character behind a curtain. Tide stays behind and notices a large group of people entering the premises and crowding the bar. "Siboney" continues. Two individuals sit down and look intently toward the back of the room, as if watching over what is happening behind the curtain. Tide looks in the same direction, too. Cut to Yuddy and the local gangster. They are shown first in an extreme close-up and then as reflected on a dusty glass pane. The music continues in the background. In a mocking tone, the dealer explains that making imitation passports is his job, he does it well, and he expects to be paid in full. He speaks in Tagalog (subtitled) and comes across as hostile. Yuddy confesses to having no money. The music has by now finally stopped, signaling the imminent resolution. He stabs the man and quietly walks

3.4–3.6 *Days of Being Wild*: denouement.

back to Tide's table. Suddenly, the incongruously languid beginning of "Solamente una vez," in the instrumental cover by Los Indios Tabajaras, appears in the soundtrack, very nearly drowning out all sound effects (fig. 3.5). The music lends a quasi-surreal character to the aftermath of what turns out to be a botched murder. Is Yuddy hallucinating? Is the imagined music part of an attempt, as botched as the murder, to quickly regain composure? As Yuddy tries to walk his way out of trouble, the dealer, albeit injured, manages to shout out a signal to his comrades. A furious fight erupts, captured in an extremely elliptical editing style that conveys the dazzling velocity of the resolution. Sound effects and the actors' voices drown out "Solamente una vez." Yuddy more than holds his own. Barely aware of what is happening, Tide is injured. Quick on his feet and putting his policeman's training to good use, he swindles a gun out of one of his adversaries and murders them all (fig. 3.6). The two escape via a window leading to the station's corrugated rooftop, accompanied by the fuzzy whistle of a departing steam locomotive.

THE ABSENT FILIPINO MUSICIAN

Cugat's 1955 big-band arrangement of "Siboney" is roughly contemporaneous with the setting of the story. It evokes not so much the swing era, a ground his earlier big-band version of the same song had covered already, but rather the more eclectic and genre-bending big-band compositions for the concert hall (e.g., Stan Kenton). Cugat's particular arrangement also ties the film—via jazz—to crime and romantic longing as evoked in some well-known soundtracks of the 1950s. Wong is situating the late 1950s and early 1960s not simply by signaling the era through the choice of props, clothing, and location but also by reviving a topos of that era's film style, namely a striking choice of jazz-inflected scoring.[36] The musical choice also resonates with the role of the Philippines in the musical imaginary of the era. As a formerly Spanish and subsequently US colony, the Philippines have long acted as a conduit between the Caribbean Isles, Mexico, and the United States on the one hand and the Greater China region on the other. This applies to porcelain, textiles, and minerals as well as labor. Migratory but also enforced movement of people was facilitated by the perfecting of ever more efficient routes across the Pacific. Music became party to this exchange since at least the late nineteenth century. Doubtless due to exposure to both musical repertoires and the relevant languages, Filipino musicians became coveted members of marching bands and subsequently performers of Tin Pan Alley, jazz, crooning, and, of course, Latin dance genres in Shanghai and subsequently Hong Kong as well.[37] In setting the action in the Philippines, therefore, *Days of Being Wild* complicates the meaning of "Latin" as applied to "Siboney." The Philippines are, to a Hong Konger, the vicarious source of this music as it was through Filipino musicians, as much as recordings, that much of this repertoire was encountered for the first time, especially live—whether in hotel "tea dances" (a staple of Hong Kong social life at the time), bars, or nightclubs. This vicariousness cuts two ways. By appropriating their sounds and honing decades' worth of experience as migrant musicians, Filipino musicians passed as their Western counterparts for an audience of mostly local Hong Kongers. The latter entertained the illusion of witnessing an authentic performance of (primarily) US repertoires or at any rate repertoires sanctioned by the US market.[38] Yet the nature of the repertoire bespeaks a subaltern position on the part of the performers to begin with: to former colonial entities on the one hand, and elite members of their audiences as well as market imperatives on the other. For these musicians had to learn a musical idiom not their own in order to be accepted as legitimate members of the Hong Kong music scene. The fulcrum of these musical activities were the individuals running the venues where the performances took place, for whom the music was merely the vessel for a profitable enterprise.

If I dwell on the socioeconomic matrix that presides over the success of a Latin tune in the Hong Kong of the 1960s, this is to show the complications arising from tying a character to a locale and a song with a long history: what we might call, in keeping with the intrinsic open-endedness of the signification process, the "unintended consequences of borrowing." Wong's mixing and matching is productive as much as reproductive, though. Wong delegates Yuddy to choose the music on his behalf (via a jukebox). Yuddy's agency is Wong's tool in his effort to complete his portrait of the protagonist. The music casts Yuddy as dance-loving, abreast of current trends, and cosmopolitan. His carefree, reckless, and self-destructive behavior at this pivotal narrative juncture affects the music's identity in turn. Wong has enrolled "Siboney" to stigmatize Yuddy's Philippines as a place of licentiousness, unruliness, and ultimately menace. This is consistent with the racially insensitive, us-and-them portrayal of the gang members. In *Days of Being Wild*, Filipinos are engaged with, only insofar as crime and the underworld is concerned.[39]

The underpinnings may be unpalatable but they do add new dimensions to Cugat's arrangement of "Siboney" as it soaks up the tropical climate, decrepit architecture, and anarchistic vibe of the old Manila station.

The plot associates "Siboney" with the Philippines via the simple fact of one young man carrying his own music wherever he goes. Except that it just so happens that the Philippines have historically been an important stopover in the music's long journey toward Hong Kong in the first place. There is a stark irony to this. Yuddy's command of the charts and disposable income enable him to bypass Hong Kong's local venues and their Filipino musicians to enjoy US releases in their original, pristine form: he buys and enjoys such recordings in the comfort of his home. Dancing, the social art par excellence, is for him a solo affair. If he eschews the conventional routes toward romance and sociability, this is because he can afford it. His wealth, social network, and good looks ensure a constant supply of friends, acquaintances, and girlfriends. Yuddy's predicament is the photographic negative of Wong's modus operandi. Wong, too, bypasses the Filipino musicians responsible for making Latin music a staple in Hong Kong. His reconstruction of the sound of 1960s Hong Kong is not literal but plastic, indirect, metaphorical. A portent of things to come, in *Days of Being Wild* Wong adopts a recording rather than taking the trouble of staging a live performance as part of the mise-en-scène. At stake in this choice is the erasure of the role of the Filipinos in his reimagining of the city. Yet the same choice also opens up potential meanings that a realistically staged performance might not afford. Filming a whole chunk of the story in the Philippines, where Yuddy's mother has ostensibly moved, he implicates "Siboney" in a stereotyped representation of the locale. In doing so he frees the song from the contingencies of the Hong Kong context. What began as a borrowing evocative of the Hong Kong soundscape, then, is refashioned after the striking iconography of its intermediate, if not original, place of provenance, as glamorously conjured by Chris Doyle's Steadicam-like cinematography.

DOWNWARD SPIRAL

Wong's appropriation of "Siboney" continues in *2046*, where its adoption signals an internal recurrence on two counts: as a mark of Wong's style but also, and just as importantly, an integral element of his cycle about 1960s Hong Kong.[40] For all its loose ends and inconsistencies, the cycle itself—*Days of Being Wild*, *In the Mood for Love*, and *2046*—is almost Wagnerian in scope and ambition. Across all three films, Wong spins a web of visual and auditory motifs around a cast of actors whose roles in his films and those of other directors he builds on and cannibalizes. The cycle is the primary means through which any internally repeated element, no matter what its provenance may be, is swallowed up into the "Wong Kar-wai franchise." Serialization and franchising expose the structural inconsistency that underpins Wong's approach to the cycle: do unto you what you don't want done unto others, one is tempted to say. Predicated on superseding the borrowed music's prior history, his franchise equips it with a fresh history of its own, reframing it within a world that extends beyond his films through such merchandise as souvenirs, gadgets, and special CD or vinyl releases.

In *2046*, Wong uses Connie Francis's memorable 1960 version (sung in Spanish).[41] Francis begins with little more than a whisper, like a crooner, her voice cast against a bare rhythmic pattern on the congas. As the bass and what sounds like a flamenco guitar join the texture and spell out the underlying harmonies, the voice soars with an almost operatic crescendo in the highly reverberating studio space conjured by the recording engineers. It is a riveting arrangement, one that not only retains but also amplifies the song's most recognizable features: the admixture of major and minor, syncopated rhythms, and the rousing melodic line. To recognize Francis's cover and Cugat's arrangement as being "the same song" is to posit the existence of "Siboney" as a musical work that transcends its individual, concrete instantiations. This enhances the reach of Wong's cycle, which is seen as capacious enough to contain different versions of music that marked an era and whose significance to his evocation of the 1960s his films are both a symptom and an endorsement of.

This is not to say that the specific qualities of Francis's recording are incidental to the specific effect Wong has in mind for it in *2046*—to the contrary. Her shrill, wide-ranging, genre-defying vocal work adds a sense of urgency to her strongly gendered, individualistic interpretation of Lecuona's heartfelt declaration of love. The original, written while the musician was in Hollywood, is tongue-in-cheek about its true recipient. As mentioned above, aside from Cubans, only Spanish speakers of a certain age and education will know that "Siboney" is a moniker for Cuba; fewer still, that it speaks to the island's indigenous past. To the extent that to an international audience the reference is opaque, "Siboney" is intrinsically ambiguous or, better, underdetermined. Most listeners will hear it simply as a love song. In keeping with this broad interpretation, Francis's version invests "Siboney" with an unequivocal erotic charge, which culminates with the operatic rendering of the chorus: "Siboney si no vienes / me moriré de amor" (Siboney, if you don't come, I will die of heartache).

Wong doubles down on Francis's conversion by associating this particular recording with Bai Ling, one of the central female characters in 2046. As a single woman in search of love and, by film's end, the heartbroken heroine of an affair gone awry, Bai Ling tags an unhappy ending to Lecuona and Francis's cri de coeur. "Siboney," in turn, adds a presentational dimension to Bai Ling. We first see her in room 2046 screaming, moaning, and smashing objects against the flimsy wall that separates her room from Mo-wan's. The flimsiness of the wall is hardly coincidental. Mo-wan has brought home a girlfriend and Bai Ling makes it clear she will not tolerate noise in the wee hours. Not without delay, Mo-wan, who remains unseen throughout, eventually stops. The vignette cleverly frames the imminent affair between them as the most efficient way of putting an end to what would otherwise be an unending case of neighborly strife. But it also offers a precious glimpse into Bai Ling's personality: vocal, direct, and uncompromising. "Siboney" takes over from where Bai Ling leaves off (fig. 3.7). Having Bai Ling forcibly silence the noises produced by Mo-wan's vigorous lovemaking, the whisper of Francis's voice can emerge with pellucid clarity. Cut to a shot of a green lamp. At this, the sound of a percussion set insinuates itself into the mix. The sync point indicates the passage of time, as does the costume change. Bai Ling is readying herself for an evening out. "Siboney" is a presage of things to come. It points metonymically to a restaurant or club where she will be entertaining a gentleman. Hot on the heels of her flamboyant silencing of Mo-wan, a struggle in which Bai Ling is not only the undisputed winner but also the sole protagonist, the song is instantaneously subsumed under the audiovisual portrait Wong is making of her. Francis's voice shadows her every move, as if breathing down her neck as she tries a pair of earrings, looks at her makeup, and admires the lines of her dress at the mirror. The soft-spoken delivery of the song's beginning pairs well with Bai Ling's quiet confidence. As the camera insists on her obvious appeal as the target of the male gaze, and the care she puts into maximizing it, the music would seem to work in a complementary fashion by "going under her skin" and revealing not merely a sensual, fiercely passionate

3.7 Bai Ling in *2046*.

woman but also, as per the song's lyrics, a deeply vulnerable one (vulnerability being something that Bai Ling is loath to acknowledge).

This much may seem uncontroversial but entails possessing something like an ex post facto précis of the film. In the course of a film, the unveiling of a character's personality is a piecemeal process during which spectators are in flux, building a picture of the people who populate the screen as they go along. The scene is introductory rather than summative, and the music's role in it is to signal, like a curtain opening, the appearance of a major character: a phatic, or ritualistic, function as much as a gnostic one. Short of being cued up ahead of time, one is unlikely to cordon off the song and read the lyrics as a capsule account of Bai Ling's personality. Even when attended to, and understood, the lyrics are not a transparent window onto her predicament. The shift in register from a comic rant to a portrait of rare concision and sophistication on the one hand, and from unadorned to fully corseted on the other, wraps up Bai Ling in a thick cloud of cultural signifiers.[42] Not only is the song in Spanish but it is merely one aspect of a configuration in which the dominant element is a fully costumed, made-up actress intent on embodying an elaborate feat of self-presentation. Is the song integral to this effort? In keeping with the sartorial theme, songs, like clothes, are temporary items in one's evolving "closet" of personas, attitudes, and dispositions. That "Siboney" turns out to be pertinent to the trajectory of the character does not imply that it is a prima facie symptom of the kind of person that Bai Ling will turn out to be (though it is in a sense predetermined by the conventions that permeate characterization in mainstream narrative cinema).

In fact, the role of "Siboney" is complicated as soon as the third phrase of the song begins ("Ven a mi, que te quiero . . ."). Formally, the line is the "B" verse of an AABA stanza. Here the melody moves to a higher register, one that is less comfortable for the singer and therefore calls for a more dramatic delivery. Francis's line is more akin to a cry of pain than the measured expression of desire. The passage is marked, too, by an expansion into a dominant seventh harmony and the shift from a stripped-down to a full instrumental accompaniment. As we hear this, there is a cut to an extreme close-up of Mo-wan looking through what seems like a spy hole in the wall.[43] The sync point marks yet another stage in our acquaintance with Bai Ling, as well as the role music plays in shaping it. Through the pinhole, Mo-wan is looking at Bai Ling furtively and with apparent relish. Is he, one wonders, contriving his own imaginary soundtrack to a voyeuristic fantasy scene? Should the entire episode be reinterpreted in light of Mo-wan's intrusion? Given his drastically confined perspective, our initial sighting of Bai Ling could not possibly be a literal representation of what he actually sees. Yet the impossibly seductive and polished poses struck by her speak to his obvious curiosity—and desire. As in so many other key junctures of the film, point of view is diffuse. To make matters worse, just as the chorus of the song begins, Wong doubles down on his deception and cuts to a shot of yet someone else: Ah Ping, who is promptly and hypocritically being chastised by Mo-wan for peeking in on her from the very same pinhole (albeit via a camera angle that stresses the comic side of the situation). As the flamenco guitar wraps up a cadence, the music suddenly stops.

"Siboney" returns twice more, striking a balance between the ornamental and the generative. It is almost as if the song were prodding Bai Ling to fall for Mo-wan, whispering words of love into her ears like a prompter or "putto" and covertly choreographing the ballet of advances, mock rejections, and retreats that would come to shape the romance between them. The second time we hear "Siboney," Bai Ling is striking what is perhaps the most memorable image in the whole film: alone, cigarette in hand, on the rooftop of the Oriental Hotel and staring into (offscreen) space (fig. 3.8). The truncated neon sign and orientation of her gaze further widen the noticeably elongated widescreen format that is one of the film's defining characteristics. Whether it features Bai Ling or her elusive foil, Wang Jing-wen, the shot has enjoyed a wide circulation in books, magazines, and promotional materials. Iconic as it is, its meaning is utterly contingent on context. To begin with, by the time

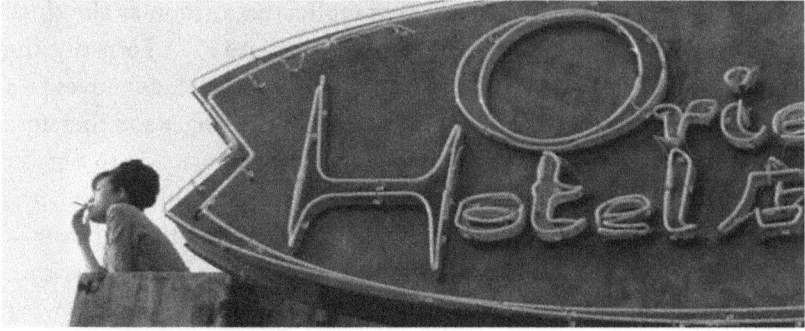

3.8 Perched facing off-screen in *2046*.

we see Bai Ling in this now-famous shot, the image is already a repetition. Earlier in the film, a similarly composed, albeit closer, shot of the same rooftop at dusk shows Jing-wen gesticulating and rehearsing bits of speech. In the words of Mo-wan, who is keeping a not uninterested eye on her, she is "talking to herself" following the breakup with her Japanese suitor (Takuya Kimura). The image is accompanied by the instrumental introduction to Bellini's "Casta Diva." Like Bai Ling, Jing-wen is the object of Mo-wan's gaze. Yet she remains, punning on Bellini, "chaste."

Heard over a strikingly similar image, "Perfidia" is consistent with the change of character (in both the literal and metaphorical sense). Bai Ling not only entertains men as a matter of course but will fall in love with Mo-wan himself. Compared to its precedent, this shot is both longer and wider, a reflection, perhaps, of the different light conditions (we are at a slightly earlier time of the day). "Siboney" appears as soon as we see Bai Ling. It is as if the music were "switched on" by the cut. It starts up from the third verse. Bypassing the introduction to begin in medias res conveys a clear sense of a process underway, a process that had begun when the same music was first heard. The meaning of the shot, therefore, depends on not one but two repetitions (the iconography, notwithstanding the change of actress, and the music). Where the first iteration of "Siboney" ends with the fourth verse, the second begins from the beginning of the third. There is a partial overlap between them. This choice follows from what I see as a stylistic consideration. The length of the music cues needed to match the aggregate length of the shots so that the episode can end with yet another straight cut: a marked sync point between the cadence at the end of the song's fourth verse and the appearance of white intertitles on a black screen. As with the Nat King Cole tracks in *In the Mood for Love*, the demonstratively neat and pointed editing at this juncture underlines yet another key moment in the new, emerging plotline—their cat-and-mouse game—while also lending a comic tone to it. This particular audiovisual treatment of Bai Ling and Mo-wan's collision course betrays Wong's justifiable attempt to lighten the mood of what would otherwise be an oppressively melodramatic presentation of their relationship. The repetition of the third verse, moreover, offers the opportunity for a symbolically charged contrast: where in the first case we saw the extreme close-up of Mo-wan spying on Bai Ling, we now hear the same music underscore Bai Ling in the act of looking—significantly—at nothing in particular, and in the full glory of an almost exaggeratedly open space.

This change of point of view, and the repudiation of voyeurism it entails, proves illusory, however. As soon as the flamenco guitar marks with a characteristic strum the end of the third verse, there is a cut to Mo-wan looking at her from the pantry of the hotel while refilling his thermos flask. Once again, the previous shot was a representation of his point of view. Bai Ling's gesturing toward a nonlocalizable and unquantifiable offscreen is contained, indeed made possible, by someone else's act of looking. This is not so much an active, and surreptitious, instance of voyeurism on Mo-wan's part but rather the unexpected—and welcome—catching sight of the object of his desire. And though his eye falls in the direction of Bai Ling, driven by the erotic impulse, the attention this time is directed inward. As in the previous scene, Bai Ling is unaware of being seen. At the same time, she presents a less constructed side of herself. Her hair partially undone, wearing a night robe, and smoking, she is in the best position to reveal the outline of a naked soul as much as her beautiful figure. As he continues to manage his simple chore, Mo-wan catches himself pondering the sort of person she may be.

The relationship between the two leads has by now evolved. Following Mo-wan's first, insidiously oblique attempt at seduction—an unsolicited gift of expensive stockings—the two of them have kept an eye on one another with an admixture of curiosity and anticipation. As we witness Bai Ling's tragic descent into unrequited love, the music changes aspect not merely in the sense that it feeds—and feeds off—an evolving narrative but also that the outcome of this narrative invites us to revisit its prior appearances. What had initially seemed like the atmospheric ingredient of her manicured, urbane beauty turns out in retrospect to be the surest sign of the predetermined course of her trajectory. As we have seen, in its first and second iterations, Francis (Cupid) whispers into Bai Ling's ears what to do and how to respond. Bai Ling obliges and eventually capitulates. She is sacrificed on the altar of both narrative interest and also Wong's relentless pursuit of his actors' commitment to his characters, and with good reason: Zhang Ziyi's wide-ranging performance very nearly steals the show in *2046*.

In hindsight, "Siboney" is less a Greek chorus than a shadow-character acting as proximate cause. Wong pioneered this ingenious use of preexisting songs in *In the Mood for Love*. The film's Latin tunes, delivered in passable Spanish by Nat King Cole, likewise straddle a middle path between sheer catchiness—the melodies will sound familiar to many, as will Cole's highly recognizable voice—and unobtrusiveness. They comment on the events but at the same time also spur the characters mischievously into action. Cole's diction is clear enough, but only native speakers of the language know what the text actually means. Titles such as "Quizas, quizas, quizas" (perhaps, perhaps, perhaps) notwithstanding, then, the songs also straddle the middle line between vocal and instrumental or, at least, vocalise (a melody without words). The innuendos that hold the key to the unfolding plot remain dormant, as if *secreted* by the singer's diction: rendered inaccessible, like secrets—hence their being whispered—but also discharged into the ether for the attentive or repeat spectator to catch.

By the time we hear the third, and last, iteration of "Siboney," the terms of the relationship between Bai Ling and Mo-wan will have drastically changed. The number three enables all sorts of symmetries as well as a final, and bitterly ironic, chiasmus. Bai Ling is eloping with another persistent suitor. Mo-wan, for his part, has relapsed into his old ways. As in the scene in which we first became acquainted with Bai Ling, he remains offscreen. The appearance of "Siboney," playing once again from the beginning, is fastidiously timed to coincide with the cut to a shot of an old lover of Mo-wan's, whom we've seen in a restaurant frequented by both, paying a visit to his room. Bai Ling is in the lounge talking on the phone. Having duly taken note of the female visitor, she is stung. She suddenly hangs up and rushes to her room to be alone and subject herself to the indignity of hearing Mo-wan make love to another woman next door. As this masochistic and, one hopes, cathartic ritual unfolds, "Siboney" does not cut but fades out.

FOUR

REDRESSING

The only film in the Wong Kar-wai canon that does not make use of existing music is, ironically, also the most derivative. I say "derivative" not in the pejorative sense of unoriginal or imitative but rather in the technical one of "originating from" and "being influenced by." While many have touched on Wong's debt to the martial arts novels of Louis Cha (aka Jin Yong), and *The Legends of the Condor Heroes* in particular, few have gone as far as to say *Ashes of Time* (1994) is an adaptation— and with good reason. While it draws on the world of Cha's legends, *Ashes of Time* spins a story that is not only new but also out of character relative to the protagonists of the source novel. The film reimagines Cha's troubled heroes as young men unsure of their calling whose life has been derailed by existential angst. Nominally a prequel to Cha's novel, *Ashes of Time* bends the martial arts genre to Wong's now-all-too-familiar themes of longing, nostalgia, and regret. While there is action aplenty, this is not only elusive—direct physical contact is nearly always elided or rendered figuratively—but also inconsequential. The main driver of the narrative is the gradual unveiling of the net of relations that tie the protagonists in ever tighter knots. In keeping with the film's focus on subjectivity, the fighting sequences are set pieces that complete the depiction of a character as much as propel the action forward. Notwithstanding their stylishness and innovative look, they are merely a means of credentialing a given character as a martial arts hero, sometimes even de post facto.[1] Moviegoers expecting a conventional martial arts flick were quick to recognize this and walked out of the theater in droves.

Its genetic relation to Cha's novel notwithstanding, it is therefore fair to ask: Is *Ashes of Time* a martial arts film? Whether answered in the positive or negative, the quagmire of assigning the film a genre has loomed large in the film's critical reception.[2] Genre is naturally a fertile perspective in which to read the film, and to an extent it will inform my own analysis of the film's rich soundscape. Yet genre is folded within another and just as significant dimension of the film, one that follows from Wong's penchant for playing cinephile, music lover, storyteller, and producer—all at once. *Ashes of Time*, I wish to argue, is first and foremost a work of fan fiction by a Cha aficionado who happens to have become a professional filmmaker. The film satisfies two essential conditions of classic fan fiction work. First, it extends the reach of the source text across media. Second, it is a freshly conceived backstory that "rights" or "redresses" what the fan perceives to be flawed, incomplete, or otherwise amendable aspects of the source story.[3] As if filling a void, the film depicts Ouyan Feng and Huang Yaoshi as young men (that is, prior to their appearance in Cha's source text as aged warriors). Wong adds a psychological, indeed highly personal dimension to their trajectory as tainted warriors by grounding their inability to act for the greater good in their failure to fulfill their romantic longings. This is not to say that he was dissatisfied with Cha's model—to the contrary. In the words of Wimal Dissayanake, one often "transforms what one loves most," the very act of transformation pointing to a most intimate sort of engagement with a beloved novel, film, or piece of music.[4] But where Dissayanake views the transformation through the lenses of Jacques Derrida's notion of "supplement," I understand the intimacy of Wong's engagement with the source novel as symptomatic of the visceral nature of fandom. Such a symbiotic relationship naturally also calls to mind Harold Bloom's celebrated theory of the anxiety of influence with its attendant assumption of the intertwinement between reading and writing summed up in the term *misprision* (Bloom's term for "defensive, or expedient, distortion").[5]

Wong's misprision of not only Cha but a whole tradition of Buddhist aphorisms that underpin the martial arts genre is encapsulated in the first intertitle of the film, the one that marks the end of the title sequence. It is a subtle but decisive modification of a statement made in one of the Chan Buddhist scriptures: "The flag is not swaying, nor is the wind blowing. It is the mind itself that is in tumult." Bending the drama in the direction of romantic angst, Wong, ever the close reader, changes "mind" into "heart."

Wong's tendency to build on his literary sources in the manner of a fan is in evidence in his treatment of Julio Cortázar, Manuel Puig, or Liu Yincheng (to name but three). But Cha looms large in Wong's career in ways that transcend his (re)modeling of the protagonists of *Ashes of Time* after those from *The Legend of the Condor Heroes*. His considerable debt to Cha manifests itself not so much in borrowing motifs and characters as what appears to be a sustained attempt to re-create Cha's stellar and in some ways unrepeatable career trajectory of wildly successful writer-cum-entrepreneur. Modeling himself after Cha, Wong makes a bricolage of his own professional persona. In the Hong Kong of Wong's youth, Cha was the driving force behind a printing and financial empire. He was therefore a worldmaker in the literal sense.[6] It is no surprise that his figure cast a shadow on Wong's own struggle for self-fashioning and definition, success as an artist, and the establishment of a franchise empire. The venerable writer is a tool in Wong's creation of his own myth. This might explain why he eschews too explicit an adaptation of the older master's work. The choice of Cha as a terrain in which to prove his own worth paves the way to an attempt to supplant the model. Wong emulates Cha not to stand on the proverbial shoulders of a giant who preceded him, let alone to pay homage, but to unseat and make tabula rasa of the model's legacy: bricolage as erasure.

The unfolding of Wong's relationship with his role model is paradoxical. The departure from the narrative and linguistic register of *The Legend of the Condor Heroes* is for Wong a way of both acknowledging his love for the model and carving a space for the affirmation of his own prowess as worldmaker. While they are self-standing works in their own right, adaptations relish the challenge of inviting those in the know to weigh their merits against the source (or sources) that inspired them. Like fan fiction, *Ashes of Time* is to the contrary a self-contained work that extends the reach of the source across the mediascape while at the same time preempting a direct comparison with it (one more reason why viewers expecting to see Cha on the big screen were sorely disappointed). The film behaves like a classic transmedia work in a franchise: more a self-standing piece signed by an author as part of a "spread" of branded products than the retrospective look at a prestigious precedent. On the flip side, *Ashes of Time* revealed the existence of Cha's work to a global audience wholly unaware of it prior to exposure to the film in something like the way a *Matrix*-themed videogame reinforced the *Matrix* franchise despite the departure from the specifics of its plot and characters. And while it is true that the film failed miserably at the box office, it is also the case that its critical success endowed Wong with a certain cachet among a thin but influential cross-section of the cinephile community both in Hong Kong and elsewhere, including, perhaps most importantly, film festival organizers, critics, and the arthouse circuit.

Wong's emulation of his model extends to the attempt to shape the reception of his films. Cha's work resonates through *Ashes of Time* in something like the way Wong's own work is extended by the transmedia products that sprang from it. Cha built a persona revolving around a franchise encompassing his serial novels, of course, but also the newspapers he published, the books he endorsed, as well as the many radio and television adaptations (some of which mediated Wong's own understanding of Cha's literary output).[7] With *Ashes of Time*, Wong pays his dues to Cha by joining in the common, cross-generational—and now also posthumous—effort of perpetuating and enlarging the universe first crafted in the older writer's serialized novels. But in doing so he is also advancing his own brand. A plethora of cleverly designed and strategically placed products, ranging from chapbooks to stylish T-shirts, project Wong's own world into the mediascape—and the marketplace—reinforcing the notion that Wong's films are the source, the germinating seed of a whole new universe shaped by a set of memorable characters and a distinctive sensibility. While it may have begun in the vein of a work of fan fiction, then, *Ashes of Time* also came to partake of the logic of the franchise.[8] The soundtracks, marketed as both a CD and, in the case of the *Redux*, also a collectible anniversary vinyl, have been central to this effort. Aside from their appeal as a marketing tool and source of revenue, the soundtracks continue to play a key role in the reception process in that they perpetuate the illusion that the film for which they serve an ostensibly ancillary role is a "source text" of its own (and not merely a spin-off of Cha's novel). On creating a product that is patently derivative of his film, by a sleight of hand Wong unseats Cha as the point of origin of the world evoked by the music, as well he might. For in adding a footnote to the literary giant's opus magnum, the fan-turned-filmmaker has enrolled a musical score that, in concert with the cast and the desert setting, propelled him into a territory that is far removed from Cha's own. *The Legend of the Condor Heroes* trilogy aside, the world of *Ashes* is also marked by John Ford, *jidaigeki*, spaghetti Westerns, and Tsui Hark's (then recent) smashing success *Once upon a Time in China*. In keeping with Wong's extraordinary ability to metabolize the most diverse sources, this wide range of influences is made to serve the rendition of an utterly original and stylistically compelling vision.

Drawing on topical analysis, in what follows I examine how the music of *Ashes of Time* plays a constitutive role in the conjuring of this vision. I will then move on to consider *Ashes of Time Redux* (2008) as a choice example of the formidable impact of new developments in sound technology and a changed distribution landscape (as Wong himself stated a number of times, the unsalvageable condition of the soundtrack is what prompted him to rework the film in the first place). I will offer a sobering assessment of the results of Wong's response to these changes above and beyond the practical necessity of restoring his film as a material object. For I view the restoration/rebranding of *Ashes of Time* as the key moment in the emergence of what I uncharitably call Wong the "also-ran," as opposed to the expedient—and winning—fan artist of the 1994 original. Where the low-budget score of the original *Ashes of Time* borrows profusely in order to transfigure, the *Redux* version features an orchestral suite that apes musical utterances of such films as *Crouching Tiger, Hidden Dragon* (1999) and *Hero* (2001). For all the polish of the signal, nuances of the mix, and exquisite detail, *Ashes of Time Redux* rings conventional in the context of the global film culture of the late 2000s. At the same time, and ominously for Wong's commercial ambitions, it retained the narrative opacity of the original release.

MUSIC AND WORLDMAKING

Is the "martial" a musical topos and, if so, should one expect it to pervade the music for a martial arts flick? Thus formulated, the question may seem frivolous. In fact, it pertains to the age-old practice of combining music and choreographed action both on- and offstage. It is a question that resonates with what appears to be a universal need to regulate such a combination, a need that takes culturally distinctive forms. In the Chinese tradition, for example, the choice of repertoire is informed by Confucian ideas on the use of music in rituals and ideas about the constitutive role of music in the production of sociality.[9] Invoking musical genre, style, or register—what music is appropriate to what type of action or subject—is, of course, important but risks begging the question of why the presence of music is so pervasive in combat and military rituals as well as fictional representations thereof. Music underpins the display of religious, political, and military power in processions, parades, ceremonies, and inaugurations. It is called upon to delineate the stages of the action and the roles of its actors. But in crossing over from the battlefield or the training ground to a parade, a fanfare sheds its primary mode of existence—as a call to arms, for instance—to acquire a distinctly symbolic dimension. It partakes in the effort of celebrating a state of affairs (the crowning of a king, for instance, or the promotion of a colonel to general). Rituals construct neither an abstraction of the world as seen from a certain perspective, such as one sees in diagrams or scientific theories, nor an alternate and imaginary world in the manner of fiction.[10] Rather, rituals stage the conferral of a certain role on an individual, group, or institution. In so doing they provide not just the stamp of authority but a sensorial dimension to a social situation: a fuller impression of, for lack of a better word, their social reality.[11]

Worldmaking amounts to an elaborate effort to persuade that something is actually the case.[12] In a ceremony one is made king or magistrate just as a child is, in a manner of speaking, "thrown into the world." Worldmaking of this sort endows social relations with the semblance of inevitability and unquestionableness with the aim of making them seem a reflection of natural or divine order. Needless to say, not even the most established, elaborate ritual will mask the underlying instability of the social fabric. There is nothing final or irreversible about the roles assumed by individuals and the relationships they strike with other members of their group. A given kind of social organization is one among many, not merely in the sense that one can entertain or contemplate others but also, and more importantly, in the sense that it can be upset, subverted, and even torn apart (in a revolution, for instance). That is why there always lurks a moment when a musical peroration can ring false or, worse, turn into a parody of the very thing it is meant to celebrate. It is a question of tone, to be sure, but above all the symptom of the breaking down of the social contract, and with it the worldmaking abilities of music.

Theater and cinema are proof of the constitutive—as opposed to reflective or symptomatic—role of music in worldmaking. If decades of contrarian, ironic, or blatantly against-the-grain music scores have taught us anything, it is that to strike the appropriate tone is not just a matter of decorum, compliance with conventions, or, worse, redundancy; it is bound up with the very ability of music to conspire in the worldmaking powers of film by embodying a certain sonic environment, endowing the spoken word with a particular expression, or cueing the spectator to read the image in a certain manner. Replete with explicit references and overt citations from older films, the compilation scores of Quentin Tarantino's films are exemplary in this respect. His compilations are appropriate to a fault, each track reading with the grain of the image to the point of winking to the knowing spectator in apparent self-satisfaction at the "cleverness" of the selection. The point is especially apparent in his parodies of martial arts movies (*Kill Bill: Vol. 1* [2003] and *Kill Bill: Vol. 2* [2004]) and the war film (*Inglourious Basterds* [2009]).[13] But it also applies to the pop track heard in the most gruesome sequence of *Reservoir Dogs* (1992), the notorious hacking off of the cop's ear. Stealers Wheel's "Stuck in the Middle with You" is played by Mr. Blonde as a deliberately jarring, against-type soundtrack to the horrific proceedings, of which he is at once director, set designer, actor, and music compiler. A brilliant musical oxymoron, the catchy tune is simultaneously motivated and gratuitous, intensifier and anesthetic. Tarantino deploys it to draw us into the action while simultaneously distancing us from it. As such, it is an object lesson in the use of music in the construction of a storyworld.[14]

FILM MUSIC AS WORLD MUSIC?

At stake in my opening salvo is not just worldmaking as a cultural practice but also the world as a physical and political entity. What is the cross-cultural reach of certain categories of experience and their codified representations? Is the appeal of the "martial" shaped by the global circulation of goods and consequently the cultivation of a global audience? How does the music of a film like *Ashes of Time*, in both its first incarnation and its subsequent and widely publicized *Redux* version, speak to its audiences?

It could be argued that the kind of dramatic scoring that has graced film since practically its inception, itself a legacy of theatrical as well as nontheatrical forms of spectatorial address, is the first instance of a truly global musical tradition. Film music is global not in the sense that Esperanto is (that is, as an artificial medley of languages from around the globe which everyone begins to learn as it were from scratch). Nor is it global the way American rock 'n' roll is, namely as an appropriated idiom capable of voicing the particular situation of people from around the world, despite its distinctive qualities and circumscribed origin. Film music is global, rather, the way global pop is, namely as a family of practices, an expanding field of technical innovations and musical tropes and conventions that are quickly adopted as their own by practitioners and consumers alike. Like global pop, film music is in this respect an example of a musical technoculture, namely a genre "whose styles have evolved in an inextricable relation with their dissemination via the mass media and their marketing and sale on a mass-commodity basis."[15] In the so-called silent period, scoring practices from one part of the world made inroads into other regions primarily via the exchange of personnel. Recorded sound meant that films traveled with a fixed musical soundtrack, thus galvanizing the imitation of examples deemed admirable or hits whose success could be replicated. Hollywood films enjoyed a robust distribution both before and especially after World War II and thus became the most imitated models the world over. The symphonic scores of classical Hollywood cinema, however, have long come to sound like the expression of a particular moment of one particular, if admittedly dominant, film industry. To be sure, American models remain dominant within mainstream cinema. But the way in which the influence of Hollywood plays out is best described as a form of indigenization (rather than wholesale imitation or appropriation).

This is not to say that film soundtracks are not replete with music from highly distinctive traditions—ranging from bluegrass to *bhangra*, and baroque opera to *enka*.[16] Whether or not their compiled music is adapted, plagiarized, or bowdlerized, films have become a formidable vehicle for the distribution of music from virtually all corners of the world. Their scores register an encounter. But their mode of employment conceals the radical recontextualization any such encounter entails. Notwithstanding the various hats worn by a film soundtrack before, during, and after a release, music listenership at the cinema is situational and subsidiary, driven by the desire to comprehend and appreciate a narrative. Acquaintance is facilitated, indeed forced on the audience, by the function the music plays in the film. The sounds of a *pipa* or a Punjabi track, after all, are more easily apprehended when served alongside a languorous landscape or a chase in a bazaar, all the more so if they are backgrounded as a mere element of the setting. Even when reliant on esoteric sounds, unfamiliar to all but a minuscule portion of the target audience, a film score differs from so-called world music in that it is embedded in an entity that in justifying its presence also contains it: the film as narrative.

Or does it? Casting a musical citation within a larger organism, albeit not one as straightforwardly representational as a narrative film, is a strategy adopted by musicians, too. This is most commonly done through sampling. Music scholars have illustrated the ways in which this practice has been a key engine of the absorption of folk, traditional, and exotic repertoires on the part of the urban middle class that is the main target of the music industry. They have also exposed and documented the thorny ethical and legal issues facing sampling of this sort.[17] Less remarked on is the fact that cinema provided an important precedent or at least counterpart to this process. The driving factor for the inclusion of esoteric or difficult-to-access repertoires in the cinema has long been the evocation of a locale. This understandably widespread tendency has been made to serve a host of diverse aesthetic and ideological agendas: the search for the verisimilar that underpins Hollywood studios' research departments; irony, as exemplified, for instance, by Stanley Kubrick's memorable use of the Chieftains' own brand of folk revivalism in *Barry Lyndon*; or the Third Worldism of a Pasolini, who scavenged recordings in search of novel sounds for his films as far back as the 1960s.[18]

World music is conspicuous for its absence in Hong Kong cinema. Rarely have Hong Kong filmmakers harbored the ambition to capture the world beyond their adoptive city. Bound by political, logistical, and financial constraints, they have drawn heavily on the territory for both inspiration and resources. In one sense, then, Hong Kong cinema may be said to be parochial rather than global in outlook. But Hong Kong is a city like no other, and the parochialism of its film industry has taken surprising forms. In a shipping center and migrating hot spot, rich in regional traditions but also utterly open to influences from the then so-called free markets—the British Commonwealth, North America, and Japan—indigenization and pastiche, if not outright plagiarism, were the order of the day in the media industry throughout Wong Kar-wai's formative period (the 1970s and 1980s). Such a modus operandi served eminently practical purposes but also suited a major slice of the target market: the growing migrant communities with strong ties to Hong Kong across Southeast Asia and North America, themselves savvy consumers of global products and therefore also tastemakers.[19] Much as it developed a penchant for documenting the city's social and economic changes, Hong Kong cinema has historically always also drawn heavily on ready-made cinematic sounds and images, giving rise to an exhilarating and broadly accessible film language, derivative to boot yet replete with innuendos to a fiercely local audience, and capable of gripping with its feistiness and stylistic flourishes a global audience as well.[20] This is particularly true of the one genre that cast its eye beyond Hong Kong to look at a distant, mythical Chinese past: the martial arts film.[21] In its 1994 version, Wong's *Ashes of Time* is a choice, if idiosyncratic, manifestation of the local-global nexus I have just described. In fact, it avoids Chinese music altogether. The Silk Road–esque flavor of the soundtrack of the 2008 version marks instead a rupture in the trajectory of Wong's cinema and its cozy reliance on Japanese and Western models. In the 1960s, producers such as the Shaw Brothers drew inspiration from global cinema. The Wong of the early 1990s relied on recent Hong Kong hits and the memories of a lifetime watching cinema and television. A decade and a half later, the soundtrack of *Ashes of Time Redux* was instead conceived in the shadow of a new, flamboyant, and internationally minded form of pan-Chinese production.[22]

MUSICAL GAMBIT

The ease with which martial arts movies lend themselves to parody and contamination points to what I see as a structural instability of the genre (instability that characterizes its Western counterpart as well, the chivalric romance, from old French models to *Don Quixote* and beyond). Think of the wonderfully digressive nature of not just Wong Kar-wai's film but a whole tradition of ostensibly martial arts films, such as the Zatoichi series, centered around a tavern as a place of rest but also reflection and social interaction; the forays into Zen mysticism of a King Hu and of course the backhanded celebration of rural Japan in Akira Kurosawa's *Seven Samurai* (1954), scored by Hayasaka Fumio; or again, Takeshi Kitano's recent take on the blind swordsman in *Zatōichi* (with music by Keiichi Suzuki [2003]). The instability of the genre and indeterminacies of translation notwithstanding, the quality or property referred to as "martial" in the West is also a preeminent element of such systems of combat technique as kung fu (or its Japanese counterpart, *bujutsu*). When applied to cinema or literature as a modifier, however, "martial arts" is a loose translation of a Chinese term—*wuxia*—with a rich history that bears other meanings as well. The Chinese original is a compound and encapsulates a reference to both a martial skill—typically sword fighting sublimated into superhuman, extravagantly implausible virtuosity—and a condition, that of a righteous wanderer, complete with its attendant existential baggage (uncertain identity, solitude, and—especially significant to a filmmaker like Wong Kar-wai—a doomed love life).

Listening to the opening credits of *Ashes of Time*, one may be forgiven for thinking that the music maps all too neatly onto the dual nature of *wuxia*. The film begins with a simple yet menacing quadruple barrel-drum pattern and a drone at the low strings, soon enriched by a simple descant at the cellos. All parts are rendered through a synthesizer, as was common practice in Hong Kong cinema in the early 1990s. As a theme of sorts, the drum pattern would be sufficient to carry the credits. Yet it soon slips into the background, retreating into its ranks as the accompaniment to a solemn statement of the taut title theme proper: a foursquare exhortatory chorus in minor of undisguised Leone- and Morricone-esque derivation. The musical relay neatly summarizes the dual nature of the score and by implication the film genre through a vivid play of rhythmic versus melodic thematicity. Duality neither assuages nor reassures, however, but creates tension, pushing the boundaries of the genre. As the pretitle sequence begins, an expansive, plaintive theme upsets the all-too-soon achieved balance (fig. 4.1). The male choruslike sonority of the previous theme is replaced by a softer and brighter timbre in the soprano register. The texture breaks open and the ostinato of the barrel-drum pattern dissipates into widely spaced metric accents (because the pulse is no longer marked explicitly by the martial drums, the illusion arises that the tempo of the music is slower, which is not the case). The shift is synced to the image of the open sea bathed in dark copper hues in what appears to be dusk (or is it early morning?). Cut to two extreme close-ups of the heroes Ouyang Feng, also known as Malicious West (Leslie Cheung), and Huang Yaoshi, or Evil East (Tony Leung Ka-fai), respectively (figs. 4.2 and 4.3). Leung's head is barely contained within the frame; Cheung's is half-obscured by it. The rising antecedent of the theme maps rather neatly onto the shot of Malicious West, while the descending is consequent to that of Evil East. Acting as

4.1–4.3 Pretitle sequence from *Ashes of Time*.

their unofficial anthem, the musical peroration is consistent with their colossal, copper-hued portraits.

These images also capture the onset of an action. Malicious West and Evil East appear to be looking intently at one another just before a duel. Relational editing—an eyeline match—imbues their gaze with a direction and a target, conjuring the sense of a physical proximity we will never be able to ascertain in fact (they never share the same frame except in two extremely fast cut-ins of them in a field full of weeds surrounded by crumbling rocks). They then proceed to engage in a duel that is at once larger than life (entire hills are dislocated as they wield their swords) and wholly abstract (no blood is spilled). The episode is so compressed as to verge on the epigrammatic and is redolent of the opening sequence of a television series. The same large close-ups of the two heroes, seemingly unharmed, return to bookend the duel. The chiasmic structure accentuates the exemplary nature of the episode. It is a classic presentation piece, a way of establishing the martial credentials for both the characters and the film. Yet it is folded within a larger scheme. Images of vast expanses of water and earth point to the sea and the desert as the geographical boundaries of the action. Like wind and fire, water and earth are also extensions of the heroes' weapons while simultaneously grounding their seemingly supernatural powers to the realm of the physical. The image of the sea appears three times at regular intervals—like a refrain—imparting to the episode not only a poetic rhythm but also a decidedly meditative dimension that is at odds with the tumult of the battle (little do we know at this point in the film that the image of the sea is a reference to what one of the protagonists sees from her window). The literal and metaphorical distance of the sea from the site of the battle finds a musical correlative in the apparent lack of sync between the score and the fighting. It isn't just that the music is nondiegetic but also that it moves of its own accord, independent of the logic of the onscreen action.

The clattering of swords colliding, clanking of blades clashing, and swishing of the swinging arms, torsos, and weapons are to the contrary ostentatiously synchronized to the corresponding gestures of the actors. Near the middle, the score is nearly engulfed by the booming sound of the hills collapsing under the force of Malicious West's and Evil East's strikes. Yet the length of the entire pretitle sequence coincides with that of the theme, forcing one to wonder whether the former is cut to the latter. The pretitle sequence, put another way, applies the principle of synchronization in the elemental sense of "same duration." In doing so, it invites us to grasp synchronization not as taking place punctually but rather unfolding across a long stretch of screen time (in something like the way hypermeter or harmonic rhythm can connect events distributed across a temporal span far greater than the single beat). As is the norm with pretitle sequences, the most explicit sync point falls at the appearance of the title, which appears with the suitably emphatic final cadence.

Opening with a duel is appropriate enough for a self-described martial arts film. The pretitle sequence, moreover, tallies nicely with the ending of the film. By then, Malicious West, in similar garb and sporting the same hairdo, will have resumed his career as a swordsman after a long spell as a middleman. Along with the Nine-fingered Hero, Evil East and Malicious West are the most important characters drawn from the film's literary source (Cha's *The Legend of the Condor Heroes*) and as such deserve pride of place. This is due to them not only as a concession to the spectators familiar with the novel but also because it is against their background of swordsmen that their love-forlorn past makes sense. If it is clear that what interests Wong in the martial arts genre is the space it opens for imagining a new kind of romantic longing in an exoticized past, it is also the case that the love stories he yarns around his heroes' youth feed off one's familiarity with the same characters as old people in the source novel. More than an adaptation, then, *Ashes of Time* is a spin-off. When the fighting resumes at the end of the film, it strikes one as the return of the repressed—the source novel—following a long digression into the intimate lives of these otherwise very public, indeed legendary, figures. It is a parody of *wuxia pian* (heroic chivalry) in the form of intimate melodrama in the same way that *The Eagle-Shooting Heroes* (created by Wong's coproducer, Jeff Lau [1993]), made to cut the losses *Ashes of Time* was incurring, is a parody of the same in the form of a spoof (the two films were made by the same production team and released as a foil to one another).

THE *REDUX*

Following the realization that the print of the 1994 release was in dire condition, some ten years after the original release Wong Kar-wai started work on a new version of *Ashes of Time*, eventually released in 2008 as *Ashes of Time Redux*. In a characteristically lucid and informative essay comparing the two versions of the film, David Bordwell puzzles over the retention in the *Redux* version of the short duel between Malicious West and Evil East in the pretitle sequence.[23] Though to his credit he mentions the Louis Cha novel as a possible factor, Bordwell may be underestimating not only the literary background to the film but also the status of Cha's novels in the public imagination of the Chinese-speaking audience. Given that for the *Redux* Wong edited out two subsequent sequences that help "establish the solo prowess," in Bordwell's own words, of the two characters, the combat scene in the pretitle sequence is all he had left to stress their role as pillars of the story (and link to the novel).

Bordwell's query, however, is more than justified if one considers the new context for which *Ashes of Time* was restored and recut. Despite bagging a last-minute slot at the Venice Film Festival, where it also won an award for cinematography, the 1994 *Ashes of Time* was made for the region around Hong Kong, the Chinese-speaking audiences of Taiwan, and the migrants living or dwelling in the many Chinatowns scattered around the world. To be sure, work on *Ashes of Time Redux* was driven by the desire to revive material on the brink of irreversible decay. Some of the trimming—we do not know which—was dictated not by artistic choice but by the fact that certain images and sound tracks were unsalvageable. This is not to say that Wong did not eye for his new release a global audience already familiar with his international successes, however. This was an audience for whom, crucially, acquaintance with Wong's style and thematic preferences and the awareness of such global hits as *Crouching Tiger, Hidden Dragon, Hero,* and *House of Flying Daggers* (2004) were to inform the encounter with his film far more than the knowledge of the source novel.

Consider again the beginning credits and the pretitle sequence in *Ashes of Time Redux*. Gone are the original black credits laid matter-of-factly over a white background; a slicker, more stylish visual presentation has taken their place instead, one that conjures a link between computer graphics and that most universally appealing signifier of East Asian visual culture: ink painting (fig. 4.4). Wong adds the recurrent image of the moon on the brink of obscuring the sun—the special occurrence of an eclipse and the seasonal cycle being key to the reframing of the story—now working in tandem with the familiar shot of the sea (figs. 4.5 and 4.6). He changes the color scheme, deepens the shadows, and adjusts the framing of the close-ups of the two heroes. Gone, too, are the hill explosions. And gone is the synthesizer. We hear instead a chamber orchestra enriched by Chinese instruments, most prominently the Chinese zither

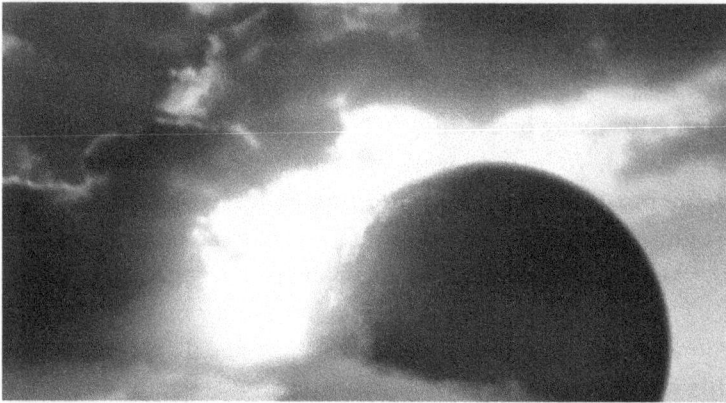

4.4–4.6   Titles and pretitle sequence from *Ashes of Time Redux*.

(*guzheng*). The use of instruments in lieu of a synthesized score is made more vivid by perceptible room acoustics. Reverberation and close miking underline the attacks, thus making the contact between fingers and strings, and hence the presence of the soloist, almost palpable.

As in the 1994 version, the corresponding music cue is neatly divided in two. The first part, newly composed, runs through the credits. Over a string drone, at first the zither intones a dialogue with a cello whose glissando calls irresistibly to mind the Yo-Yo Ma of *Crouching Tiger, Hidden Dragon* (scored by Tan Dun). As the cello ceases to play, it soon becomes clear that the remainder of the section will be a cadenza-like solo at the *zheng*. The explicitly martial flavor of Frankie Chan and Roel Garcia's 1994 exordium, mediated by Ennio Morricone's influence, gives way in the *Redux* version to a sonic world shaped by the impact of the Silk Road Ensemble. Given that the main story is set in an area consistent with the trade route—location shooting took place in southwestern China—the choice adds a layer of geographical specificity that makes the score participate in the effort of constructing the setting. In the arrangement for the *Redux* version, the martial element—the ostinato rhythms, pounding percussions, swelling strings—is reserved for the pretitle sequence, during which we hear a variant of the male chorus theme, which in the original appeared over the written credits instead. As in the 1994 version, no attempt is made to synchronize the music with the specifics of the combat scene. The most significant sync points are a loud strike of the barrel drum made to coincide emphatically with the first close-up of Malicious West and the sudden retreating of the orchestra with the appearance of the title, the music literally thinning out into a mere whisper (the chorus makes a belated appearance at this point). The gimmick is standard, if impeccably executed, Hollywood fare, as is the doubling of the main parts with horns and trombones at the cue's climax. To my ears at least, the result stands in curious contrast to the ethnic vibe of the *zheng* solo, reminding me of Miramax's rescoring of Hong Kong martial arts films for the American audience.

Another key difference is that in *Ashes of Time Redux* the second, more expansive theme is nowhere to be heard—not, that is, until the first evocation of Malicious West's own love life, some twenty-five minutes into the film, at which point we will first become acquainted with it as opposed to recognizing it. It is replaced by martial music of sufficient gravitas to convey the seriousness of the characters. Playing genre-appropriate music over images of sword fighting redresses what may have seemed, in the 1994 original, an incongruous combination. At the same time, it further insulates the pretitle sequence from the rest of the film, making Bordwell's query about its retention, ironically, seem even more urgent. In the 1994 version, the deployment of an expansive, highly expressive theme in the context of a spectacular fight sequence introduced an element of instability. The special kind of music/image combination posed a question about the thematic center and even very genre of the film, creating an expectation that simultaneously also provided a link to what followed, precisely on account of the tension that the remainder of the film was to solve.

THE 2008 SOUNDTRACK

Despite their significance, there exists no complete account of the differences between the soundtracks of the film's two versions. They may be summarized as follows. The Mandarin of the Brigitte Lin characters (Murong Yan / Murong Yin) is restored in the *Redux*. Also in *Ashes of Time Redux*, the voices of all characters are enhanced with regards to tone color, dynamic range, and spatial specificity. The new soundtrack is in Dolby Stereo, which also means that it is suffused with ambience, which further contributes to situate the voices within a specific spatiotemporal frame. As to the music, in Bordwell's apt capsule account, "There is a little less of the Morricone flavor now; the music coaxes rather than hammers. Other stretches of music have been dropped altogether."[24] Take the sequence in which Maggie Cheung's character tells a contrite Evil East about her failed marriage to Malicious West. The melancholy version of the first theme from the credits, carried here by the synthesizer imitating a Hawaiian lap-steel guitar, is nowhere to be heard in the *Redux* version (where the whole segment is underscored by no music at all). This follows from the de facto elimination of that very theme from the credits (where it is replaced by a more symphonic cue, redolent of Hans Zimmer's scores, heard over the pretitle sequence mentioned earlier). Because of this substitution, a few short cues derived from the original theme, and retained in *Redux*, no longer betray any connection to a source melody (as they do in the 1994 version). The decision to lift the underscore during Maggie Cheung's quasi-monologue doubtless also reflects the new color scheme of the score. With almost no exception, the characteristically spaghetti Western–inspired lap-steel, surf, and slide guitar timbres heard at various points of the 1994 version give way to either a wind or a string instrument, most prominently the cello as enshrined by such instruments as the *dizi*, *pipa*, and various kinds of traditional percussions. Again, this change gestures toward the soundtrack of *Crouching Tiger, Hidden Dragon* and with it the world evoked by Yo-Yo Ma's Silk Road Ensemble. The cello moreover figures prominently in the elegiac orchestral suite that ends the film: a signal technical improvement over the patched-up sequence of prerecorded midi cues, which are noticeably stitched together in the 1994 precedent. The role of yet another throwback to the Leone and Morricone collaboration—the male chorus—is also drastically curtailed. The pan flute, a product of the world music wave of the 1960s if there ever was one, and another Morricone staple, is replaced by Chinese instruments. Hand in hand with more vivid color tones and deeper shadows, room acoustics and the use of original instruments mute the unabashedly citationist, postmodernist flair of the original film.

The changes are all-encompassing and far-reaching, as they reflect, too, the different nature of the exhibition venues. In a movie theater with a subpar audio system in mono, a theater where the majority of *Ashes of Time*'s intended audience most likely experienced the film in the 1990s, the harsh, relatively undifferentiated, and more grating sonorities of the synthesizer would project more effectively than a finely calibrated orchestral score recorded for Dolby.[25] Writing about the 2008 *Redux* version, Bordwell claims that "the most pervasive change has involved the color tonalities."[26] His analysis is illuminating, but the emphasis on color underplays the extent and impact that the new soundtrack has on those of us for whom cinema is an intensely aural, and not just visual, experience. Bordwell's emphasis on color unwittingly obscures the extent to which, in *Ashes of Time*, color tonalities and musical timbres are mutually implicated in the creation of the setting. In the original version, the two are of a piece with the dry, bleached-out desert setting. This was a nod to not only Sergio Leone but also Leone's own source, the Kurosawa of *Yojimbo*, a film shot, significantly, in black and white, and featuring a score that juxtaposed a pastiche of Japanese traditional music and Henry Mancini.[27] By the same token, in the *Redux* version it would be difficult to separate music and cinematography in the evocation of the luxuriant setting of Zhang Yimou's *Hero* and especially *House of Flying Daggers*—evocation that is central to Wong's reimagining of South China and southwestern China as tropical locales and the repositioning of the tavern from where Malicious West conducts his business as but one stop along the Silk Road.

To bear this out, let's consider the *Redux* version of Evil East's encounter with Peach Blossom (fig. 4.7). Redolent of the sparse textures and naturalistic timbres of Béla Bartók's "night music," the newly composed score functions initially as stylized soundscape. The music makes palpable a field of action larger than the one captured onscreen, evoking a whole climate or region, as opposed to a singular locale. This is apposite at this juncture, as the female characters, be they stationary or mobile, mark the geographical boundaries of the story. The musicalization of the physical world also tells us that the wet, tropical marshland that provides the setting of the encounter is rooted in fantasy. As the music regroups and assumes the form of a more conventional solo, the underlying string tremolo is almost onomatopoeic in its suggestion of clouds of insects and other flying creatures. The solo features bends and leaps that are loosely synchronized to Peach Blossom's frustrated embrace of the horse. It is written for the *bawu*, a flute-shaped reed instrument whose low register is so rich in harmonics as to create a buzzing timbre in keeping with the hazy, almost hallucinatory visuals of the episode. The *bawu* can be heard in countless scores and popular recordings and is indelibly associated with southwestern China. Aside from adding a layer of geographical specificity, its lovingly rendered timbre evokes, intersensorially, the instrument's principal construction material—the cylindrical bore is made of bamboo, which closes off on one end with a natural node. At this juncture, the difference between a synthesizer and original instruments is most acutely felt.

The use of a specific instrumental sound as the conduit for an almost haptic sense of the presence of a natural setting is not uncommon in martial arts cinema. A significant precedent is the celebrated sequence set in a bamboo forest that ends part 1 of King Hu's *Touch of Zen* (1971). As combat begins in earnest, the bamboo flute solo is faded out. Its illustrative music is replaced by a complex orchestration of sound effects and a rhythmically inspired choreography of bodies in flight.[28] The King Hu precedent is significant—indeed, prescient—in other respects as well. While conceived and shot entirely in Taiwan, *A Touch of Zen* was the culmination of a revival of martial arts cinema that began in Hong Kong in the mid-1960s. Spearheaded by the Shaw studios, such a revival followed from the global success of Japanese *jidaigeiki*, the Zatoichi or "Blind Swordsman" series, Leone's spaghetti Westerns, and the James

4.7 Cherry Blossom from *Ashes of Time Redux*.

Bond franchise. The Shaws' commercial imperative was both channeled and hindered by the artistic imperative guiding such directors as Zhang Che and King Hu himself. Artistic and commercial imperatives sit uncomfortably next to each other in the Hong Kong revival of martial arts of the early 1990s as well. In drawing liberally on Louis Cha's novels and referencing with such abandon the global sources of the Shaws' martial arts films, the Wong of *Ashes of Time* engaged in an act of re-creation of the Hong Kong 1960s as totalizing as the one found in *Days of Being Wild* and, especially, *In the Mood for Love*. But such a re-creation was contingent on the reenactment of the circumstances that drove the Shaw Brothers to revamp martial arts in the first place, namely the desire to bank on a wave of recent hits. It is no secret that *Ashes of Time* sought—in vain, as it turned out—to replicate the success of Tsui Hark's *Once upon a Time in China* (1991–97) and *The Swordsman* (1990). For its part, *Ashes of Time Redux* was conceived in the wake of the above-mentioned global hits (*Crouching Tiger, Hidden Dragon*; *Hero*; and *House of Flying Daggers*). Running counter to Huang Yaoshi's own mantra, both versions of the film are haunted by memories of films of the distant, as well as the more recent, past, and a keen awareness of their commercial success.[29] Similar commercial imperatives bore similarly lukewarm responses from the box office, however. Notice, moreover, how dramatically the cinemascape that nurtured these cyclical attempts at reviving martial arts had changed. In the 1960s, the Shaw Brothers drew inspiration from global cinema; in the early 1990s, Wong learned from Hong Kong precedents and a lifetime of listening to the radio and watching film and television; but in 2008 a new, flamboyant form of pan-Chinese production provided the impetus. It is therefore unsurprising that Wong's second major venture into the martial arts genre—his 2013 release *The Grandmaster*—was conceived and executed for distribution in the PRC. Such a move is symptomatic of the role of mainland Chinese audiences in reshaping the cinema and with it cinema's role as a global incubator and vehicle of musical experiences.[30]

THE GRANDMASTER

Though obviously a remake of his own work, *Ashes of Time Redux* signals a discontinuity in Wong's cinema. Rather than enhancing the status of the original and strengthening the mythology of Wong's persona as the source of a distinctive, instantly recognizable musical sensibility, the *Redux* version lays bare his attempt to adopt a musical aesthetics not his own. If Wong the bricoleur can revive even the most unpromising track or worn-out hit, Wong the also-ran ends up commissioning unoriginal, if technically immaculate, scores. It's a state of affairs that permeates the original music of the soundtrack of *The Grandmaster* as well. While appealing, well crafted, and deserving of detailed analysis, Shigeru Umebayashi's score is conventional in both design and realization. The cues accompanying the most conceited moments of the action—think of the opening duel, set in a dilapidated neighborhood in impossibly heavy rain—would not be out of place in standard Hollywood fare. They are kinetic, percussive, and punctuated by sound effects that render, in hyperbolic fashion, the fighters' movements, punches, and near misses. As to the pensive, lyrical passages of Umebayashi's score, they, too, harken back to Tan Dun's scores for Ang Lee and Zhang Yimou of the early 2000s. The telltale sign is the texture of solo cello levitating over a string orchestra to sketch recitative-like passages that flirt with melody without quite delivering a fully-fledged theme. The result is a quasi-vocal lament, seemingly inarticulate yet lyrical. Redolent of Zhang Yimou's films, too, are the extreme sound close-ups that monumentalize the faintest sound by pushing it temporarily into the foreground of the mix.

One especially fine example of this approach to sound occurs halfway through the duel in the brothel between Gong Er and Ip Man. Initiated by the former to vindicate her father's defeat at the latter's hand, the duel is unusually charged as it pits the Northern school against the Southern, a senior against a junior master but also a female against a male fighter. The sexual tension is implicit in the gender—and casting—of the protagonists, yet on the whole Wong refrains from sexualizing the admittedly relentless contest. One exception is the extreme close-up of Gong Er's face brushing past Ip Man's as she pirouettes around him to escape his grip (fig. 4.8). Their stoic demeanor and the fierceness of their eyes can hardly conceal the suggestion of a kiss. As the action slows down, the drums fall silent. In their stead, we hear the "schwing" of two imaginary swords moving quickly through the air—or is it an echoed, subtle "clang"—complete with a human whisper that in shadowing the sound also helps delineate it as a line with a beginning, a middle (corresponding to the point of maximum proximity of the two actors), and an end. Be it a schwing or a clang, the sound of metal swords is at least nominally martial in tone but is so treated as to suggest breathing and even touching, in a word, the establishment of a contact zone between the two preordained lovers.

The other notable instance of imaginative sound design is the duel that acts as the preamble to Gong Er and Ip Man's duel: the famous challenge between Ip Man and Gong Er's father, Gong Yutian. The challenge posed by Gong Yutian seems simple enough: Ip Man is to break a round cake perched on the palm of the older master's hand. This is prefaced by Gong's statement to the effect that Northern and Southern schools should pursue unity rather than conflict, all the more so at a time of national emergency (the events narrated in the film roughly coincide with the Sino-Japanese War). Aside from the physical difficulty of snatching away the round biscuit or at least gripping it for long enough to break it, then, Ip Man faces the added burden of countering the symbolic significance his elder challenger has assigned to its breaking with a clever, and persuasive, motto of his own. He is being invited to align his bodily prowess with a stance he genuinely believes in and therefore needs to search for a properly articulated counterstatement to go along with the gesture that will—in the event he succeeds—put a dent in the cake. This Ip Man eventually does, not without taking his time to formulate a strategy. As he sizes up his opponent, the distant yet perceivable sound of *taikos* marks emphatically the beginning of the confrontation. Their subsequent, sparser interventions build suspense. As the two men finally begin to encircle one another, all sound effects recede into

4.8 Love in midflight in *The Grandmaster*.

the background, giving way to an atmospheric texture of synthesized sounds that mimic the whooshes of their bodies while also signifying the concentration of the duelists on their task (at the expense of their surroundings). The soundtrack unfolds cyclically, in sync with the bodies, the rise and fall of the overall volume lending a temporal dimension to the circular motions we see onscreen (themselves an elaboration of the round shape of the cake itself). Cut-away shots of the absorbed audience, among them Gong's daughter, Er, enhance the suspense. The onlookers' rapt attention is rendered via a hushed silence that resonates as it were with the inner struggle concurrently on display in the fighting ring, where all the two masters can hear, if at all, is their robes whooshing past one another.

NEITHER A CITATION . . .

Unlike *Ashes of Time*, *The Grandmaster* also features preexisting music retooled by Wong with the usual dexterity. The borrowed music ranges from the well-known yet decidedly unmartial tune by Morricone, "Deborah's Theme," to two older compositions, also more elegiac than martial, by Umebayashi himself ("Epilogue I" and "Moyou" [pattern]). Wong lifted Umebayashi's compositions from the soundtrack of *Sorekara (And Then)*, a 1985 adaptation, little known outside Japan, of Soseki Natsuke's eponymous novel directed by Morita Yoshimitsu.[31] For the occasion Umebayashi rearranged and rerecorded the two pieces. Aided by cellist Nathaniel Méchaly, he appears to have thickened the texture of

"Epilogue I." Umebayashi also added a solo cello for Méchaly in "Moyou" (the solo is not heard in any of the released versions of *The Grandmaster*, but is on clear display on the soundtrack album). Doubtless, too, the new recordings were enhanced, equalized, and calibrated to blend seamlessly in the final mix of their new host film. The result is an almost identical, if somewhat more polished, rendering of the old tracks, their main features clearly recognizable, their identity intact (or almost: more on this below). While the re-creation is strictly speaking allosonic rather than autosonic, it is validated autosonically, so to speak, by the involvement of the composer himself in the process of re-recording his own music.

It would seem intuitive to link Wong's borrowings to his desire to evoke or allude to the 1985 film (and, indirectly, the novel on which it is based).[32] The circumstances surrounding Wong's borrowing and the specifics of the two films' stories are such, however, that they cast into doubt the idea that *The Grandmaster* is using the music of *Sorekara* to cite or allude to the source film. Wong's borrowing indicates not citation but intertextuality only in the most general sense, namely as the "actual presence of one text within another."[33] The motive behind a citation is, particularly in literature, self-evident. In a literary text, the quoted portion is typically signaled. As such, it invites the reader to account for its presence as either a deliberate rupturing of the textual flow or, as is the case in traditional epic poetry, drama, and narrative, as a means to support or augment the text at hand. In the latter case, a citation invariably buttresses and as such also seamlessly blends into its textual surroundings. In *The Grandmaster*, the music from *Sorekara* blends in because of its topical qualities, thanks to its lack of renown (excepting the happy few familiar with Yoshimitsu's screen adaptation of the novel). It is a quotation in the material, not functional, sense of the term. And it is necessarily partial at that, for music is but one component of the film (to cite *Sorekara*, Wong would have to lift a shot or scene in its entirety).[34]

In Gérard Genette's taxonomy, quotation is only one of three possible outcomes of the "actual presence of one text within another." The other two are plagiarism and allusion.[35] In literature, the full-blown reproduction of a passage from another work is manifestly a citation because of long-standing editorial and typographical conventions. To be sure, the quoted text may drive a wedge between insiders and outsiders. One may not fully appreciate the full import of a citation qua citation— its role as homage to a figure well known to the target readership, for example. Even when aware of its significance, the same readers may not be able to grasp the full force of its meaning. But they will know that it is a quotation. Allusion is different in two respects. First, it is less literal. The presence of one text may be so fleeting or indirect as to be noticed only by the most attentive of readers or those in the know. Not coincidentally, allusion is often the prerogative of esoteric poetry. But allusion differs from quotation in function as well. Allusion is primarily a bridge, a gesture that temporarily points to another text, and with it another world. Where the primary function of a quotation is to support, enrich, and expand the host text with the full force of its unique articulation, the main point of allusion is to evoke the work from which it is lifted and with it a milieu or sensibility.

The corresponding scenario in a film soundtrack would play out quite differently. To know that a given musical passage has been lifted from another film, and that it is an allusion to it, its presentation must be supported by an explicit, and didactic, reference. A character may mention its provenance, for example, or conveniently bend a record or CD cover in the direction of the camera as she plays it on the hi-fi, or click a link on the display of a mobile phone. The sheer fame of the selection, at least within a film's target audience, will also do the job. But even assuming the music is recognized by a large-enough slice of the audience, is the end result an allusion proper? Consider *Airplane!* (1980). The film borrows John Williams's notorious "shark motto" written for *Jaws*, the goal being parody by way of allusion to another film. The hyperbole turns the notorious "shark motive" into mood music of a sort, only upside down: the invitation not to take the onscreen events too seriously.

. . . NOR AN ALLUSION

Given the definition of allusion sketched above, let us consider a particularly thorny example of borrowing, one that has a direct bearing on my discussion of *The Grandmaster*. In *Casino* (1991), Martin Scorsese borrows the main theme from George Delerue's score for Jean-Luc Godard's *Contempt* (1963) and deploys it as many as five times.[36] The choice may seem consistent with allusion. Scorsese cuts Delerue's music to scenes in which relationships deteriorate or fail (*Contempt* putatively tells the story of a disintegrating marriage: I explain my "putatively" below). But what would the function of the allusion be? Is the music meant to clarify what the mise-en-scène, dialogue, or camera work conveys only insufficiently or ambiguously? If so, recognition of the reference to *Contempt* would be an obligatory passage in the construction of the story. But this is far from being the case. We know that the marriage between Ginger and Sam (Sharon Stone and Robert De Niro) is failing and that the working relationship between the latter and Nicky (Joe Pesci) is faltering. The scenes in which Delerue's music appears are comprehensible, irrespective of one's prior knowledge of where the music has been lifted from. And as well they might, for Scorsese must have known that a large section of his potential audience wouldn't have recognized the music anyway. To be sure, *Contempt* has a solid following the world over. Its presence in the minds and hearts of many cinephiles was revamped by a restoration effort for the large screen sponsored by Scorsese himself (1997), a sumptuous Criterion DVD release (2002), and yet another Technicolor restoration on the fiftieth anniversary of its release (2013).[37] Yet the film can hardly be said to command the kind of popularity that would make its soundtrack broadly recognizable. Delerue's simple yet lush harmonies, string sonorities, and slow-moving melody lend undeniable pathos to the film, whether one recognizes the track or not.[38] For all its presumed aura as "homage," the music works because of its generic, not specific, qualities: its proven track record—no pun intended—as a solid piece of score writing at the service of generic expectations.[39]

Scholars and critics alike are keen on allusions as they offer them the opportunity to set into motion and showcase their investigative skills. Because allusions are oblique, not to mention esoteric, their unveiling turns the glosser into a cocreator of a sort. Partaking of this long, venerable tradition, Jonathan Godsall stresses how preexisting tracks in Scorsese's films function "on multiple levels and in multiple ways."[40] In the case of *Casino*, Godsall writes, Delerue's "Thème de Camille" is "paradigmatic of the kind of cue one might find in a romantic melodrama," the "musically appropriate" soundtrack to "scenes of failing 'marriages,'" but also an "invocation of *Contempt*," which adds a level of "extra-musical meaningfulness."[41] What is extramusical about the invocation of *Contempt*? The reference to the film is contingent on the identification of certain features of the music—its instrumentation, texture, and hieratical, slow-moving melody—as uniquely ascribable to "Thème de Camille." The processes subtending the understanding of a cue as a token of a type or as a preexisting, and uniquely identifiable, piece of music depend equally on musical competence and the pool of memories of the pertinent music/image relationships one has built over years of watching films. To be sure, such a hypothetical invocation of *Contempt* would bypass the kind of musico-theoretical conceptualization Nicholas Cook refers to as musicological listening: "any type of listening to music whose purpose is the establishments of [musical] facts or the formulation of theories."[42] But does this make the invocation extramusical? Perhaps what Godsall is hinting at is that the target of the allusion is not a musical object but another film (the allusion as bridge, in other words). On recognizing it, to paraphrase Arthur Danto, Delerue's music "pulverizes" into a reference to *Contempt*.[43] Or, put yet another way, we hear an allusion *in* the music.[44] But isn't this how film music routinely operates? Unless we posited that meaning is "musical" only when it is reflexive or self-referential, the invocation of *Contempt* is more simply a fine—indeed, paradigmatic—example of how music produces meaning.

The larger question posed by Scorsese's retooling of "Thème de Camille" is the following: What is the added value of this extra, if not extramusical, bit of meaning—if any? The allusion to *Contempt* via Delerue may invite a comparison between Godard's film and Scorsese's own. Yet I don't see that doing so enhances appreciation of either. In fact, it runs the risk of glossing over their impossible-to-overestimate differences. When all is said and done, the allusion—if any was intended—is little more than a flourish: an oblique address, perhaps, rather like a wink to a fellow cinephile.[45]

UNQUOTABLE

If Delerue's music functions in "multiple ways," this is because it is bent on changing face along what we might call the horizontal dimension of time: like a leitmotif, it is *metamorphic* as much as multilayered. This is observable not only as it moves from *Contempt* to *Casino* but across its various iterations within *Casino* itself. Scorsese uses the cue five times, which is also why the music can easily pass as an original film score (recurrent themes, after all, are a staple of film soundtracks).[46] The first occurrence of "Thème de Camille" is perhaps the most symptomatic. The music is synchronized to a short series of shots of the Nevada desert outside Las Vegas, where Sam and Nicky are to have a short meeting. Despite being the main locale, the desert is made to look unusual, surreal even. Scorsese obtains this quality by drawing on the famous crop-dusting sequence, set in the corn fields of Indiana, in Alfred Hitchcock's *North by Northwest*

(1959). Like the protagonist of the latter, Sam looks utterly out of place in his arch-urban outfit and ridiculously large shades. The younger director borrows from the older master more in the manner of troping than allusion, however. Sam's predicament is similar to Thornhill's (Cary Grant) in more ways than one. Perhaps touched by grace, like Thornwall he narrowly escapes ruin and even death at the hands of the mob and overcomes the formidable hurdles that befall him during the journey toward his (admittedly anticlimactic) redemption.

The surreal quality of the location strengthens the comic premise of the situation. The two pals are unable or perhaps too paranoid to meet in a more convenient place because of the massive amount of surveillance to which they are subjected. At this juncture of the narrative, however, Sam's trajectory is decidedly a downward, perilous one. As befits the fastidious manager that he is, he arrives exactly on time and for this gravest of sins he is having to wait for the chronically tardy Nicky in what to him, a creature of the East Coast, begins to look and feel like a strange and hostile environment. His discomfort, and the fear he articulates in a voice-over, foreshadows the stunningly curt dismissal he is about to suffer at the hands of Nicky and the rapid deterioration of their partnership. We first hear Delerue's music over an aerial shot of Nicky's car driving toward the site of the meeting. The effect is lyrical, uplifting even, the grandeur of Delerue's line and the expanse of the desert reinforcing one another. Except that Sam is simultaneously pondering his chances of coming out alive of the meeting ("50–50," he opines). A cut to an extreme close-up of the upper half of Sam's face affords a most unusual view of Nicky's approaching car, namely as reflected in the lenses of his glasses, a trail of dust blazing across (fig. 4.9). As the music changes harmony and the majestic theme begins to pick up speed, a Ginger Baker drum solo, from Cream's "Toad," is also heard (a representation of what is playing inside Nicky's car, perhaps?). The cacophony punctures the admittedly puzzling idyll conjured by the combination of the music and the landscape. As Nicky approaches the meeting point and gets out of the car, finally, music gives way to an eerie silence and eventually the animated discussion between the two.

The outcome of the meeting would seem to reinforce the notion that Delerue's music is, in Godsall's words, "appropriate to scenes of failing 'marriages.'" But we must resist the temptation to project knowledge acquired by decoding the homage to Godard back onto a segment of the film in which the music appears to resist it. Scorsese uses "Thème de

4.9 Sam is thinking "50–50" in *Casino*.

Camille" in such a way that it must *earn* the association to disintegrating marriages (both literal and metaphorical) rather than wearing it like a tag from the outset. As an easily identifiable quotation with an explicit semantic mission, the appearance of "Thème de Camille" would be far less puzzling than it sounds. It is precisely by wearing the hat of a conventional film score that Scorsese's borrowing strikes a most unconventional note. In the context of the desert meeting, the music is expressive of the landscape and partakes of the gliding motion of the smooth aerial shot of Nicky's car. It strikes a decidedly lyrical tone that sits ill at ease with the tone of the episode at hand, and as such poses something of an enigma, the suspicion of a portent, and is therefore as yet far from unveiling its destination (and the destiny of the characters around whom it is woven).

The first repetition of "Thème de Camille" is propelled by the reunion between Sam and Ginger following the latter's eloping to LA to meet her lover Lester with their daughter, Anne. The cathartic potential of the scene is soon undercut by a conversation that delivers us Sam at his most prickly and profane. The music almost feels cast against type. Its linkage to the onscreen action is not intuitive; it must be excavated. As Ginger makes a desperate phone call to Lester in the middle of the night, we hear a second repetition of "Thème de Camille." Sam overhears her words to the effect of wanting to see him dead. A furious fight ensues. Playing for a third time and in close proximity to its latest appearance, "Thème de Camille" is hard to miss and will have been by now recognized as a recurrent element. As animated dialogue gives way to unrepeatable profanities and even physical abuse, once again Delerue's chorus of strings cuts against the action as much as reinforcing it. The cue embodies a sympathetic, magnanimous perspective on the action that the images of Sam and Ginger's frenzied fight belie. Following a brief interruption, finally, "Thème de Camille" makes another appearance as Sam kicks Ginger out of the house, accuses her of being a "junkie," and refuses to let her take Anne with her.

As my précis suggests, the thematic link between Delerue's music and Sam and Ginger's broken marriage can be fully grasped only in retrospect (and contemplated after subsequent encounters with the film). This much is implied by Godsall himself when he draws attention to the significance of its fifth, and very last occurrence, over the end credits. There, the association between "Thème de Camille" and failing relationships is at last cemented. A true culmination, the music's last iteration, in Godsall's apt words, "forward[s] the notion that these disintegrations are a central strand of *Casino*."[47] Prepared by strategic repetitions, this consummation shows that Scorsese is sensitive to the instability of the music he's borrowed and the contingency of its impact. In *Contempt*, the endless repetitions and deliberately rough editing of "Thème de Camille" call to mind the actor's tests evoked by Walter Benjamin in his famous reproducibility essay.[48] Godard's provocative manner folds the music within a reflection on the filmmaking process; it stages a refusal to anchor its meaning, thereby making "Thème de Camille," in a sense, unquotable—hence the need for Scorsese to reinvent it.

SOREKARA REMIXED

Recognizing that a cue is taken from music one is familiar with—what Carolyn Abbate, in a verbal bricolage of her own, calls a "synapse"—is not simply the result of the reproduction of the original music's structural components (its rhythm, melodies, harmonic plan, instrumentation, "sound," etc.).[49] Recognition is made possible by a specific realization of the borrowed excerpt as made possible by a set of concurrent circumstances: the dramatic situation, position of the track in the mix, and relation to the soundtrack—in short, the allocation of one's attention. Consider the intratextual resonances, in *Sorekara*, of "Epilogue I." The cue plays over the crucial conversation that unveils the aborted love story between Daisuke and Michiyo, and it underscores his hopelessly belated attempt to revive it (fig. 4.10). The music derives explicitly from "Prologue," which plays briefly near the end of the pretitle sequence and

4.10 Untimely confession (I) in *Sorekara*.

segues into the credits as the title theme proper ("Prologue" also plays, virtually identically, as the closing theme of the film). On hearing "Epilogue I," put another way, one also hears the recurrence of the title theme (albeit in a different form). We are, as it were, set up for recognition. It isn't just that the latter is the (genetic) source of the former. It is also that, in retrospect, the credits will foreshadow the appearance of the same musical material, suitably altered, at what is arguably the very climax of the film.

Except for a brief pause halfway through the sequence, "Epilogue I" underscores the entire conversation between Daisuke and Michiyo. In the first segment, the cue features a new theme scored for a small string orchestra. This accompanies the ill-starred lovers' reminiscing about happier times and nodding to one another about details of dress and decor. The theme is derived by inversion—descending, rather than ascending—from the title theme, with which it shares tempo, phrase length, harmonic rhythm, and range. This first half of the cue, then, reeks of "Prologue" without being too obviously modeled after it. There follows, unaccompanied by any music, Daisuke's confession of his still lingering love for Michiyo. As she responds to him, the second half of "Epilogue I" continues as a much more recognizable version of the title theme (scored for the same ensemble). The scene ends with her sobering assessment of the situation, the soundtrack repeating a phrase but aborting it before the cadence.

Whether through variation, subtraction, instrumentation, or augmentation, the title theme provides the core ideas out of which much of the soundtrack of *Sorekara* germinates. Notwithstanding the sometimes-glaring similarities, the CD release of the soundtrack lists each cue with a different title. This is common practice and may well reflect the working title the cues were given during the production of the film. Doubtless, too, the titling responds to the need to fill out an album so as to justify its release (and price tag). But it also points to a long-standing tenet of the aesthetics of film music, namely that the identity of a cue owes as much to its placement within the narrative as the intrinsic features qua composition. It follows that placing the same music in another film transforms its identity even further.

This is exactly what happens in *The Grandmaster*. In Wong's film, "Epilogue I" plays over a segment—or two, depending on the version—in which the music is the dominant (and in one case sole) element of the mix. This placement throws into relief the main melody, which ironically is not the prerogative of the piece (as noted, the main melody is the germinating element of the soundtrack and as such it pervades *Sorekara* as a whole). What is unique to "Epilogue I," rather, is the instrumentation, which *The Grandmaster* also showcases to fine effect. Also unique to "Epilogue I" is the above-mentioned new, opening theme (whose contour is the inversion of that of the film's main theme). Wong omits it, however, as it stretches for far longer than he needs in either the US, European, and, indeed even the Chinese version (the longest). In the US cut, a truncated "Epilogue I" plays over a touching flashback sequence in which Gong Er, inebriated with opium, suddenly revisits the key stages of her introduction to martial arts (fig. 4.11). We first see her practicing in the snow. She is already a grown-up, and a master in her own right, but the setting is a clear indication of her life as a younger woman in Manchuria. This segues to images of her as a child perched on a windowsill to spy on her father as he practices in the snowy courtyard, and a shot of her learning under his careful guidance. The cut for the Chinese (including Hong Kong) market only retains the initial segment of this extended flashback, creating an ambiguity as to whether Gong Er is remembering a precise moment of her past life or fantasizing about herself practicing in the snow. While the digression and correspondingly the music are cut short, the latter returns in the form of a short cue somewhere else as well: the scene in which Ip Man leaves Jiang's dwelling, having been told that Gong's legacy will be forever lost. In the US version the music is an elegy for a dying Gong Er, but in the cut for the Chinese market the emphasis is on (dis)continuity and the dying of a tradition as the result of people's

4.11 Opium-inspired reminiscence in *The Grandmaster*.

passing: elegies both, to be sure, but with a very different emphasis. Alternate versions of the same film shave meanings off the music while adding others. If this is possible, it is thanks to the most broadly recognizable, hence adaptable, characteristics of the music: its mode, melodic contour, tempo, and instrumentation. Put succinctly, in *The Grandmaster*, "Epilogue I" functions perfectly well in its camouflaged role as a memorable, somewhat haunting yet ultimately generic piece of film scoring (rather than an allusion to *Sorekara*). As we have seen several times in this book already, Wong invests the track with new meanings by tapping into the generic aspects of what he's borrowed instead of its uniquely identifying features and particular history. Key to this effort, one suspects, is sourcing and hence listening to much of this music on an LP or CD first, the music freed, at least temporarily, from the binding context of the film for which it was written: like a soundtrack for an unmade film—his own.

WARRANTY VERSUS LEVERAGE

Wong's invitation to listen to Umebayashi's music without prejudice is doubtless also helped by the obscurity of his borrowing outside a relatively narrow, and aging, slice of Japan's domestic market. Given the intended reach of a film like *The Grandmaster*, it is fair to assume that Wong did not expect a global audience to recognize the tracks he had lifted from *Sorekara*. It is, of course, conceivable that the music played a role in an esoteric program that only the director and a few intimate friends or collaborators were privy to.[50] This seems far-fetched in the context of a body of work where the point of a citation or allusion, if any, is that it be grasped immediately and unambiguously by as many members of the audience as possible.[51] Let us, nevertheless, for the sake of argument, entertain the possibility that Wong deployed Umebayashi's past tracks as citations in the full sense of the term. We would first have to establish what the purpose of the citations is. What is it about the two chosen Umebayashi tracks that prompted the director to re-present them in the context of his own film? Is the borrowing a form of homage? What the significance of Wong's homage might be we cannot know—even when asked, the director would most likely respond evasively—and it does not matter, unless we took the other, and decisive, step of claiming, in line with author-centered criticism, that the main, indeed preferable, route toward understanding *The Grandmaster* is to unpack these esoteric, deliberate, and therefore symptomatic citations. This would align film music criticism with the venerable tradition of, for example, Dantean or Miltonian hermeneutics (albeit not, significantly, the interpretation of Shakespeare's borrowings, which are a lot more expedient and transformative and, just as important, have long been recognized as such). But it would also show the warping effect of confusing an expedient borrowing for a citation: our experience of a film is reshaped in such a way as to assume a shape that can conveniently accommodate the meaning of the purported quotation.[52]

Wong comes to our rescue by making it hard, if not impossible, to rationalize the presence of the music in his film in light of its history prior to the borrowing. Consider, by contrast, Scorsese's *Casino*: the thematic parallels are such that one may mistakenly hear "Thème de Camille" as carrying the tag "broken marriage" from its very first appearance. That is far from being the case, as we've seen; still, the music does eventually reach the point where its semantic mission is precisely that. Scorsese uses Godard's precedent as a warranty. Wong turns to Umebayashi as a form of leverage instead. Central to both *The Grandmaster* and *Sorekara* is the renunciation of love (whether as the result of a vow, as in the former, or an admixture of arrogance and naiveté, as in the latter). Yet profound differences not just in setting but also emotional tone between the two films remain. This lingering gulf makes it easier to see that the thematic similarities between the two films are not the raison d'être of Wong's borrowing. Wong not only recoups the financial costs of the borrowing by marketing the soundtrack as his own (having been granted master rights). He also aims to increase its artistic and financial value.

This is most clear when we turn to "Moyou," the second of the tracks he lifted from *Sorekara*. In Morita's film, the cue is used only once. Even at first hearing, the orchestration, ostinato accompaniment figure, and angular melodies are striking in and of themselves. But the presence of the music is muted by the concurrent action it accompanies. Daisuke tells his jealous aunt that he has just broken off the engagement with the woman chosen for him by his family and goes on to admit in no uncertain terms that he is committed to Michiyo (fig. 4.12). Unlike the main theme and its various derivations, this cue is unmemorable in the literal sense of being hard, if not impossible, to remember. This is not a matter of acoustical signal but, again, allocation of the attention. Blasted at full volume during the outdoor funeral of Gong Yutian, in *The Grandmaster* the same music is by contrast showcased as the dominant element of the mix (fig. 4.13). Wong's retooling has a curatorial, almost didactic dimension. He draws attention to features that Morita's editing had obfuscated. Indeed, it is almost as if he were reproaching his Japanese counterpart for misidentifying the genre of the music and muddling its affective qualities. The solemnity and repetitiveness of the onscreen action encourage the appreciation of the tempo and also the haunting quality of Umebayashi's main melody. The color white is in line with tradition (the Chinese traditionally wear white in funeral rites, as the color has long been associated with death). Wong digitally "painted" the mountain range in the background to play up the contrast between the almost blinding brightness of the locale and the darkness of the mood. The contrast implicates the music, its dark tones teased out by Wong's antiphrastic use of the color white. The images of Gong Er as a child lend the piano of "Epilogue I" the air of playfulness and innocence, inflecting the presence of the color white of the snow with a sense of innocence. Here, the grandiosity of the occasion and vast expanse of whiteness that engulfs the ritual reposition "Moyou" not merely as a funeral march but as a monument in sound to Gong.

"DEBORAH'S THEME" AND THE SEARCH FOR A PREEXISTING AUDIENCE

Tracing something like an outward spiral-like path, Wong builds musical alliances with local, regional, and transnational audiences. Insofar as he expected someone to recognize Umebayashi's music from *Sorek-*

4.12 Untimely confession (II) in *Sorekara*.

4.13 White rite from *The Grandmaster*.

ara, if at all, this was with the aim of reaching out to his Japanese audience. Musical borrowing, that is, is subsumed under a multipronged approach to distribution and marketing that relies on the selective activation the audience's cinematic memory on the one hand and on the other the appeal to professional networks that stretch far beyond what the limited Hong Kong circuit allows.[53] Though he is not systematic in this regard, Wong borrows music tracks the way he casts his actors by way of tapping into different musical and cinematic traditions.[54] Just as he reshapes his actors' personae he also subtly yet decisively transforms music by tying it to a whole new range of visual, sonic, and dramatic motives. In the case of "Moyou," as we've seen, Wong rescues the music from a suboptimal presentation in *Sorekara* not so much to tap into a slice of the overseas audience—the music was hardly conspicuous in the source film to begin with—but rather to unleash its full potential and, in the process, take symbolic ownership of it. This also applies to Morricone's "La donna romantica," which Wong lifts from the obscure Italian erotic comedy *Come imparai ad amare le donne* (How I learned to love women, directed by Luciano Salce [1966]) to use as an underscore to the last conversation between Gong Er and Ip Man. Like Salce's film, the music is utterly unknown and as such hardly material for an allusion (no matter how esoteric). Nor can it be the tool to deepen a relationship with or generate interest for his film across a particular section of his potential, and potentially global, audience. Nor, finally, is the borrowing the vehicle for a commentary or gloss. The narrative contexts are simply too divergent.

In the original film, Morricone's romanticism sounds almost out of place as we see images, now graphic, now oblique, of the young protagonist's sentimental education. Visually, the register is comical throughout, the plot an excuse to string together a number of gags and showcase young faces (and bodies) in a manner consistent with the licentious comedies of the time. In *The Grandmaster*, by contrast, the same tune underscores the first full acknowledgment that Gong Er and Ip Man had repressed their mutual feeling of love for the sake of their families (and the preservation of the martial arts traditions they were first in line to inherit). The new context is not merely more dignified; it is also enabling. Freed from the shackles of a limiting and somewhat indecorous presentation, "La donna romantica" morphs into a heartfelt if admittedly long-winded elegy to missed or, worse, dodged opportunities. It plays in *The Grandmaster* the role that Wong's other Morricone borrowing, "Deborah's Theme," had played in *Once upon a Time in America* (1984) (where the music strikes us just as Noodles meets Deborah after a long separation and finally comes to see the love that could have been but wasn't). The substitution frees up the much more famous "Deborah's Theme," allowing Wong to use it elsewhere as a wordless elegy for Ip Man's wife and with it a whole way of life before all hell broke loose with the Japanese invasion. "Deborah's Theme" also evokes the couple's past life in Guangdong as against the novelty and disorientation of Ip's new life in Hong Kong. Morricone's famous cue plays throughout what is in essence the film's coda. A montage of evocative images—the arrival of new immigrants, Queen Elizabeth's 1953 coronation, New Year celebrations—places Ip Man in Hong Kong in the protracted postwar period. As his martial arts school earns new students and grows in reputation, we see him settle into a comfortable life and make Hong Kong his new home. The sudden appearance of Gong Er speaking from beyond the grave ("Mr. Ip, all encounters in this world are a kind of reunion") launches a short, magnanimous reflection, in voice-over, about his legacy and the meaning of life.

Ip Man's new home is nothing like the cradle out of which *Wing Chun* emerged, however. It is a haven for refugees run by the British. It aspires to be modern. The unmistakably nostalgic quality of Morricone's music is central to capturing the condition of nourishing the old (the values associated with *Wing Chun*) in the new (Hong Kong) as both an aspiration and a delusion—a condition central to all migrant cultures. Then again, in typical Wong Kar-wai fashion, the stylistic markers of the montage— slow motion, elliptical editing, black and white cinematography—are sufficiently ambiguous to signify not merely the passing of time during Ip Man's own life but also a nostalgic, retrospective look at the Hong Kong of old from the present time of the film's release (2013). Morricone's music is just as effective in folding the epic of Hong Kong's last seventy years into that of the unlikely survival of *Wing Chun* in a geographically marginal outpost of the decaying British Empire. In short, "Deborah's Theme" would seem to be Exhibit A in our long, frustrated quest for a garden-variety musical allusion in the Wong Kar-wai canon. It is internationally famous, hence highly recognizable. Its affect and thematic associations are indisputable and most important pertinent and indeed necessary to the delivery of the meaning of the segment it accompanies. Having infused *Ashes of Time*, via a Morricone pastiche, with the lurid aesthetics and cynicism of spaghetti Westerns, Wong turns to Morricone's romantic manner to call up Leone's weaving of violence into a nostalgic re-creation of a time period. It's a classic instance of the metonymic function of allusion and a much-delayed send-up of Tsui Hark's *Once upon a Time in China* (which it ridicules as it were by inversion, by showing what an actual remake of Leone's film might look like). "Deborah's Theme" is also the farthest point, culturally and geographically, in the outward spiral-like chain of sonic and visual motives that fill out the film's texture. Whether a heartfelt homage, facile concession to international taste, or marketing ploy, Wong's blatant gesturing toward Leone's epic is symptomatic of his outward-looking approach in his attempt to revive the martial arts genre. Ang Lee reframes the martial via old Chinese melodrama and *huangmei diao*. Zhang Yimou taps into the depths of Chinese history and redeploys the resources of Chinese opera as transfigured via special effects. Wong Kar-wai, for his part, looks unabashedly westward, toward not so much Hollywood but American cinema as reimagined by an outsider (Leone) whose career was improbably jump-started by a remake of Kurosawa's *Yojimbo*.

The melodic contour, chord progressions, and orchestral colors of "Deborah's Theme" betray the inspiration of the romantic symphonic repertoire. Morricone takes his models seriously. In *Once upon a Time in America*, he does not limit himself to marking the reunion between Noodles and Deborah with a ready-made melody or striking sonority; rather, he takes time to build the main line via recurring and ever-expanding leaps. In keeping with the scope of Leone's film, moreover, the music moves at a leisurely pace and features moments of pure texture, anchored by a dominant pedal, all of which contributes to its expansive, almost rarefied quality. In *The Grandmaster*, the main melody is carried by Nathaniel Méchaly's cello (not the upper strings and the voice as in the original). It is accompanied first by the piano and then a string orchestra, almost in the manner of a double concerto for piano and cello. The arrangement is almost identical to the one used in the recording Yo-Yo Ma made with Morricone in 2004.[55] Yo-Yo Ma's cello, of course, also features prominently in Tan Dun's soundtrack for *Crouching Tiger, Hidden Dragon*. Notwithstanding Tan's playful bending of the sound of Ma's cello in the direction of the sonority of the *ehru*, the preeminence of the cello and the warm, translucent envelope of the string orchestra in that memorable soundtrack are too significant as similarities to pass as coincidence. Again, in a curatorial vein, Wong is gesturing toward Tan Dun's successful precedent not only to emulate it but to point to Morricone as the model of both. Tan Dun's use of percussion instruments, which *Ashes of Time*, through Chan and Garcia's expedient rewriting of the Morricone of Leone's spaghetti Westerns, predates by almost a decade, offers indirect corroboration of Wong's curatorial argument.

This musical argument is clinched in the film's postlude. Ip Man's final statement, "We are all part of the same quest. It all comes down to two words—horizontal or vertical," propels us from the historical time of postwar Hong Kong into the suspended time of a hall filled with impassible yet, one surmises, also infinitely compassionate statues of the Buddha. There follows a wordless montage of images of Buddha statues featuring, over a low drum ostinato, Méchaly's agile cello lines against the broad brushstrokes of Umebayashi's orchestra. Umebayashi's music is texturally and harmonically derivative of Tan Dun's soundtracks. But its juxtaposition with "Deborah's Theme" draws attention to the ever-present cello and with it the just-heard Morriconean model, which *The Grandmaster* implicates in the spiritual struggle over human passions and the taming of evil impulses, which the statues so powerfully symbolize.

FIVE

OBLIVION

In the early 2000s, the American DJ and record producer DJ Shadow commissioned Wong Kar-wai to shoot a video of his remix, "Six Days" (Wong's own company, Block 2, also coproduced it). Released in 2002 as both a track on the LP *The Private Press* and a single, "Six Days" fared reasonably well on the charts.[1] To date, the music video has racked up more than sixteen million views on YouTube.[2] As such, it is one of the most widely seen works directed by Wong. Yet it bears no explicit indication whatsoever that he, the celebrated Hong Kong auteur who justifiably counts among the most recognizable "hands" in contemporary cinema, is in fact the director. How could this come to pass?

The story of DJ Shadow's "Six Days" begins with the 1971 pacifist hit "Six Day War" by the British band Colonel Bagshot.[3] Built on a bare-bones accompaniment consisting of bass pedal and pulsating timpani redolent of a march to the gallows, the song relates the experience of war from the (impossible) vantage point of dead soldiers for whom, as per the refrain, "tomorrow never comes until it's too late." The refrain completes the melodic arc launched by the chorus while simultaneously bookending each of the six strophes of which the song is composed, one two-stanza strophe per day (from Monday to Saturday). Repetition and the cumulative form add to the suspense and heighten our sense of the anguish of being in the trenches awaiting near-certain death. At week's end, the song, and with it presumably the war, comes to an unceremonious end. Colonel Bagshot's sole hit, "Six Day War" has enjoyed broad appeal since its release, as also indicated by the many covers and remix versions (at least three). The piercing vocal line, repeated as many as six times with nary a variant except in tone color, retains throughout an unerring sense of urgency. Fear and frustration are expressed in verbal images that are at once concrete and intuitive. While the title provides the premise for the form and the number of strophes, it also doubles as a reference to the Arab-Israeli conflict of 1967 (famously known as the Six-Day War). Still fresh in the collective memory at the time of the song's release, the conflict handed to Israel territories—most notably the West Bank—whose sovereignty remains still hotly disputed today at huge human and political cost.

Whether intended or not, the reference to the Arab-Israeli conflict shaped the reception of "Six Day War" then and continues to do so today—unless, that is, one comes across the song for the first time in the context of Wong's music video. Where the medieval minstrel replaced the original text of a religious hymn with an ode to beer, Wong recasts the entire piece as the working out of an inner conflict between a spurned lover (Chang Chen) and his better self as he battles the impulse to seek revenge on her female lover (Danielle Graham). In keeping with my remix of Wong's cinema and the minstrel tradition, a male, lyrical "I" equates love and combat. The video revisits in an extremely compressed form many topoi of the love-as-tug-of-war tradition: prelapsarian bliss, betrayal, heartbreak, aggression, and finally despondency. Images of a young woman bathing in a shallow pool against a bright cobalt-blue background are crosscut with red-hued shots of her and the male character locked in an enveloping embrace on a suitably unmade bed. Their union is sanctioned by the ritualistic carving of a tattoo bearing the figures 426 on the female character's left shoulder. The same artificial seascape provides the set for the betrayal. Preying like a voyeur on the scene, he sees her make love to another man. All hell breaks loose. Bright, saturated blues and reds give way to paler, grayish, charred tonalities (figs. 5.1–5.3). The fast cutting projects the aimless panting of a

5.1–5.3 Love as contest in "Six Days" (MTV Video, 2001).

shattered mind. The refrain ("Tomorrow never comes 'til it's too late") points to a painful stasis, a condition of being stuck in a horrendous present despite the nominal passing of time signaled by the litany of days— Monday, Tuesday, Wednesday—and a clock running backward (4:27 is followed, tellingly, by 4:26). In a classic bit of Wong Kar-wai scramble, the female figure moves from one partner to the next and then back again. She also engages in a showdown of sorts with the male character in an empty industrial space. Both the imagery and choreography nod to the martial arts tradition. Despite proving more than a match to his prowess, she comes across as observer as much as participant, and refuses to strike. For all this, she remains an elusive target to his half-hearted attempts at physical violence. Is the duel imagined, merely a cathartic delusion? The video ends with images of destruction, followed by a quote. The only way to "unlock" time is to erase the sign that had marked, literally and metaphorically, the relationship. Unable to remove the original tattoo, forever carved on the skin of his vanished lover, the male character settles for a second best: the "426" drawn by her on a mirror, which shatters under the force of his high kicks. The last kick, and with it the last image of the video, is reserved for a lone light bulb hanging from the ceiling. An exquisitely timed close-up, just before the bulb busts, shows the design of the filament to be the inspiration of the tattoo's font style. The light fading out in fine detail before our very eyes, we read the following on a painterly, tattered wall: "The Possession of anything begins in the mind" (Bruce Lee).

Despite the somewhat conventional—and distracting—fast-paced cutting, the video for "Six Days" is replete with vivid reminders of Wong's collaboration with Chris Doyle: tilted angles, selective focus, off-balance colors, and a plethora of sensuous details. Did DJ Shadow get more than he had bargained for? The video pays off with repeated viewings; indeed, its indirect style and intricate plotting demand it. This serves the song well. After all, repeat encounters are key to the success of a music video (especially so in an age of click-through rates). As my summary has attempted to indicate, however, Wong delivered not only a complex and seductive piece of work but also one whose plot and iconography bear little relation to the song that it acts as the ostensible vehicle for: an antiwar song, at that! To add insult to injury, the impetus behind Wong's cavalier sidestepping would seem to have been the promotion of his epic, 2046, then still in production and possibly within view of release (the film would eventually open globally in the fall of

2004). Though at the time of the video's release the insistence on the numbers 2, 4, and 6 would have been an oblique reference at most, with the benefit of hindsight it is a fairly obvious borrowing from the then film-in-progress, as is, of course, the casting of Chang Chen in the role of a jealous man catching his lover in flagrante delicto. A very similar episode marks one of the highlights of Chow's science-fiction novella in 2046. In the latter, the female figure is played by Carina Lau, and she is murdered to the strains of Vincenzo Bellini's opera *Il pirata*.[4] The sequence rhymes with "Six Days" in other important respects: the depiction of the betrayed party as a voyeur, his murderous impulse, the cage elevator as a conspicuous element of the setting, and, of course, the presence of Chang Chen himself. The impulse to rehearse the same material in the context of different forms—a feature film in the making on the one hand and a music video on the other—may follow from temporal proximity, the music video being produced roughly at the same time as the shooting of that portion of the film. Whatever the reason, what interests me here is that self-borrowing from a film concurrently in production handily overruled any attempt to engage with Colonel Bagshot's song on its own terms. Presented with a new music track, Wong draws from a familiar repertoire of visual and narrative motifs. As a result, DJ Shadow's remix mediates Wong's own remix of his own work.

But isn't it callous in the extreme to refuse to acknowledge that the song is about the tragedy of being a front-line soldier? To transform a pacifist hymn into the soundtrack to yet another iteration of Wong's obsession with time passing and heartbreak?[5] Truth to be told, the obfuscation of the song's original meaning begins with DJ Shadow's remix itself. He changed the title of the song into "Six Days" and shortened the text in such a way as to muddle its message. Just as important, he spliced Colonel Bagshot with "While I Cry in the Morning," a forgotten 1968 track by the late musician and sometime-actor Denis Olivieri. If one is to believe DJ Shadow, the idea came quite by chance as he had a headphone on his right ear playing "Six Day War" while simultaneously playing "While I Cry in the Morning" on his turntable. Circumstances enable perception; an awkward posture morphs into a winning musical gesture. Lifting the rhythmic section from the latter and the vocals from the former, a new song emerged. If the final product does sound like a version of "Six Day War," rather than a blend of both source tracks, this is doubtless due to the strong identifying function of the title and the preeminence of the vocal line. The instrumental riff from "While I Cry in the Morning" does alter the texture, however, lending it a clubbier, more contemporary feel (which is remarkable given that Olivieri's song is even older than Colonel Bagshot's 1971 hit). DJ Shadow achieved this effect by isolating the introduction to Olivieri's track: a slick ostinato in duple meter carried by a syncopated bass drum pattern and punctuated on the downbeat by a downward arpeggiation at the electric guitar "smeared" with a delay pedal. Where in the original this basic pattern is transposed and repeated two times at different pitches before returning to the original key, DJ Shadow extracts only the first presentation and repeats it, seemingly ad libitum. The move eliminates a sense of harmonic motion and effectively turns Olivieri's intro into a glorified break beat. DJ Shadow also prefaced the basic pattern with a curtain raiser of sorts, namely a string tremolo in crescendo cut from a very different cloth. He then filled out the texture with echoes of the guitar arpeggio as well as the sustained sound of a bass flute. Finally, he digitally modified Olivieri's original to obtain brighter timbres, boosted dynamics, and a subtle reverb. Having thus modified the borrowed material, he remixed the vocals and the basic rhythmic pulse, also played by a bass drum, from "Six Day War."

It's brilliant DJ work. DJ Shadow digs out two oldies, one of them very obscure, and creates a new entity without adding new material but only by reconfiguring elements that are (literally) on record for all to listen to. The motive behind the remix is not textual but the wish to create a new texture and feel, revel in the delight in the discovery of a new sound, and boast about the ability to make two oldies sound as if they were a contemporary track. Admittedly, "While I Cry in the Morning" is sacrificed at the altar of "Six Day War" yet not without inspiring a "sabotage" that alters the latter's original frame of reference. Given the new sonic outlook of the remix, DJ Shadow must have decided that the antiwar ethos and seriousness of tone of the original text had to be muted. Circumstance—holding a headphone to his right ear while playing something else, and realizing the two channels blend—trumped his respect for the original. Bricolage trumped quotation. Be it poetic license or commercial calculation, he was correct in identifying a mismatch between text and the resulting music. The shortened text is vague, if not lacking, however, and a video realization was evidently called for. Wong, for his part, does not so much make a video of a remix song but completes the remix work itself. He does so more in the manner of a dramatization than that of a vehicle (as is the norm with most music videos).

DJ Shadow's bricolage gives Wong carte blanche and propels the video even further away from Colonel Bagshot's original conception and well into the director's own world.

"WHO'S HERE BECAUSE WKW DIRECTED THIS?"

Think of Wong's video as a *contrafactum*. Where the medieval poet/musician would have replaced the old text with a new one, or added a second text, in the case of "Six Days" the process of transformation takes place in two steps. First, the text is not so much replaced as camouflaged. The result is consistent with the new effect imparted onto the music by the remix. In keeping with the aesthetics of remix, however, DJ Shadow transforms as little as possible of the original material. The sole license he takes is the subtraction of a portion of the text and, of course, retitling. Wong's images complete the camouflaging job, effectively playing the role of a new, or added, text grafted onto the music.

Wong's decision to revert to personnel, visual tropes, and dramatic situations associated with his own oeuvre is facilitated by the fact that there is no need to showcase the presence of a performer or band (as is the norm in many music videos). A DJ/mixer as distinct from a conventionally styled performer, DJ Shadow revels in his invisibility. He is content to project a sense of his presence at one remove, that is, solely through the sheer force of his skill as a mixer (as well as his considerable renown among members of his fan base). This gives Wong considerable latitude in shaping the final product of the collaboration. Yet the "Six Days" video is hardly even mentioned as a "Wong Kar-wai film" nor is the song associated with his cinematic world—to the contrary. Wong makes a pastiche of his own work, creating images and situations that remain staunchly unmoored. Rather than being firmly situated in a storyworld that subsumes the music within a dramatic arc, as is the case in a film, the Chang Chen and Danielle Graham characters remain nameless and operate on a two-dimensional stage whose plausibility as the setting for a full-blown story is as weak as its grip on the soundtrack. In completing the work of freeing Colonel Bagshot's original text of any references to the war, his images further the agenda of DJ Shadow's remix rather than dislodging the primacy of the music. Last but not least, Wong is not credited. That acknowledgment alone would have cued up a sizable number of—if by no means all—viewers to not only see telltale signs of a known director in the shooting style but also hear the music under a different frame of reference. Wong's free, loose engagement with what remains of the original text does not quite achieve the kind of bond that will by itself unseat any meanings or associations that DJ Shadow's remix accrued before and especially after the release of the video.[6] And this the remix did. Albeit in another version—a remix of a remix—DJ Shadow's "Six Days" has had an illustrious history aside from its release as a music video as well, most notably as the title music for *Tokyo Drift* (2006), the third installment of the *Fast and the Furious* film series. And it is thanks to *Tokyo Drift*, not Wong's work for DJ Shadow, that the remix is now for the most part remembered. Thousands of YouTube users continue to enjoy the official video release in relation to their memory of that film, blissfully unaware of the identity of its director or the place of its images in the director's universe.[7]

As hinted, this ought to be surprising. But it says less about the niche following of Wong Kar-wai's work than the difference between cinema and MTV. If "Six Days" is more readily associated with *Tokyo Drift* than Wong's art and video direction in the corresponding MTV video, despite it having been seen by millions of people, it is also because *Tokyo Drift* is a film (itself part of a franchise). As both an art form and an institution, MTV gives the lie to the notion that the "image" occupies a dominant relationship relative to sound. For all their visual dazzle and sophistication, music videos are a vehicle for the sale of recordings and are a showcase for the musicians they immortalize. Through their characters and narrative arc, films such as *Tokyo Drift* reshape a piece of music much more forcefully and irreversibly than a music video does (or any form of visualization unmoored to a narrative, such as a video game). Films leave a more permanent mark on the music they host, reverberating with it. And this explains why Wong the worldmaker is, in this particular instance, the loser. The medium speaks through him more than he does through the medium.

DOUBLE AGENTS

Moving from "Six Days" to Wong's film work demonstrates why the oft-mentioned claim that Wong is little more than "a glorified MTV director" does not hold water.[8] This is not a matter of defending Wong from what is meant, derogatorily, as something of a slide. I do not see the art of directing music videos as intrinsically inferior or less creative—to the contrary. I reject the claim, rather, because the difference between the two forms is too significant for the claim to make much sense.[9] Film is a long form; an MTV video, a short one. The latter is presentational while the former is representational.[10] But before we dismiss the comparison as wholly irrelevant, let me consider the moment that, in Wong's oeuvre, comes perhaps closest to the rhetoric and imagery of music videos: the montage sequence in *Chungking Express* (1994) in which an infatuated Faye (Faye Wong) cleans cop 663's Soho flat to the strains of Wong's cover of "Dreams" (a hit song by the Irish band the Cranberries).[11] The sequence shows "Stage Two" of her makeover of her love object's living quarters. Where "Stage One" unfolded to the notes of the Mamas and the Papas' "California Dreamin'," this time the musical source is Hong Kong's contemporaneous mediascape, namely the singer/actress's 1994 release of her cover in Cantonese of the Cranberries' hit song (as part of the album *Random Thoughts*).[12] The sequence consists of a scrambled collection of shots accompanied by a long stretch of music unadulterated by sound effects or voice-over (fig. 5.4). The insertion of what to all intents and purposes looks and feels like a music video does create a discontinuity in the narrative flow that encourages an interactive relationship with the filmic presentation—such as singing along—reminiscent of a KTV as much as an MTV aesthetic.[13]

As my analysis of the "Six Days" video has indicated, the viability of MTV as a business and consequently artistic model is, to Wong, rather limited. But if by a thought experiment we thought of the promotion of the song as the rationale for Faye Wong's presence in the film, and her role as a freebie for the promotion of *Chungking Express* in turn, we would be better positioned to understand the already-mentioned claim that Wong is a glorified MTV director. The charge, if such can be called, has less to do with filmmaking style per se than his demonstrative use of stars and the ability of his work to spur singers and actors on to success. Taking the "Dreams" sequence as representative of the entire film, we could think of *Chungking Express* as a staggered or diffuse music video, as if "Dreams" had retroactively invaded the very body snatcher that preyed on it, permeating it with the logic of MTV. This would be consistent not only with the success enjoyed by Faye Wong as a singer following her appearance in the film, which propelled her to fame, but also the intense interest generated by the soundtrack among the film's global audience.[14] *Chungking Express* registers a rare convergence, in Wong Kar-wai's

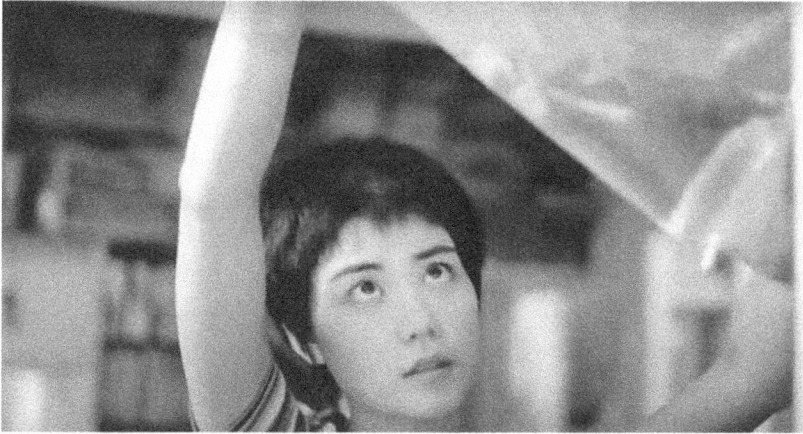

5.4 Faye Wong as herself in *Chungking Express*.

career, between the film as vehicle for his own cast of characters and situations and the film as vehicle for a star singer. The appeal to MTV as a frame of reference is only applicable to this film, however. And it fails to capture other aspects of the director's modus operandi. While it is true that he does nothing to conceal the star appeal of singers like a Faye Wong, Leslie Cheung, or Andy Lau, Wong Kar-wai is, in the end, after the glow of celebrity culture from across the Hong Kong mediascape. He is a savvy manipulator of the star power of nonsingers as well as singers. And although Wong the director could only dream of the success enjoyed by Wong the singer, in the last analysis he comes across not only as the Pygmalion figure in her rise to fame but also the producer of Faye Wong's own recording of the song. For much as the "Dreams" sequence shares a great deal with a conventionally styled music video, it is embedded in a narrative that not only transcends but also subsumes it within its folds. The film endows the episode with a specific function and inflects the meaning of the song's title and its lyrics. Featuring Faye Wong so centrally in the episode makes palpable the gulf between the unassuming snack-bar worker and stewardess wannabe the singer impersonates in the film and the pop star that she is.

Playing with identities serves *Chungking Express* supremely well and reverberates across the film. Every character is a double agent. Be they well-known stars, budding young actors or singers, they all play cameos of themselves playing at being big film stars, impersonating improbable

167

characters or sporting the most egregiously implausible costumes. Preexisting music is an essential ingredient in the film-inspired self-branding of these down-on-their-luck characters (or, which comes to the same thing, the image-making their presence in the film entails). As has been the norm so far, we should resist from calling such borrowings citations. It is more accurate to say that Wong Kar-wai stumbles on the music and makes do with it the way his characters do. Other than its being a moving-enough expression of infatuation, "Dreams" offers little in the way of intertextual resonances anyway. The director's choice owes more to Wong's recent release than any interest in the original or its band per se. As a vehicle for Faye, the character of *Chungking Express*, Faye Wong the star performer, and Faye Wong the media celebrity and public persona, the song is repositioned in such a way as to make its provenance immaterial—so much so that we may view the success of the Cranberries in Hong Kong as a posthumous reflection of Wong's cover as inflected by Wong Kar-wai's film.

A textual link between "Dreams" and Faye's first encounter with Cop 663 (Tony Leung) further justifies its presence in the film and thus mutes the presumed significance of the provenance of the original. Reading almost like a stage direction and echoing the accidental nature of Wong's own encounter with the song, the first stanza of her cover stresses the "serendipitousness" and "suddenness" of the appearance of the "dreamed" one. Moreover, "Dreams" likely led to the selection of the exceedingly well-known song that marks their first meeting, the Mamas and the Papas' "California Dreamin'." As if out of respect to their chronology, and the true genealogy of the dream trope in pop history, in the film the latter appears well before the former. This order also results in the desirable masking of the true trajectory of the process of selection of the film's tracks. The scene is set off by Cop 223 (Takeshi Kaneshiro) delivering his last soliloquy as he brushes past Faye: "This is the closest we ever got. Just 00.1 of one centimeter between us. I knew nothing about her. But six hours later she fell in love with another man." The words echo the ones he utters at the very beginning of the film after nearly crashing into the drug dealer. Here they function as a bookend and hint at a new narrative and new group of characters. Cut to Cop 663 signing off his duty card opposite Midnight Express, captured by a telephoto lens against the Lan Kwai Fong blur (fig. 5.5). The warm tones of the image of the district at night, alongside the sight of what promises to be a new protagonist, reinforces the status of this moment of the

5.5 Tony Leung against the Lan Kwai Fong blur from *Chungking Express*.

film as a major narrative caesura. But it is "California Dreamin'," blasting from a stereo inside the shop, that propels the viewer into a new zone and marks the space as the site of a different stage of the film.

The song heralds the entrance of Cop 663 onstage, wrapping him in new and colorful sounds, and associating him with a dream of a journey to a sunny, faraway place (the California of the title). The iconic descant between two acoustic guitars that opens the song is cued in near the end of the freeze frame of Cop 223 looking at Faye. The first vocal line ("All the leaves are brown / and the sky is gray") is neatly synchronized to the appearance, in the following shot, of Tony Leung. Shrouded in the red and amber lights of the sloped alley, his figure is already in focus but his identity remains unclear. As he approaches the counter, in a slightly menacing manner, he takes off his hat. A luminous medium close-up of Leung's clean, finely chiseled face, wearing a benevolent expression, brings the shot to a reassuring end. Already a recognizable matinee idol, Leung receives here proper star treatment, complete with the trappings of an elaborately staged entrance: the striking new iconography; suspense generated by the gradual, finely calibrated unveiling of his identity; and a new soundtrack.

The music may serendipitously frame Cop 663's appearance but it is not, strictly speaking, meant for him. It is Faye who is playing it on a stereo near the counter. The acoustics are the first hint. As Leung approaches the counter, reverberation, a faint echo, and slight yet perceivable sound

169

distortion betray the presence of a source positioned in the proximity of the action. As we cut to Faye we not only see the shop where the music is coming from but also realize, in a classic variant of the standard, tripartite point-of-view shot structure, that we had been furtively looking at Cop 663 through her own eyes (she feigns being absorbed by her chores when, about to place his order, his gaze finally crosses hers). It is, as per convention, love at first sight. But her "sighting" him comes dressed up—again, serendipitously—with the hopeful strains of "California Dreamin'," which, having been caught in the current of her nascent feeling, will from now on be played ad nauseam.

The song's calculated reappearance every time he stops by, is a covert message, but one that only Faye can be privy to. Though Cop 663 is initially bound to miss its import, he cannot fail to notice it as Faye constantly plays it at an annoyingly high volume; she is, as it were, hiding her dream in plain sight. Because of the volume, the song also becomes the occasion for comedy as it drowns out Faye's and Cop 663's voices as they laboriously try to get past pleasantries and engage in something like a real conversation. But the biggest joke is that Faye, as if the victim of a self-inflicted conditioning experiment, ends up doing what is implied by the lyrics. Toward the end of the film, she packs up and moves to California. She manages her feat by becoming a stewardess and, in this way, takes in Cop 663's heart the place previously occupied by his former girlfriend (also a stewardess). It is her hyperbolically circuitous, convoluted way of delivering her feelings at his heart's doorstep, more oblique still than her other expression of interest in him: the clandestine trips to clean up, incognito, his apartment.

MUSIC AND PLACE

Faye's mimetic impulse cannot be faulted, for Cop 663 does fall for her in the end. The insistence on the stewardess theme is not fortuitous for other reasons as well. In secluded Hong Kong, air travel has been a necessity of life, and its imagery has permeated the culture to an extent rarely matched in other parts of the world. Its ports of call have drawn maps of both circulation and desire and the history of Hong Kong cinema bears witness to this. Air hostess films constitute a small but respectable subgenre in the history of the local film industry. The most famous of them all remains perhaps *Air Hostess* (*Kong zhong xiao jie* [1959]), a now-cult classic featuring Grace Chan (also known as Ge Lan).[15] In the film the stewardess is depicted not only as a privileged member of society with access to a burgeoning global community, but also as an agent of change. Frequent flying was a rare, envied opportunity. Among its perks came the ability to bring all manner of gadgets and trendy, hard-to-find artifacts—including music records—from all sorts of exotic locales, including the perceived centers of what was new and fashionable (in the cold war world order, this meant the United States, with Japan a distant second, as well as Britain). Somewhat improbably, this also turned hostesses into trendsetters of sorts, holders of a cultural cachet no longer obtainable nowadays, at a time when new products and trends are launched—via media events—almost simultaneously in every corner of the world.

Andrew Jones has argued that the association between stewardesses and musical imports in Hong Kong—mambo, rock, or, later, surfing—encapsulated in an appealing and effective manner the stewardesses' status as privileged members of the flying class, and their partaking of the global circuit (hence his captivating metaphor of "circuit listening").[16] Compare this to the at best belated charm of "California Dreamin'" (released in 1966) in *Chungking Express*. The song may indicate Faye's intentions, notwithstanding the emotionless, inscrutably mechanical way in which she goes around parading it; but it is devoid of any cultural capital whatsoever—hence its endearing, melancholy even, appeal. By a significant parallel, Faye's dream of becoming a stewardess, thirty-some years after the job was most sought after, is at best quaint. By the middle of the 1990s, the profession had suffered the proverbial, if the pun may be excused, fall from grace, acting and modeling having taken over as professional images of globe-trotting success for the young and beautiful. Yet Faye seems unselfconscious about her condition of young, disempowered youth chasing an out-of-date dream. Like many characters in Wong's oeuvre, she is a latter-day, urban bricoleur grabbing sounds, images, and ideas that serve her immediate purposes (irrespective of their provenance). The logic that controls her choice of profession, and "California Dreamin'," is purely associational. Midnight Express, the food joint where she works, is nearly opposite to California, the iconic bar in Lan Kwai Fong's California Tower (a building that, though it remains largely unseen, the film has now come to commemorate because it no longer exists). True, the association may be facile, thoughtless even; yet that is precisely its point, for it is consistent with the copy-cat mentality that seems to dominate the building industry—from planning to execution and, of course, naming—across the city.[17] If a developer sees fit to name an estate "Sorrento" or a tower "California," why shouldn't Faye play a song that celebrates it? After all, if the expiry date of the stewardess dream is long past, so is that of the building just across: naming it California as late as the early 1990s, when it was erected, was like short-selling local dwellers and tourists alike a dream that no one was buying anyway.

In response to developers' underestimation of their patrons' wit, Hong Kong saw the emergence of a uniquely local form of ironic distance from the city's celebration of out-of-date objects of desire, as also expressed, in the realm of music, in the winking embrace of all manner of foreign hits of yesteryear in the clubs of Lan Kwai Fong and Tsim Sha Tsui (an embrace that differed markedly from the deliberate, expertise-driven and campy cultivation of music of the 1970s and 1980s in American clubbing culture, or the growth of period-specific radios on the internet). In one important sense, then, "California Dreamin'" underscores Faye's partaking of the culture at large and vulnerability to the dreams sold to her by the commercially driven environment she is part of. The compulsive nature of her playing the track shows the dream to be stifling, and it will cause her to drift off. But it also bespeaks the focus, bordering on obsessiveness, that is Faye's strength and that, to an extent at least, enables her to be more than just a passive vessel of whatever her surroundings feed her. The song is like an exercise she must conduct daily, and the volume at which she plays it indicates the determination and formidable strength of her will. It is self-inflicted Muzak on steroids, a mantra of sorts, which she uses to instill in herself the resolve to leave. Her approach is radically utilitarian, one in keeping with her own predicament: going to California, seducing Cop 663, drowning out other people's conversations, and so forth. It is the epitome of solipsistic listening, one that assimilates a pop song to off-the-shelf, globally distributed products purchased to serve one's most immediate needs, like a deodorant, can of fruit, or carton of milk in a Circle K store.

UTOPIA EXPRESS

Faye uses "California Dreamin'" this way because she feels she owns it. But so does Wong Kar-wai. Like many of the characters in his films, Wong comes across music from the mediascape and makes do with it in ways both expedient and imaginative. To give his musical discoveries filmic reality, however, he must rise above the status of these down-on-their-luck characters. He must act rather like the elite professional with a healthy budget that he actually is. In doing this, he takes a page from the DJ's book. Having stumbled on a track, whether by design, through a member of the cast, or sheer accident, he proceeds to comb the relevant artists' catalogs and musical genres, obtain licensing rights, and finally remix the music he's chosen. I use the term *remix* in its literal, not metaphorical, sense. The tools of the trade are the same: playback equipment ranging from turntables to tape and, of course, digital players, amplifiers, mixers, and equalizers. Of course, Wong calibrates the qualities of the existing track not against those of another track (or tracks) but dialogue, sound effects as well as images—their narrative import and visual qualities as well as role within a certain editing pattern. As part of this new context, the music *sounds* different. It isn't just that it is now part of a mix that sonically envelops it, or cut up into discrete sections, only some of which are deployed in the final edit, reassembled, or re-equalized. It is also that narrative considerations push certain dimensions of the recorded track—say, the singing voice—or connotations (its status as hip-hop, or Italian opera) to the foreground (and vice versa). The music finds itself implicated in a dramatic situation that masks its existing identity and forges a new one.

The analogy with DJ-ing goes further. Wong fishes out of obscurity a track the way a DJ Shadow picks old gems or discarded catalog items and reinvents them. Take Michael Galasso's "Baroque," played over the pretitle sequence of *Chungking Express*. Galasso's work for film and especially the theater is well known among the cognoscenti.[18] While generically cinematic in its striking sonorities and coarse textures, however, "Baroque" first came to light as part of a 1992 curated CD meant to celebrate the creative freedom and crossing over of genres of the US postwar scene. Called *Utopia Americana*, the recording features the likes of Allen Ginsberg, Pauline Oliveros, Steve Reich, and John Cage (among others). The music website and crowdsourced database Discogs labels the work's genre "electronic, jazz, non-music, and classical" and the style "contemporary, experimental and poetry."[19] I stress the significance of personnel and the generic rubrics of the recording to indicate that to the extent that "Baroque" undergoes a transformation in *Chungking Express* this is in respect not of some broadly shared idea about the piece—the music lacked a reception history when Wong came across it—but rather in respect of its being a track in a recording: which is to say the physical, curated CD release. The latter is a wholly different vehicle for the delivery and consumption of music to a film soundtrack, as is the musical argument offered by its compiler, the Italian writer and producer Renzo Pognant Gros. Gros, it will be noted, felt no inhibitions in juxtaposing Galasso with the music of some of the high priests of postwar American modernism and jazz experimentalism.

Wong's own recontextualization could hardly be more drastic. Intriguingly—and misleadingly—enough, *Chungking Express* begins in the manner of an action film. The pretitle sequence is a sustained parallel montage sequence of Cop 223 chasing a wanted man simultaneous with a blond-wigged dealer (played by Brigitte Lin) rushing through the arrangement of a deal—both in or near the Chungking Mansions in Tsim Sha Tsui (figs. 5.6 and 5.7). When the two main characters accidentally run into each other, 0.01 of a centimeter from each other, to be precise, in Kaneshiro's now-celebrated voice-over formulation, we realize that we are seeing events as recounted from a point in the future ("This was the closest we ever got / Just 0.01 centimeter between us").[20] The corollary to this is that, contrary to our initial impression, the pre- and posttitle sequences are an instance of crosscutting rather than parallel montage: the two narrative threads, besides being simultaneous, converge toward a single place. Unlike standard crosscutting, however, we experience no suspense prior to the meeting because we do not know where the sequence is leading to until the very end. On whether two simultaneous actions presented onscreen are mutually implicating sides of the same event—as in a classic chase—hinges the difference between crosscutting and parallel montage. In the latter, the director cuts back and forth between two distinct, separate events to draw out an analogy or instructive contrast between them, whether they occur simultaneously or not. Speaking from the future or, put another way, in the present of the film-viewing experience, Cop 223's voice-over also tells us that crosscutting—that is, the teleological orientation of the sequence toward that fateful brushing off one another in the cauldron of the Chungking Mansions—is an artifact of retrospection. The convergence of the physical and existential trajectories of two characters, who until then were merely associated by the fact of sharing the same space at the same time, albeit in the contrasting roles of criminal and police enforcer, such converging is made explicit—it is fated, one is tempted to say—by the voice-over. Every randomly chosen pair of actions is potentially material

5.6 and 5.7 Brigitte Lin and Takeshi Kaneshiro in the Tsim Sha Tsui cauldron in *Chungking Express*.

for a crosscutting sequence, provided a plotline makes the linkages explicit. Kaneshiro's voice-over chronicles that process of emplotment.

The relationship between the chase and the proceedings of the drug deal is initially ambiguous—is it crosscutting or parallel montage?—because they are segments of a film of his own life that Cop 223 is making before our very eyes. Or is Cop 223 merely remembering? The question is moot. When memories run past his mind's eye, they do so with the look and sound of movies. Recalling is not cinematic for the fact that its products are delivered to us, by some third party, in the form of a film sequence; its cinematic nature is one with the act of remembering. It would seem impossible to rehearse things in one's mind, in Wong Kar-wai's world, unless one can make them up to look like movies. Memory is productive and, just as important, restorative of one's bruised ego—hence the need for the glamorizing effect provided by movie imagery and music. Short of falsifying the outcome of the events, especially those that left a scar, Cop 223 re-creates them in a form that redeems, and soothes, him. This explains why after stumbling on a drug dealer—the ideal target for his searches and a possible stepping stone for a promotion—he egregiously glosses over his gross act of incompetence and goes on to inform the viewer instead that "fifty-seven hours later [he would] fall in love with this woman."

That the title sequence is a fleshing-out of a cinematic fantasy, and not some unmediated representation of a past event, is made clear by the plethora of references embedded therein. To begin with a chase already in progress is itself a classic trope, an effective means to plunge the spectator into the heart of the film, be it a chase on foot on dangerous ground as in Alfred Hitchcock's *Vertigo* (1958); one on a car, like the opening sequence of Arthur Ripley's cult film *Thunder Road* (1958); or a virtuosic multitransport extravaganza, such as one sees at the beginning of many James Bond films and their progeny. The casting is also significant. Kaneshiro's tall, slender-yet-muscular figure and generically handsome features have the uncanny ability to recall, at the merest tilt of the camera, not one but many past glories of Japanese cinema—ranging from the young Mifune through Seijun Suzuki's unwitting heroes all the way to more recent matinee idols (doubtless this quality of his, along with his sex appeal, has played a role in his success). Lin herself, of course, sports a much-noted Marilyn Monroe wig, Lolita shades, and, in a wonderfully cross-genderish gesture, and oblique gesturing toward martial arts cinema, a Humphrey Bogart raincoat.[21] As an attempt to conceal her identity, this costume is, frankly, improbable; it is, in fact, the conspicuously unconcealed evidence of the intent to reference former starlets and movie characters. The blonde wig does not merely give away an intertextual link. Its very preposterousness and cheap appearance convey the gulf separating original from copy, even in the realm of images (Monroe's blonde hair was itself a quintessential image department creation, if ever there was one). Combined with the Lolita glasses on the one hand and the Bogart raincoat on the other, the outfit betrays a certain rush. It's as if the drug dealer had walked into a film costume store off Nathan Road in Tsim Sha Tsui and put together a disguise at the last minute. That she might have, in fact, mistaken a movie-themed store for a standard clothing boutique perfectly captures the confusion between films and the real world. But there is a poignant, bittersweet dimension to this piece of clownery. The distance between knowingness and naïveté is, for these characters, infinitesimal (another instance of 0.01 of a centimeter?). Their daily imaginings and routines are fed by the detritus of media-hyped artifacts—clothes, fast food, songs—reaching them through channels they can hardly control: their bricolage is born out of helplessness as much as the mastery of the milieu they find themselves in.

From beginning to end, the title sequence is underpinned by Galasso's mock-baroque music. A pastiche timidly redolent of Wendy Carlos's work for Stanley Kubrick, and distant echoes of Emerson Lake and Palmer, the music is written on and for the synthesizer. It is built on a dynamic minor-mode ostinato that strengthens the impression of having stumbled on the action in medias res. It opens steadfastly with two statements of a standard harmonic progression, voiced like a Vivaldi orchestral refrain: treble against a pedal bass in a quick call-and-response pattern. Moving steadily in three, this musical nucleus provides much of the sequence's kinetic impetus. The top part sketches something like the skeleton of a melody. To this, Galasso soon adds a flourish in the alto register, which continues, marching on its own, as an inner part until the end. As the drug dealer enters a seedy establishment bathed in a ghastly red light, a new part—in the upper soprano register—begins to draw a solo in an ostentatiously bluesy manner. The crossover of different idioms is tempered by the fact that the solo moves within the rigid bounds of the meter and harmonic rhythm established by the ostinato as well as the uniform palette of timbres of the synthesizer (here heard in its string, oboe, and electric guitar registers). Ambient sounds are faded out as the solo comes into its own, preparing for the climax of the pre-title sequence, the title card. The card is a collage of "Chungking Mansions" and "Midnight Express," not just linguistically but graphically as well: the two halves of the title correspond to distinct graphic elements. As the title appears onscreen, the solo swells above all the other elements of the mix, acquiring in the process a certain pathos.

The posttitle sequence begins with pillow shots of the city rooftops, followed by a chase involving Cop 223. A thunderstorm is underway in the skies of Hong Kong, and thunder figures prominently in the mix. Cop 223's voice is heard for the first time. Images of the chase are supported by the same music throughout. The music partakes of the construction of the chaotic, somewhat threatening but ultimately compelling microcosm, replete with startling juxtapositions, of the Chungking Mansions. As this is, in classic Bond tradition, a chase about which we as yet know precious little, we soon find ourselves in the position of having to weave the thread of the narrative ourselves, piecing together vital information as to who is chasing whom, along the way. The repetitive—indeed, soon predictable—pattern of the music confers unity to the rather fragmented succession of images. Its reassuringly consistent strains, for all the ominous minor-mode inflections, drive home the point that it is one and the same locale that we are looking at and that the initially confusing array of images will in some way coalesce into a coherent picture. When, in the heat of the race to catch a wanted man, he rubs shoulders with the drug dealer, Cop 223 announces laconically that he will fall in love with her within fifty-seven hours. It was her, not the criminal, that the elaborate chase was all about.

The iconography and editing betray the influence of comics: think of the use of strip-printed images, the hyperbolic turns and twists involving the chaser and the chased, and the jolting cuts from one climactic moment of the action to the next. It soon becomes obvious that instead of following the action step by step, we are being shown a curtailed sequence, composed of evocative, if somewhat elusive, images of it. The absence of a master shot is in keeping with the fact that Cop 223 is mentally projecting a private film of his own past (he is naturally familiar with the locale as he revisits what has happened there). The sound effects are, too, cleverly modeled after comics. Instead of a complexly orchestrated mix, punctuated by the occasional climax, we hear discrete sonic events: a crash, a sibilant screeching or thumping sound, a siren (and so forth). Sifting through the music and a paper-thin, almost perfunctory, background texture, these sounds strike us at somewhat interval regulars, rather like the cinematic translation of the panel-by-panel, grapho-linguistic transcription of sounds one sees in comic books. There is nothing cartoonish, let alone comic-book-like about the editing of the music. Ostinatos are common in music for action scenes (where it is often reinforced by percussion). The music's martial element, key, and its kinetic drive make Galasso sound rather like an instance of mood music cueing the spectator to the correct interpretation of what we see: this is a dangerous situation, and the fate of the protagonists is at stake. In standard action cues, the recognition of affect depends on not only such features as key and tempo but also sonority and texture: action music often veers toward a zone where music and sound effects overlap. This is not achievable here, as the textures are clearly readable and the part writing, foreshadowing perhaps the love interest that is the true destination of the sequence—and subject of the film—too delicate. The synthesizer, moreover, occupies its own discrete zone of the mix, separate from the sound effects. The score, in one word, exhibits a disengaged quality. This is the only hint that it is a preexisting track rather than a tailor-made, original composition. The ostinato pattern heightens the impression of disengagement, exact repetition precluding the possibility of fine-tuned sync points—lest one cut the images to the music, an option that Wong did not find workable here. Loosely synchronized to the incidents of the action, its tempo neither consistent nor in striking contrast to the blur of the onscreen antics, Galasso's score moves at its own pace and of its own accord—as befits a retrospective, summative soundtrack.

By the time we hear Cop 223's voice-over again, near the end of the sequence, we know we have seen events long past as retold by him. The synthesizer has played the role of both the baroque orchestra (the Vivaldi-like part writing) and the soloist. Galasso's choice of the synthesizer can only be speculated about. But it fits the ethos—and budget!—of *Chungking Express* like a glove. The film was, after all, made under a famously tight timeline and even tighter budget. Ever since synthesizers became readily available, the Hong Kong film industry embraced the instrument to add the semblance of symphonic grandeur to the mix. Of course, the use of a synthesizer in lieu of flesh-and-blood players has primarily been motivated by economics. There is no doubt that this was the case for the film's original music as well (written by Roel Garcia and Frankie Chan). The director and his team seem to have made virtue out of necessity. Like the wig, toy weapons, and minimal sets, the synthesizer score redeems its limitations by refusing to disavow its middle-brow quality as it engages in imitation of learned musical registers (the high baroque) and impassioned, highly expressive ones (the R&B solo). Whether Chan and Garcia's choice of the synthesizer is chronologically prior to Wong's decision to employ Galasso's music is moot. What matters is that the presence of the synthesizer harmonizes the latter's preexisting work to the former's freshly composed score.

Plunged into the world of the Chungking Mansions, therefore, Galasso's music comes across as a pastiche of a film score: specifically, a Hong Kong film score.[22] It gestures like a serious, self-important soundtrack, one complete with a strings section and highly paid professional musicians: the phantom score conjured for a film running in Cop 223's mind and to which we are privy like unwitting soul mates. With this, the dizzying transformation of Galasso's original, self-standing composition into the soundtrack to *Chungking Express* is complete, as is its migration to a different media vehicle and a new distribution channel, network of listeners, and affects. In a telling reversal of the popular response to "Six Days" on social media, the comments to the YouTube release of "Baroque" is replete with references to Wong's film. Though a still image of the cover of the original recording graces the streaming video for the song, *Chungking Express* has all but overwritten *Utopia Americana*.

FINALE

A similar process of ex post facto assimilation invests Galasso's music for *In the Mood for Love*, albeit in reverse fashion. Where Wong uses Galasso's "found" track to open *Chungking Express*, he withholds the original composition Galasso writes for *In the Mood for Love* until the very end. As a result, instead of a preexisting track foreshadowing the sound of the original score and becoming confused with it, as in *Chungking Express*, Galasso's celebrated original track for the film's Angkor Wat finale mimics retrospectively, in both texture and instrumentation, a preexisting track (Umebayashi's even more celebrated "Yumeji's Theme"). The respective weighting of the preexisting tracks is also reversed: where in *Chungking Express* Galasso's preexisting music is a one-off, in *In the Mood for Love* Umebayashi's "Yumeji's Theme" plays incessantly.

The set for the finale of *In the Mood for Love* is prepared by the acknowledgment of the sheer size and complexity of the world as a physical and

5.8 Su Li-zhen in *In the Mood for Love*.

political space, and Hong Kong's place in it. Three years after her separation from Mo-wan, Lai-chen returns to the old flat where her aborted romance had started, only to find it empty. Upon asking the landlady, Mrs. Suen (Rebecca Pan), about her plans, Lai-chen is told that because of the "situation" in China—a reference to the 1966–67 riots—Mrs. Suen is planning to leave Hong Kong to join her daughter in the United States. Lai-chen, looking out the window toward the apartment Mo-wan used to live in, can hardly contain her tears (fig. 5.8). It would seem intuitive to interpret her reaction as an expression of regret, frustration for a missed opportunity, or nostalgia for happier times. But the dynamics of Lai-chen's breakdown are even more complex. Subsumed within her tears is a grasp of how the private sphere is enmeshed with a social situation. Her sorrow is tinged, made deeper and more devastating, by understanding that the departing Mrs. Suen, driven away from Hong Kong by political and economic instability on the mainland, was the objective (if unwitting) enabler of Mo-wan and Lai-chen's encounter and she had come to stand for the environment—personal, social, and political—that had both nurtured and repressed their feeling of love. With Mrs. Suen gone, and with the disappearance of a whole communal and societal network associated with her, symbolized by the intricate close quarters of her flat, Lai-chen now understands that the love story has truly come to an end and can only exist in the form of memory—hence her despair.

The image of her looking out and quietly shedding tears may well chronicle the first time that she experiences the aborted love affair with Mo-wan as objectified within the social matrix of her milieu.

The overwhelming power of social and political structures over the individual is so obvious a fact as to be prima facie utterly uninteresting as an object of representation. *In the Mood for Love* manages to give this obvious yet obviously important truth the noteworthy, poignant expression it deserves by referring to it off-handedly, through Mrs. Suen's remark about the 1966–67 disturbances in China and their reverberations in Hong Kong. Held back until very late in the film, the appearance of the broader social and political context is a seismic shift in point of view, rather like a sudden awakening after a long period of lethargy. The breathtaking speed with which the film changes gears takes us to Singapore first and then Cambodia via TV footage of French president Charles de Gaulle's arrival in that country in 1966, the grainy images of which, not unlike the horrific footage of a self-immolating monk in Ingmar Bergman's *Persona* (released, coincidentally, also in 1966), break through the lavish, sensual, lacquered surface of the film with considerable force. This reversal of perspective sheds new light on everything seen up to that point, suggesting that politics had been there all the way through, hidden in plain sight, buried under the obvious truth about its crushing power, a truth that the film defamiliarizes not only by holding it back until the very end but presenting it in the form of an absence. Though in a manner not quite as chilling and gruesome as in that other tale of solipsism and eroticism, Nagisa Oshima's *Ai no corrida* (1976), politics in *In the Mood for Love* are nowhere, because politics are everywhere.

But while Oshima ends with images of Japanese soldiers and flagrant symbols of nationalism, Wong returns to Mo-wan's predicament as a path to transcendence. The TV footage of de Gaulle's visit to Cambodia is blown up until it is no longer readable. Out of the blur there emerges an image of a monk robed in orange perched quietly by the corner of a yard door in Angkor Wat (figs. 5.9 and 5.10). Following the commotion of de Gaulle's warm welcome in Cambodia, the image looks like a still tableau. The air is crackling with environmental sounds—birdsong, monkey calls, the buzz of various insects. We see a hole in a stone wall, garlanded with dry scrub blowing in the gentle wind (fig. 5.11). Integral to the fabric of the now-ruined temple, the hole is a vestige of bygone time but also, as we will soon learn, a vessel. A finger rests on it, as if taking its measure. A close, side-angle shot shows Mo-wan facing the

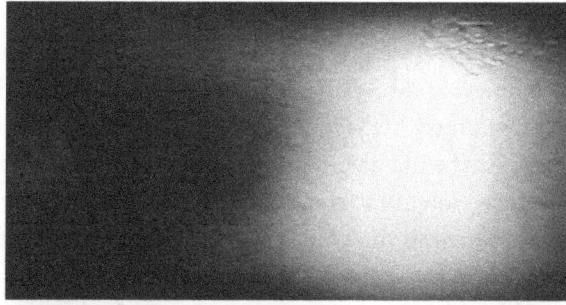

5.9–5.12 Mo-wan in Cambodia: from *In the Mood for Love*.

wall where the hole has presumably been carved to accommodate a thin beam or bolt. Having reached Cambodia on an assignment to cover de Gaulle's visit, Mo-wan is visiting Angkor Wat in his off time. The grave expression on his face suggests the intention to carry out a ritual, perhaps. As the image lingers, we are privy to a degree of hesitancy as well. Galasso's solemn variant of "Yumeji's Theme" appears just as he makes a move toward the hole. The sync point signals his resolve to whisper a secret into it (fig. 5.12).

Whether lifted from a record or, as is the case here, expressly composed for a film, Galasso's music ends up being the assimilated, not the assimilating, element of the soundtrack. This is not just a matter of how frequently it appears (and, consequently, its exposure). Galasso's "Angkor Wat Finale" betrays a clear compositional relation to "Yumeji's Theme." Indeed, as already noted, it comes across as a leitmotivic elaboration thereof.[23] In a telling reversal of his usual practice, Wong Kar-wai wants us to hear one track in terms of another: an overt, deliberate case of infratextual relation. The cello pizzicato ostinato rhythm, in triple meter, outlines a C-minor triad that unfailingly recalls the waltzlike pizzicato that underpins "Yumeji's Theme." The exacting rhythms and clockwork quality of Galasso's finale also add to the similarity, as does the dominance of string instruments. The key (C minor) and consequently mode is the same. Without hindering the perceived similarity of Galasso's music to "Yumeji's Theme," C minor is admittedly implied as much as affirmed. The arpeggiations that open the piece and run through it outline a C-minor chord in the second inversion (thereby stressing the dominant sonority G). The dominant G is further stressed by the double bass outlining a G / D, a pendulum-like motion, quasi-percussive in nature, neatly spread across a 4 + 4 phrase, and keeping at the same time the whole piece both anchored to a strong hyperbeat in the low register and off kilter harmonically. Above this almost mechanical rhythmic and harmonic foundation, Galasso lays it on thick by adding not one but two more cellos playing rhythmically simple yet affecting lines that swap material and crisscross like a tightly textured duet.[24]

The contrast between pizzicato and coll'arco on the one hand, and between exact (the rhythmic section) and free articulation (the solo cellos) on the other further ties "Angkor Wat Finale" to "Yumeji's Theme." Yet Galasso, in keeping with the leitmotivic principle of development, departs from his model by stubbornly, and for that very reason also memorably, insisting on a monochromatic sound palette: one double bass and three cellos playing in a relatively narrow range (as opposed to Umebayashi's more even spread and hence traditional, quartet-like distribution of the parts). The resulting tone color offers up a striking match to the faded browns and dark grays of Angkor Wat. Monotonousness of color also provides the appropriately stable background against which the cellos can sketch their impassioned lines. Abstracted from the plot, Galasso's animated lament would seem to have been cast against type, as in an extravagant montage of attractions with the images of the temple ruins at dusk (whose subtle soundscape of gentle breezes and distant tropical bird sounds the music so unceremoniously overrides). Understood in context, however, the music hits the spectator with the force of a foregone conclusion one can no longer pretend not to acknowledge. The emotional restraint that pervades the film, and the main characters' subdued, somewhat soporific demeanor throughout, has the effect of postponing the inevitable. Should anyone have failed to appreciate the depth and finality of the tragedy that has befallen Li-zhen and Mo-wan, the finale is the moment when any lingering doubt is dispelled. The pain of unfulfilled love is at long last articulated in tones at once apposite and shocking—through music. The brisk tempo and brief, recursive, stepwise or small-leap motives evince a groan-like sonority from the solo instruments that stands in clear contrast to the stern immutability of the temple complex and calls to mind Alberto Savinio's comparison of the voice of the cello to the "cry of an ass."[25] A sonic metaphor, perhaps, of the "tumult in Mo-wan's heart"?

The disorderly texture and fuzzy boundary between the cellos, busy as they are climbing over each other's lines, quickly establish a tone that will soon clash with the subsequent image of Mo-wan's resigned, almost indifferent attitude as he casually explores the grounds of the temple complex. Following the last shot of Tony Leung, seen in a long shot walking through a characteristic axial gallery, the film opens up to the reality of the spectator watching the film. With the fictional characters literally out of the picture, the onus of shouldering the pain of heartbreak falls on the spectator, whom Wong invites to whisper into yet another small hole in the image that concludes the film (fig. 5.13). Just at the point where the rhythmic section of Galasso's cue signals a return to the first phrase, the piece ends in open-ended fashion on the much-emphasized G. This is in keeping with its cyclical form, which evokes a perpetual motion device. There is no cadence proper but rather quite simply the halting of the music just as the camera's lateral dolly also stops moving.

5.13 Angkor Wat in *In the Mood for Love*.

An unmeasurable amount of time has now passed. Musicless at last, the last image of Angkor Wat at dusk is marked by environmental sound effects: insects chirping, breezes, and the sounds of night break in a subtropical forest. Following the roar of Galasso's music, our ears take a split second to adjust to the much softer sound level of the temple captured in its native sonic environment: a clear intimation of the site and its sparse inhabitants continuing to guard the land and offer ambivalent solace to their visitors well after Mo-wan will have left its grounds. At the beginning of the episode, the hum of the reverberating walls and distant tapestry of bird sounds helped establish the setting as an aspect of the film's storyworld; now, having Galasso's music been repeated until exhaustion, the very same sounds make palpable present-time Angkor Wat caught in the here-and-now of its profilmic manifestation.

Like a benevolent Trojan horse, Galasso's "Angkor Wat Finale" has paraded its debt to Umebayashi's preexisting track only to lend to it retrospectively the air of an original score. At stake in such a repurposing is nothing less than the definitive erasure of Suzuki's film as repository of the music and indeed inspiration for *In the Mood for Love*. Given a new lease on life in Wong's *In the Mood for Love*, the "Yumeji's Theme" of Suzuki's *Yumeji* is simultaneously also condemned to oblivion.

INTRODUCTION

Epigraphs: Rauschenberg and Seitz, unpublished transcript, cited in Jonathan D. Katz, "'Committing the Perfect Crime': Sexuality, Assemblage, and the Postmodern Turn in American Art," *Art Journal* 67, no. 1 (Spring 2008): 38–53; "Thirteen Questions: A Dialogue with Jorge Luis Borges," interview by Willis Barnstone, *Chicago Review* 31, no. 3 (Winter 1980): 11–28; *Ashes of Time*, directed by Wong Kar-wai (Block 2 Pictures, 1994), 1 hr., 40 min.

1   In Arthur C. Clarke's novel, written on the basis of the screenplay after, not prior to, the film, the discovery of the weapon is somewhat different. Moon Watcher uses a stone—not a bone—"as if in a dream," while within a group of warthogs (a more realistic detail, because tapirs are not known to have inhabited Africa, where the beginning of the film is set). See Clarke, *2001*, 18–19. The iconic timpani motif of Strauss's fanfare is adumbrated in an earlier passage of the novel describing the apes' encounter with the monolith (11–12). In the film, the latter is just as famously scored with György Ligeti's "Requiem."

2   It makes sense to talk about "Also Sprach Zarathustra" as being found, tinkered with, and retooled because Strauss's symphonic poem had a long life as a self-standing artistic expression before its emplotment in Kubrick's film (whether in the form of live performances or recordings). Interestingly enough, Strauss's fanfare bears striking similarities to and indeed appears to have been modeled after a composition by Danish composer Niels Gade. Christopher Reynolds leaves it undecided

whether the similarities are the result of deliberate allusion or expedient borrowing. See C. Reynolds, *Motives for Allusion*, 14–15.

3   On the role of Hong Kong Television (TVB) in the development in the new wave and especially the career of Wong's mentor Patrick Tam, see Yau, "Urban Nomads"; and Fang, "'Pity about the Furniture.'"

4   On stage production as bricolage, see Atkinson's pioneering article, "Making Opera Work." On the postproduction in film as a form of bricolage, see also the introduction to Baumgartner, *Metafilm Music*, and Cecchi, "Collaboration and/as Bricolage." Godard's relentless subversion of editing conventions produced results that are vastly different from Wong's camouflaged retoolings, summarized by Baumgartner with the term "Metafilm Music."

5   On objective hazard as "an active synthesis of the subjective and the objective," see Carrouges, *André Breton*, 191. (In the English edition of the book, the word *hazard* is translated as *chance*.)

6   Kelly, "The Anthropology of Assemblage," 29.

7   Key to my understanding of the transformative power of postproduction, therefore, is its multimedia dimension or, better, dramaturgical impetus. Nicolas Bourriaud likewise extols the productive powers of reframing and retooling in contemporary culture. Despite his clever play with cinematic metaphors, however, his vision is bound to a conventional understanding of artistic practices (and their attendant markets: the art market, music industry, etc.) as separate endeavors—an understanding that, in my opinion, cinema has irreversibly upended. See Bourriaud, *Postproduction*.

8   Hebdige, *Subculture*.

9   See Deleuze and Guattari, *Anti-Oedipus*; and Derrida, "Sign, Structure and Play."

10   Lévi-Strauss, *The Savage Mind*, 16–22. These two figures appear to map rather neatly onto those of the collagist, record mixer, or indeed the director / music compiler on the one hand and the film composer conceiving and cutting music to the images and soundtrack of a given film on the other.

11   Derrida, "Sign, Structure and Play," 231.

12   Derrida, "Sign, Structure and Play," 232.

13   The artist or musician whose works are a pastiche of other styles or practices, as opposed to a collage of ready-mades, is to an extent also a bricoleur.

14   Lévi-Strauss, *The Savage Mind*, 22ff.

15   Lévi-Strauss, *The Raw and the Cooked*, 15. On this problematic aspect of Lévi-Strauss's work, see Prieto, *Listening In*, 258ff. See also Kerman, *Contemplating Music*, 181.

16   See Brown, *Overtones and Undertones*, 10.

17 Brown, *Overtones and Undertones*, 10.

18 Pier Paolo Pasolini, liner notes to *Dimensioni Sonore I* (translation mine).

19 "As he swung his hand around, puzzled by its suddenly increased weight, he felt a pleasing sense of power and authority" (Clarke, *2001*, 18–19).

20 Kelly, "The Anthropology of Assemblage," 28.

21 Kelly, "The Anthropology of Assemblage," 28–29.

22 See Biancorosso, *Situated Listening*.

23 Derrida, "Sign, Structure and Play," 227.

24 Such privileging of logic over experience also informs the work of countless critics and scholars for whom a borrowing invariably "drags along with it" the whole of the source from which it was lifted. Iampolski refers to this process as a process of "normalization" (*The Memory of Tyresias*, 51ff.).

25 Altglas, "'Bricolage,'" 477.

26 On moving to Hong Kong, ease of access was to me epitomized by the multizone DVD player. To my delight, I could watch films from all over the world without nary a murmur or complaint from the playback system.

27 Film scoring as is sometimes still practiced today also calls to mind bricolage in the eighteenth-century sense of the term, namely "fixing" something by way of a provisional repair (the music coming to the rescue of a rough cut or providing the requisite expression, which is found to be lacking in the images and the dialogue, for example).

28 This sobering scenario is different from Arthur Danto's idea of "the end of art," which is "a declaration of artistic freedom, and hence the impossibility of any further large narrative. . . . It is a wholesale case of living happily ever after" (Danto, "The End of Art," 128).

29 S. Reynolds, *Retromania*.

30 While Reynolds considers film remakes, it does not occur to him that it is through cinema that the rejuvenation of pop may have occurred in the first place.

31 On the ideological dimension of the bricoleur/engineer distinction, and Lévi-Strauss's view of nuclear science as a background to its formulation, see Johnson, "Bricoleur and Bricolage."

32 See Markham, "Bricolage."

33 See, for instance, Fisher, "Rock 'n' Recording." For a recent summary of the debate, see Davies, "Works of Music."

34 On this, see Bordwell, *Planet Hong Kong*; and Bettinson, *The Sensuous Cinema of Wong Kar-wai*.

35 I am also thinking of the collages by such artists as Anthony Brown, Nancy Spero, and John Stezaker (to name but three). The mosaic technique has also undergone a revival in the late paintings of Chuck Close.

36 The key work in the Wong Kar-wai canon, in this respect, is the little-known short *Hua Yang de Nian Hua*, a two-minute-and-twenty-second film built by stitching together extremely short excerpts of old Chinese nitrate movies. On this film, see Biancorosso, "Popular Music"; and Ma, *Sounding the Modern Woman*, 216–17.

37 Bishop, "History Depletes Itself," 329.

38 For a comprehensive survey of the use of allusion in classical Chinese poetry, see Peng, "The Role of Allusion." See also Williams, *Imitations of the Self*, especially the introduction and chapter 6.

39 On the vernacular/cosmopolitan dialectic in Southeast Asia, see Pollock, "The Cosmopolitan Vernacular." For an account of the process of indigenization, see Arjun Appadurai's virtuosic reconstruction of the history of cricket in India in "Playing with Modernity." For yet two more scenarios specific to Chinese-language cinema, see Yiman Wang's discussion of self-conscious remakes of Western models in "Remade in China," and Hu, *Worldly Desires*.

40 "Knock-off" phones may "refer to" precedents, playfully or clandestinely as the case may be, but they supersede their status as imitations or parodies to, quite simply, work as telephones (as in bricolage, the references pale compared to the use afforded by the retooling). As observed by Jeroen de Kloet, Chow Yiu Fai, and Lena Scheen, "*shanzhai* cultures may also help to revalidate the importance of craftsmanship, as the focus is more on making than on creating" (*Boredom, Shanzhai, and Digitisation*, 17). On the "subcultural" and even militant dimension of *shanzhai* culture, see Hennessey, "Deconstructing Shanzhai."

41 "You so often obliterate the sources of the things you use, that I did not regard you as essentially an assembler but as a sculptor," wrote curator William Seitz to David Smith, in order to justify the exclusion of so many of his works in the landmark *Art of Assemblage* exhibition (at the Museum of Modern Art, 1961). Cited in Dezeuze, "Assemblage," 31.

42 The key intervention is Gorbman, "Auteur Music." For a recent critical survey, see also the introduction to Ashby, *Popular Music and the New Auteur*, 1–28. On compilation soundtracks, see Hubbert, "The Compilation Soundtrack," and "Jonathan Romney and Adrian Wootton / Interviews from *The Celluloid Jukebox* (1995)," in Hubbert, *Celluloid Symphonies*, 452–64.

43 It should be noted that the use of preexisting music predates the period that is the focus of Gorbman's 2007 essay. Godard, Pasolini, and, outside the mainstream circuit, Kenneth Anger drew on their record collections for their films starting in the early 1960s.

44 Kubrick's use of the "Blue Danube" waltz in *2001: A Space Odyssey*, to discuss a glaring example, is both a huge gamble and a rare balancing act. On Kubrick's use of preexisting music, see McQuiston, *We'll Meet Again*,

especially chapter 6, and (the sadly untranslated) Bassetti, *La musica secondo Kubrick*.

45 In *The Savage Mind*, Lévi-Strauss never makes explicit references to twentieth-century collage and ready-mades. Yet it is hard to escape the impression that whether consciously or not, dada, cubist, and surrealist artists played a role in suggesting the analogy between myth creation and the manipulation of ready-to-hand objects.

46 Warhol's career, from his Campbell's soup cans to the serial paintings, was predicated on the successful exploitation of precisely this paradox.

47 In *Remix*, Lawrence Lessig refers to this as "Read-only" culture.

48 On the performative nature of musical taste, see Hennion, *The Passion for Music*. The difference between user knowledge and builder knowledge maps onto that between bricoleur and engineer and is—or ought to be—of central concern to music educators.

49 For a sobering evaluation of music "taste-makers" under the conditions of what he calls "new capitalism," see Taylor, *Music in the World*, 155–73.

50 To use an enological analogy, famous filmmakers are like Burgundian wine *négociants* selling under their name wine whose grapes are sourced and sometimes even vinified in other premises.

51 The reverse is also true as YouTubers "play" images to a given music track. Social media have occasioned a return to the raucously and joyously anarchic scene of the early years of the medium, years in which almost any music would do, provided that it lasted for as long as the screen presentation. The main difference, of course, is that music was performed live. For a wide array of theoretical essays on sampling and mixing practices, see Laderman and Westrup, *Sampling Media*. For a nuanced historical account of the role of the DJ in the emergence of hip-hop, see Katz, *Groove Music*.

52 By clearing rights, Wong sustains the illusion of single-origin creation. To use Foucault's terminology, Wong is the author of the music not so much as its composer as the "function" of the audiovisual discourse in which the music is implicated. See Foucault, "What Is an Author?"

53 Ashby, *Popular Music and the New Auteur*, 17.

54 On parody in renaissance music, see, for instance, *Grove Music Online*, s.v. "Parody," by Michael Tilmouth and Richard Sherr, accessed June 13, 2021, http://www.oxfordmusiconline.com.eproxy1.lib.hku.hk.

55 In the case of *contrafacta*, erasing previous associations *was* the point, not a felicitous spin-off, especially when trespassing the threshold between sacred and secular was concerned. On borrowing, citation, and authority in the European Middle Ages, see Clark and Leach, *Citation and Authority*, especially the introduction and chapter 11. As described by Hon-Lun Yang, the covers of Western tunes in Hong Kong musicals come close to *contrafacta* (Yang, "Cosmopolitanism," 157ff.).

56   Iampolski, *The Memory of Tyresias*, 51–82.

57   For a reading of the sequence in terms of surveillance, see Chen, "Sonic Secrets as Counter-Surveillance."

58   For a classic account, see Kristeva, *Desire in Language*.

59   Consider, for example, Wong's exchange with Martin Scorsese regarding his homage to Sergio Leone via Morricone's music while shooting *The Grandmaster*. See Deadline Hollywood, "Martin Scorsese and Kar Wai Wong Interview," http://www.youtube.com/watch?v=xB9JvRbBZRM at 18:00ff. (accessed March 22, 2024).

60   Preexisting music is transformed as much as it transforms the environment in which it is embedded.

61   While I refuse to interpret borrowing solely or even primarily as a function of intertextuality, I also refrain from embracing the dichotomy between "interpretation" and, to quote Susan Sontag, the "erotics of art." Sensorial impact is key to the cinematic experience but so is world-making and the imaginative engagement with the medium that sustains filmmaking of the sort practiced by Wong. Interpretation amounts to more than the unpacking of intertextual references in any case. See Sontag, *Against Interpretation*, 95–104.

62   Thanks to Zhang Jingyi for the pun on Bloom.

63   Consider "topic theory," a branch of scholarship inspired by Leonard Ratner's revival and systematization of eighteenth-century understanding of musical topoi. Like intertextual readings, "topical" readings of musical works reaffirm the value of socially shared knowledge in guiding reception. At the same time, topic theorists privilege the study of topoi as dispatchers of stable meanings rather than focusing on the ways in which they are transformed or are no longer recognizable as such. See Ratner, *Classic Music*; and Allanbrook, *Rhythmic Gesture in Mozart*.

64   While I vindicate the significance of Wong's films as *representations* as against the reductionism implicit in intertextual readings bent on reading texts primarily through other texts, Rey Chow has cautioned us against another kind of reductionism, what she calls the "reflection-ism" prevalent "in the reading of non-Western cultural work in general (so that a film made in Hong Kong around 1997, for instance, is invariably approached as having something to do with the factographic, geopolitical reality of Hong Kong's return to the People's Republic of China)" (Chow, "Nostalgia of the New Wave," 49). If more obliquely, Ackbar Abbas's work on Hong Kong cinema and literature may be said to suffer from the same reflectionist tendency (see Abbas, *Hong Kong*). I also address this difficulty in Biancorosso, "Romance, Insularity, and Representation."

1 Subway Cinema News, http://subwaycinemanews.com/archives/3 (last accessed May 30, 2018). The website has since been closed.

2 On the ambiguity, see also Bordwell, *Planet Hong Kong*, 175.

3 The street is Castle Road in the now posh Mid-Levels neighborhood, just off Conduit Road, Central. Still intact despite the encroaching redevelopment of many neighboring areas, the site looks and feels the same way today (especially at night). The phone booth is no longer there, however (presuming it ever was).

4 See such well-known compendia as Rapee, *Encyclopaedia of Music for Pictures*; and Erdmann, Becce, and Brav, *Allgemeines Handbuch der Film-Musik*.

5 On this, see Théberge, "'Ethnic Sounds,'" 98; and Slobin, *Global Soundtracks*.

6 Arthur Benjamin, the composer, was an Australian who spent much of his professional career in the United Kingdom. In *Vertigo*, Bach and Mozart are marked as "respectable" but also "nerdy" via the association with the bespectacled female character, Midge.

7 Rota's arrangements, put another way, are less the stylized idealization of past tunes than a representation of their morphing into psychologically plausible memories thereof. On remembering as a constructive act, see Bartlett, *Remembering*.

8 *Amarcord* is, significantly, absent from Fredric Jameson's admittedly selective list of "nostalgia films" that, in idealizing the past, can erase the historical distance that separates us from it. Also altogether absent in his discussion is the sonic dimension of the films he examines. See Jameson, *Postmodernism*, 19–20.

9 The Morricone pastiche by Frankie Chan and Roel Garcia for *Ashes of Time* gestures in the direction of nostalgic remaking but differs from Rota's subtle reshaping of well-known hits.

10 See Sewell, "A Typology."

11 Sewell, "A Typology," 76.

12 The recording of a sound is a highly mediated re-presentation of that sound. However, the recording of a recording is its allographic iteration. On the former, and Christian Metz's Bazinian belief in sound recording as trace (or index), see Tom Levin's critique in "The Acoustic Dimension."

13 Goodman, *Languages of Art*, 99–126.

14 On the sacred dimension of Warhol's images, see Danto, *Andy Warhol*.

15 Therefore, Sewell continues, a sample is "both a sound and a representation of a particular association with that sound" ("A Typology," 76). One may quibble with the term *representation* (infelicitous in a presentational

context) as well as her use of "sound" applied so casually to lyrics. Does Sewell refer to the timbre of the rapper's voice, the mode of delivery, or the meaning of the words?

16   Zappa, *The Real Frank Zappa Book*, 166.

17   Zappa, *The Real Frank Zappa Book*, 166.

18   Zappa, *The Real Frank Zappa Book*, 166.

19   On this dimension of hip-hop, see Williams, *Rhymin' and Stealin'*.

20   On "textually signaled" versus "unsignaled" samples, see Williams, "Intertextuality, Sampling, and Copyright," 209.

21   Wong Kar-wai talks repeatedly of the soundscape of the neighborhood of Kowloon in which he grew up. See, for instance, Wong and Powers, *WKW*, 86–89.

22   See Shumway, "Rock 'n' Roll Soundtracks," 44.

23   Haruki Murakami's novel *Norwegian Wood* (1987) is perhaps the most extreme example of a single, fleeting flash of musical recognition resulting in a monumental feat of memory—so much so, in fact, that the author himself seems to have forgotten about it (the novel begins with the titular song and the act of remembering that precipitates the narrative but never quite returns to it).

24   Kassabian, *Hearing Film*. See also Vernallis's review of *Analysing Musical Multimedia*.

25   Kassabian, *Hearing Film*, 70, 139.

26   On "post-existing" music, see Godsall, *Reeled In*, chapter 4.

27   Here I adapt T. S. Eliot's view of literary tradition as expounded in his famous essay, "Tradition and the Individual Talent."

28   On the status of the record as musical work, see Fisher, "Rock 'n' Recording." On the use of recordings in coming-of-age films, see Stilwell, "Vinyl Communion."

29   It is common to introduce music via a plausible source, thereby building a realistic justification for its appearance. The tradition can be traced back to analogous practices in the spoken theater and opera.

30   In this respect, "Perfidia" is an object lesson in how the yardstick used to chart the uses of classical music does not apply to pop repertoires. In transforming the song creatively, Wong is, in a sense, merely following in the footsteps of many popular musicians. For a fascinating "multiple take" on "Perfidia" through the combined lenses of literary theory and the history of sexuality, see Buckley, "Does Betrayal Music Transform Sexual Pessimism."

31   Xavier Cugat and His Waldorf-Astoria Orchestra, *Perfidia—Canción Bolero*, Vox, 26334-A (1941), 78 RPM.

32   Xavier Cugat and His Orchestra, *Viva Cugat*, Mercury, PPS 6003 (1961), 33 1/3 RPM.

33　In "Does Betrayal Music Transform Sexual Pessimism," Buckley makes abundantly clear that while there is no question of Domínguez's primary artistic responsibility, equally obvious is the power of performers and arrangers, such as Cugat, in refashioning "Perfidia" to suit different markets and artistic agendas.

34　Eco, "*Casablanca*."

35　"[Interviewers]: Before beginning to film [*Happy Together*], did you have a particular relationship with tango music, and with Astor Piazzolla's work? WKW: Not at all. In fact, my first contact with Piazzolla was at the Amsterdam Airport where I bought his CDs on my way to Argentina!" (*Wong Kar-wai: Interviews*, 79-80).

36　On the Taipei of the 1960s, see Jones, *Circuit Listening*.

37　Even such a world-famous figure as Elvis Presley was at one point the expression of a local culture. Think, for example, of the role of Nashville's historic RCA Studio B in the forging of a recognizable sound.

38　De Certeau, *The Practice of Everyday Life*, 21.

39　Recanati, "Open Quotation," 639.

40　Howard, "On Musical Quotation," 315.

41　Metzer, *Quotation and Cultural Meaning*, 4.

42　Recanati, "Open Quotation," 639.

43　De Certeau, *The Practice of Everyday Life*, 21.

44　De Certeau, *The Practice of Everyday Life*, 21.

45　De Certeau, *The Practice of Everyday Life*, xxii.

46　On speech acts, see J. L. Austin's classic *How to Do Things with Words*.

47　In linguistics, borrowing refers primarily to loanwords from another language.

48　Small, *Musicking*.

49　I use the concepts of *trace, consummation*, and *transfiguration* as signposts in a continuum of effects. In something like the way automatic writing or the paintings of a Jackson Pollock come across as avowed traces of a past action so, in the films of Godard, the rough transitions and openly improvisatory nature of the mise-en-scène are vivid reminders of the acts and subtending operations that brought his films into being. But the degree of polish of the finished product should not blind us to the fact that, say, a Kubrick film—or a Vermeer domestic scene, to insist on the parallel with the history of painting—is, too, the product of a string of actions (belabored, staggered over time, and discontinuous as such a sequence may have been).

50　On the operations of the soundtrack as "occult," see Donnelly, *Occult Aesthetics*.

51　De Certeau, *The Practice of Everyday Life*, xi, xiii.

52　De Certeau, *The Practice of Everyday Life*, xiii.

53　De Certeau, *The Practice of Everyday Life*.

54 See Darnton, *The Great Cat Massacre*.

55 Compagnon, *La second maine*, I.3.

56 See Abbate, "Wagner, Cinema, and Redemptive Glee," 608.

57 Three directors are credited but six more hands were likely involved, including the producer Alexander Korda's brothers.

58 Abbate, "Wagner, Cinema, and Redemptive Glee," 602.

59 Abbate, "Wagner, Cinema, and Redemptive Glee," 610.

60 Abbate, "Wagner, Cinema, and Redemptive Glee," 609.

61 On allusion as a private, esoteric practice, see C. Reynolds, *Motives for Allusion*. In his review of the book, Raymond Knapp questions why Reynolds examines allusion strictly as an aspect of composition rather than reception (Knapp, review of *Motives for Allusion*, 743). The answer is that he wishes to stay away from opening the Pandora's box of reception, as tracing compositional intentions, when documented, provides a more solid terrain for ascertainable, as opposed to speculative, cases of allusion.

62 E. B. White, "The Preaching Humorist," *Saturday Review of Literature*, October 18, 1941.

63 Walton, *Mimesis as Make-Believe*.

64 Genette, *Palimpsests*.

65 See Abbate, "Music," 523–24.

66 Neumeyer, *Meaning and Interpretation*, 13.

67 Cook, *Analysing Musical Multimedia*, 97.

68 Biancorosso, "The Shark in the Music."

69 Cage, *Silence*, 13.

70 Livingston, *Art and Intention*, 6.

71 On the difference between purposeful action and mere happening, see Livingston, *Art and Intention*, 12ff.

CHAPTER 2. POACHING

1 On this formative period of the Hong Kong film industry, see Fu and Desser, *The Cinema of Hong Kong*; and Bordwell, *Planet Hong Kong*, chaps. 5–7.

2 The Morricone excerpts are not the only preexisting film tracks in *The Grandmaster*. Wong also employed new arrangements of "Moyou," written by Shigeru Umebayashi for *Sorekara* (directed by Yoshimitsu Morita [1985]), and Joe Hisaishi's "Mibuno Ookami" from *Mibu Gishiden* (When the last sword is drawn, directed by Yôjirô Takira [2003]). On *Sorekara*, see chapter 4.

3 *Come imparai ad amare le donne* is a comedy of adultery in seven episodes that enjoyed some circulation in Europe at the time of release and a

very limited redistribution, partly as a cult film, partly under the "Italian sex comedy" rubric, on both VHS and DVD formats. I was unable to ascertain whether it ever reached Hong Kong, let alone in what version.

4   *Yo-Yo Ma Plays Ennio Morricone*, Sony Classical, B003PTP4S6 (2004).

5   Following the purchasing of the distribution rights by the Weinstein Company, *The Grandmaster* was distributed under the brand "Martin Scorsese Presents." The conversation between Scorsese and Wong was part of the promotion campaign for the American cut of the film, and it took place on January 8, 2014, at the Lighthouse International Theater in New York City. See Deadline Hollywood, "Martin Scorsese and Kar Wai Wong Interview," http://www.youtube.com/watch?v=xB9JvRbBZRM (last accessed September 10, 2019).

6   Wong stated: "We sometimes called this film *Once upon a Time in Kung Fu*. . . . That's why, at the end of the film, I used some Morricone tracks. It is like a homage to [filmmaker] Sergio Leone and [his score composer] Ennio Morricone; to their epics" (Matthew Scott, "Hong Kong State of Mind," *South China Morning Post*, April 7, 2013).

7   Gary Needham interprets Tsui Hark's choice to initiate the series as an expression of the cultural and political climate in the Hong Kong of the early 1990s. See Needham, "Sound and Music in Hong Kong Cinema," 368. One wonders whether the same can be said, twenty years later, about *The Grandmaster*.

8   Franco Montini, "Festival di Roma, Il Morricone segreto: 'La musica per Leone rifiutata da altri,'" *La Repubblica*, November 2, 2010.

9   In the conversation with Scorsese cited earlier, Wong admits to using the Morricone music as a guide track. Bettinson stresses the significance in the inception of Wong's films of guide tracks, musical motifs, and metaphors as a "generative element." Bettinson, *The Sensuous Cinema of Wong Kar-wai*, 37.

10   See the beginning of chapter 1.

11   Subway Cinema News, http://subwaycinemanews.com/archives/3 (last accessed May 30, 2018). See also note 1, chapter 1.

12   Bordwell, *Planet Hong Kong*, 177. It remains unclear whether Wong shot the episode with the song in mind or if he "merely" shaped the editing around it.

13   Hu, "The KTV Aesthetic."

14   Morris Holbrook coined the term *ambi-diegetic* to denote the multivalence of source music (see Holbrook, *Music, Movies, Meanings, and Markets*).

15   In an aside that resonates with this statement, Miguel Mera writes, on the subject of Tarantino's *Inglourious Basterds*, that "Tarantino gives [David Bowie's 'Cat People (Putting Out Fire)'] a cinematic treatment that he felt was warranted but never received in its original incarnation"

(Mera, "Inglo[u]rious Basterdization?," 454). Mera's point is buttressed by various claims by the director himself.

16   Consider, by contrast, Jeff Smith's interpretation of the Coen Brothers' designation as "music archivists." This term, according to Smith, points to their films as "virtual museum pieces [preserving] the soundtrack as a space for lost or neglected moments in American musical history" (Smith, "O Brother, Where Chart Thou?," 131).

17   A trend-setting precedent, in popular culture, is the Beatles' use of the chorus of their own "She Loves You" in the coda of "All You Need Is Love." Cast in a chaotic assortment of sonic tidbits spanning a wide range of genres, media, and languages, the self-citation is both self-aggrandizing and deeply ironic. It also ruthlessly exposes the immense distance running between the Beatles of the early 1960s and the same band in 1967.

18   See chapters 3 and 5.

19   See Powrie, "The Fabulous Destiny of the Accordion."

20   A much-noted exception is the radio broadcast of "Hua Yang De Nian Hua" in *In the Mood for Love*. See Biancorosso, "Songs of Delusion," and Chen, "In the Mood for Music," especially chapter. 3.

21   Writing about Tarantino, Ken Garner makes a striking statement that may be complementary to my own: "His music is now all about recall-ing the *audio experience of viewing*" (emphasis mine). See Garner, "You've Heard This One Before," 175.

22   Truffaut adapted Jaubert's scores written in the 1930s for the follow-ing films: *L'histoire d'Adèle H* (1975), *L'argent de poche* (1976), *L'homme qui aimaut les femmes* (1977), and *La chambre verte* (1978). I first became aware of the interesting questions posed by the borrowing of film scores dur-ing an oral presentation by Mark Brill ("Truffaut's Reuse of Jaubert's Film Scores"). Mera interprets Tarantino's borrowing of Morricone's film tracks in terms of "mashup" aesthetics. He also considers at length the intertextual resonances of many of the borrowed tracks, and especially the film's indebtedness, via the music, to the "spaghetti Western" tradi-tion ("Inglorio[u]s Basterdization?").

23   Eli Marshall, message to author, November 15, 2014. Marshall added: "But this spirit of making art—if everything's locked in before the thing's actu-ally made: schedule, script, every shot, timing, musical gesture, where's the creativity? To borrow your metaphor, better that the film itself is 'bespoke' to itself, instead of each element fitting together—who wants a one of a kind prefab, designed to be unique yet predictable? Yet so much art produced is now this way. Not only can the film industry learn from Wong in this respect; classical music should pay attention, too!"

24   John Belton reminds us that *2001: A Space Odyssey* was one of the last examples of travelogues in the Cinerama format. See Belton, *Widescreen Cinema*, chapter 5.

25 On the continuities between the two films, see Teo, *Wong Kar Wai*, 136–37.

26 Of the divorce, we hear nothing: a striking counterpart to our never seeing Chow's wife in *In the Mood for Love*.

27 Tagg, "Nature as a Mood Music Category," 1n3.

28 Levinson, "Film Music and Narrative Agency," 257–58.

29 "Why should one care very much about whether . . . narrators should be acknowledged or posited or whether they should not? In the end, I cannot see that a great deal turns on this question" (Wilson, *Seeing Fictions in Film*, 126).

30 Whether out of jealousy, curiosity, or a similar voyeuristic disposition, later on Ling returns the favor. See chapter 3.

31 *5 Great Soundtracks—Truffaut & Delerue—On the Screen*, DRG Records, 32902 (1993).

32 If, by a thought experiment, we were aware of the derivation from the Truffaut film, or even recall the theme, the second iteration in Wong's own work would be tantamount to a request to abandon our preconceptions and hear the music afresh.

CHAPTER 3. OWNING

1 The analogy between filmmaking and the building of a cathedral was first adumbrated in Panofsky, "Style and Medium in the Motion Pictures."

2 McQuiston, *We'll Meet Again*. On compilation soundtracks, see Hubbert, "The Compilation Soundtrack." On the instructively unique case of Italian cinema, see Corbella, "Introduzione: La *compilation soundtrack*."

3 On borrowings that mesh and those that don't—the emergence of the latter a crossroads of sorts—see Burkholder, "Borrowing."

4 On citation as modernist device, see Mulvey, "Le Mépris."

5 Chen, "In the Mood for Music," 54–56.

6 I thank Paul Anderer for this observation.

7 Bordwell, *Planet Hong Kong*, 177.

8 Frankie Chan and Roel Garcia, *Chungking Express, Original Motion Picture Soundtrack*, Universal Music Hong Kong—Block 2 Music, 8889693 (1995).

9 See Jeff Smith's now-classic *The Sounds of Commerce*.

10 Todd Decker notes how digital editing tools put "the interaction between sound and image more concretely into the hands of the editor and the director" (Decker, "The Filmmaker as DJ," 285).

11 I examine the use of Bellini's *Norma* in 2046 in the introduction.

12 How fitting that 2046 inspired a staging of Verdi's *Nabucco* instead. Directed by Stefano Ricci, the opera was performed as part of the 2019

Verdi Festival in Parma. In Ricci's staging, the action was set on a ship sailing into a dystopian future.

13   *2046—Original Soundtrack from the Motion Picture*, EMI 7243 8 63601 0 6 (European Release) (2004).

14   *Yumeji*, Kino Video, DVD (2006). The film is also available as part of *Seijun Suzuki's The Taisho Trilogy*, Kino (2017).

15   Chen, "In the Mood for Music," 10.

16   Rayns, "In the Mood for Edinburgh." Wong might conceivably be referring to the snippets of Chinese music heard from the radio rather than "Yumeji's Theme." While they do not literally repeat, they function as sonic background and as such they sound "the same" to all but the most culturally sensitive spectator, signaling a routine—listening to radio—in Mrs. Suen's household. But his reference in the same interview to the world outside Mrs. Suen's household (the office, for example) corroborates the idea that Wong is indeed thinking of the routine activities of the protagonists as captured against "Yumeji's Theme." On this, see also Chen, "In the Mood for Music," 100–101.

17   Chen, "In the Mood for Music," 58–59.

18   Chen, "In the Mood for Music," 99.

19   In linguistics, this phenomenon is called *semantic satiation*. Following a different thread—pun intended—Chen contends that "Yumeji's Theme" is akin to "aural fabric," interpreting musical repetition as a spatial effect via Giuliana Bruno's term *intertexturality* ("In the Mood for Music," chapter 1).

20   On this particular aspect of the film, see Chiao-Yin (游巧瑩) Yu, "節奏性的影像變化—《花樣年華》中音樂與影像的互 動關係" (The transformation of rhythmic visual images—the interactive relation of music and image in *In the Mood for Love*).

21   Chen, "In the Mood for Music," 60.

22   Tony Rayns might well lay claim to being such a person, having written at length about Suzuki as well as Wong. See Field and Rayns, *Branded to Thrill*.

23   As my exegesis will make clear, Wong counted on precisely this scenario.

24   In music theory, *diminution* refers to the transformation of a melody through the substitution of long notes for smaller rhythmic values (*diminutio*, in Latin).

25   The connection to Fellini and Rota goes beyond musical borrowing. Like Fellini's, Wong's oeuvre is rather like an *opus continuum*, each new release merely a different chapter of a single work in progress. On Fellini's work as *opus continuum*, see Sala, "Palimpsest, Mediation, *Déjà entendu*-Effect," 66.

26   On the popularity of Lecuona and the "Lecuona Boys," see Moore, *Nationalizing Blackness*, 142. On the Montaner recording, see Martinez-Malo, *Rita*, 144. The Cueto version is on Victor #81213-a, 78 RPM, the Victor Orchestra's on Victor #46154-a, 78 RPM, and the Bing Crosby English adaptation on Various, *A Carnival of Cuban Music*, Rounder CD 5049 (1990).

27   With reference to *Tarnished Lady* (directed by George Cukor [1931]), Lecuona writes "La película es una americanada más, ahora nos tocó a nosotros hacer el ridículo" (The film is very much an American thing, and forced us to make fool of ourselves). In Moore, *Nationalizing Blackness*, 266 (translation mine).

28   Cited in Moore, *Nationalizing Blackness*, 182. In the same chapter, Moore also expands on such white and classically trained musicians as Lecuona and especially Cugat's own appropriation of *rumba* (173ff.).

29   On *Amarcord* as "folk opera," see Bondanella, *The Cinema of Federico Fellini*, 262ff.

30   The title of the cue is "Ti Ricordi di Siboney" (Do you remember Siboney?).

31   Young, *Cultural Appropriation and the Arts*.

32   *Dance with Cugat*, EP-1-3007 (1955) and *Xavier Cugat Plays the Music of Ernesto Lecuona*, SR 60936 (Stereo) / MG 20936 (mono) (1964); *Connie Francis Sings Spanish and Latin American Favorites*, MGM Records, E-3853 (mono) / SE-3853 (stereo) (1960).

33   For a study of covers in the context of Cold War–era Hong Kong, see Yang, "Cosmopolitanism."

34   See Holbrook's *Music, Movies, Meanings, and Markets*, in which the author develops a nuanced theory of "ambi-diegetic" music in film.

35   To the extent that he was cognizant of *Touch of Evil*, as I posit here, Wong must have been familiar with the studio-released version featuring Henry Mancini's title tune (instead of the collage of various kinds of source music unveiled by the film's restoration and subsequent 2006 release).

36   For precedents, see Welles's use of "vintage" optical techniques in *The Magnificent Ambersons* (1942) or Truffaut's gesturing toward silent film in *Jules et Jim* (1961). On jazz as film music, see Butler, *Jazz Noir*; Stanfield, *Body and Soul*; and "The Soundtrack."

37   See Jones, *Yellow Music*.

38   On considering the balancing act performed by Filipino musicians in such a fraught context, Lee Watkins sidesteps the notion of mimicry altogether. See Watkins, "Minstrelsy and Mimesis."

39   On racial prejudice in Hong Kong, particularly toward South Asians and Middle Easterners, see Mathews, *Ghetto at the Center of the World*, 99–100.

40   Teo views the return of "Siboney" as pointing directly to the "placement of *Days of Being Wild* into the narrative of *2046*" (Teo, *Wong Kar Wai*, 141).

41   Francis's cover is also featured in the film *The Island* (2005).

42   The song both enhances her appearance and puts a "corset" on her (as per Charlotte Perkins Gilman's famous metaphor).

43   I discuss the significance of the hole, and his spying, in chapter 2.

CHAPTER 4. REDRESSING

1   This applies to Ouyan Feng and Huang Yaoshi as it does to Murong Yang / Yin and above all the Blind Swordsman.

2   See Bordwell, "Ashes to Ashes"; Teo, "Wong Kar-wai's Genre Practice"; and Dissayanake, *Wong Kar-wai's "Ashes of Time."*

3   See H. Jenkins, *Textual Poachers*. That Wong's "righting" did not meet the favors of most of Cha's aficionados is, of course, an altogether different story. It bears remembering, however, that through the very process of disappointing martial arts fans, Wong simultaneously earned a small but influential cohort of admirers, both in the Chinese-speaking world and elsewhere: from one fandom to another. On the martial arts revival in the PRC and the attendant reinvention and interpretation of film stars in cyberspace, see Lau, *Chinese Stardom in Participatory Cyberculture*.

4   Dissayanake, *Wong Kar-wai's "Ashes of Time,"* 91.

5   Bloom, *The Anxiety of Influence*.

6   For an introduction to Cha's martial arts novels, see Hamm, *Paper Swordsmen*. On Cha's career in journalism, see 金庸与《明报》(Jin Yong and Ming Pao Daily) / 张圭阳. 武汉市: 湖北长江出版集团: 湖北人民出版社; and 金庸與報業 = Jin Yong (Louis Cha) and the press / 張圭陽香港: 明報.

7   On the screen adaptations of Cha's novels, as well as the role of his novels in the sprawling Hong Kong mediascape, see Foster, *Jin Yong's Martial Arts Fiction*.

8   As has been the case with Cha, moreover, Wong's own work has been adapted and referenced—hence, its reach extended—in various other media and forms, such as video art, painting, and design.

9   For a comparative assessment of the nature and role of martial and processional music in various regions of the world, see *Towards a Global History of Martial and Military Music*, a conference convened by Morag Josephine Grant. The conference was part of the Balzan Research Programme in Musicology, *Towards a Global History of Music*, directed by Reinhard Strohm.

10   On various kinds of representation as instances of worldmaking, see Goodman, *Ways of Worldmaking*.

11   On the sensorial dimension of religious rituals, see Meyer, *Mediation and the Genesis of Presence*.

12   On the conceptual confusion between "the world" and what is "actual" on the one hand, and the former and the universe as a physical entity on the other, see Gabriel, *Why the World Does Not Exist*.

13   On the evolution of Tarantino's compilation scores, see Garner, "You've Heard This One Before." In the same volume, I described Tarantino as "close to being Hollywood's Roy Lichtenstein as Wong is to being [world cinema's] Cindy Sherman." (Biancorosso, "Songs of Delusion," 123).

14   On this sequence as a defining moment "for both Hollywood ultraviolence and the role of song in cinema," see Coulthard, "Torture Tunes."

15   Manuel, "Music Cultures," 55.

16   On the diversity of musical traditions both in and outside Hollywood, see Slobin, *Global Soundtracks*.

17   See, for example, Feld, "A Sweet Lullaby for World Music."

18   On the role of research departments in Hollywood studios, see Rosenthal, *Why Docudrama?*; and Rosen, *Change Mummified*. On Pasolini's record collection, see "L'altra musica," in Calabretto, *Pasolini e la musica*, 185–87.

19   Underpinning the development of a "glocal" audience eager to consume Hong Kong cinema was the production and especially distribution network laid out by such companies as Cathay and the Shaw Brothers, particularly in Southeast Asia. On the former see, for example, Wong, *The Cathay Story*; on the latter, Davis, "Questioning Diaspora."

20   For a survey of the more recent—and diverse—work of Hong Kong filmmakers, see Cheung, Marchetti, and Yau, *A Companion to Hong Kong Cinema*.

21   On the global reach of the martial arts cinema of three filmmakers who themselves migrated to Hollywood, see Szeto, *Martial Arts Cinema*.

22   Hou Hsiao-hsien's *The Assassin* (2015) stands in splendid isolation, outside the commercial hence stylistic imperatives I have sketched here. For a critical survey of the film, see Peng, *The Assassin*.

23   David Bordwell, "Ashes to Ashes (*Redux*)," *Observations on Film Art*, posted December 18, 2008, http://www.davidbordwell.net/blog/2008/12/18/ashes-to-ashes-Redux/ (last accessed February 14, 2021).

24   Bordwell, "Ashes to Ashes (*Redux*)."

25   As an occasional frequenter of the Music Palace, the famed movie theater on the Bowery, at the northern edge of Manhattan's Chinatown, I can testify to how such venues literally called for flamboyant, hyperbolic soundtracks with a relatively simple mix. According to Brian Camp, the New York premiere of *Ashes of Time* took place nearby, at the Rosemary Theater on Canal Street. See Camp, "Hong Kong Fandom in the '90s: Chinatown Theaters," https://briandanacamp.wordpress.com

/2022/09/29/hong-kong-fandom-in-the-90s-chinatown-theaters (last accessed August 25, 2023).

26 Bordwell, "Ashes to Ashes (*Redux*)."

27 On the influence of *Yojimbo* on Sergio Leone's "spaghetti Westerns" and Morricone's music for them, see De Rosa, *Ennio Morricone*, 23–24.

28 For the lingering significance of this sequence in Chinese-language cinema, see also Steintrager, "Sounding against the Grain," 138.

29 See the epigraph in the introduction.

30 For a survey of the changes underway in the first dozen or so years of the twenty-first century, see Bordwell, *Planet Hong Kong*, chapter II; and Yau, "Watchful Partners, Hidden Currents."

31 *Sorekara*, LP, Victor Entertainment (1985).

32 *Sorekara* tells the story of a wealthy scion of an industrial family in Meiji-era Japan in the immediate aftermath of the first Russian-Japanese war. The romantic plot that forms the spine of the novel, and with it the film, might well be found to exhibit all kinds of thematic parallels to *The Grandmaster* (the theme of repressed desire, above all).

33 Genette, *Palimpsests*, 2.

34 Or re-create it, allographically, with the degree of accuracy with which Tarantino, for example, re-creates a fragment of *The Great Escape* (1963) in *Once upon a Time in Hollywood* (2019).

35 Genette, *Palimpsests*, 2.

36 For a survey of the score, see Godsall, "Pre-existing Music," 22–25; and Decker, "The Filmmaker as DJ," 286–91. For an interpretation of Godard's idiosyncratic choice in the context of what he calls "metafilm music," see Baumgartner, "Jean-Luc Godard's *Le Mépris*."

37 *Contempt*, DVD, Criterion Collection (2002).

38 Scorsese indicated that it was Robbie Robertson, a member of the Band and a longtime collaborator, who suggested the use of Delerue's music (Godsall, "Pre-existing Music," 20). The suggestion followed from Scorsese's request for something "not classical" to not interfere with the Bach chorales that bookend the film. If that is indeed the case, the impetus for the borrowing is not allusion to Godard, let alone quotation, but a concern with the "sound" of the soundtrack and its internal balance. Having said this, it is hard to believe that on suggesting Delerue to Scorsese, Robertson did not think of its thematic associations. Note that Robertson is credited as the producer of the CD of the soundtrack (*Casino*, soundtrack album, UNI-MCA 0881113892 [1995]).

39 An astute spectator, on noticing that all the music is preexisting, might speculate that "Thème de Camille" must be preexisting, too. But this would not change the facts of the matter. Absent familiarity with Godard's film, the cue will come across as an original score, even more

so as it is used, again like a standard score, as a recurrent theme. Its qualities as "film score," put another way, weigh more than its being "preexisting."

40   Godsall, "Pre-existing Music," 23.

41   Godsall, "Pre-existing Music," 22–23.

42   Cook, *Music, Imagination, and Culture*, 152.

43   Danto, "Moving Images."

44   Biancorosso, "The Shark in the Music."

45   I borrow the metaphor from Flinn, *The New German Cinema*, 43.

46   Godard takes the convention to an almost absurd limit and repeats the music a staggering sixteen times. Godard's example was an inspiration for Wong Kar-wai in *In the Mood for Love*. I speculate that Wong thought of *Contempt* after watching *Casino*.

47   Godsall, "Pre-existing Music," 22.

48   Biancorosso, "Melodrama."

49   Abbate, "Wagner, Cinema, and Redemptive Glee," 597.

50   As noted earlier, this modus operandi is well documented among romantic artists or artists working under conditions—political censorship, for example—that encourage esoterica, camaraderie, and obliquity.

51   For two examples, see "Hua Yang De Nian Hua" as used in *In the Mood for Love*, which comes complete with an explicit introduction by a radio presenter, and "Take My Breath Away" (albeit a cover in Cantonese) in *As Tears Go By*, which appealed to the audience's fresh memories of *Top Gun* (1986).

52   For this reason, my approach aligns with such endeavors as Keith A. Jenkins's work on Charlotte Brontë's seemingly indiscriminate borrowing from the Bible. See K. Jenkins, *Charlotte Brontë's Atypical Typology*.

53   Sometimes the actors are themselves repositories of musical knowledge. In Kikhaboy-Choi's *To Be Continued* (2022), Rebecca Pan reminisces how during the filming of *Days of Being Wild* she shared with Wong her knowledge of Hong Kong's Latin music scene of the early 1960s.

54   On this, see also Yeh and Hu, "Transcultural Sounds."

55   Save for the key: it is E flat major in the 2004 recording and D flat in the soundtrack of *The Grandmaster* (see the album *Yo-Yo Ma Plays Morricone* [2004]).

CHAPTER 5. OBLIVION

1   DJ Shadow, *The Private Press*, MCA Records 314 586 981-2 (2002); "Six Days," MCA Records 440 063 874-1, vinyl, 12" single (2002) (US release).

2   "Six Days," https://www.youtube.com/watch?v=eY-eyZuW_Uk (last accessed March 8, 2023).

3   Colonel Bagshot, *Oh! What a Lovely War*, Cadet Concept, CC 50010, vinyl
     (1971) (US release). "Six Day War" is the album's opening track.

4   See my analysis in chapter 3.

5   Possibly offended by the remix, or the comments of other viewers, one
     YouTube user writes, "This song is about war and death not some Holly-
     wood celebrity."

6   Compare, by contrast, the work of vidders. Editing clips from their
     favorite shows to preexisting music makes the latter an almost literal
     illustration of the onscreen action (see H. Jenkins, *Textual Poachers*,
     chapter 7).

7   See the video's comments thread on YouTube for a corroboration of
     this claim. Compare, by contrast, Wong's shrewd use of Umebayashi's
     "Efude" as soundtrack to his commercial for the French shirt maker
     Lacoste (*La rencontre* [2001]). Also lifted from the soundtrack of Suzuki's
     Yumeji, "Efude" features the same rhythmic section and texture as
     "Yumeji's Theme" (the solo violin is replaced by a vocalise). As such, it
     unmistakably doubles as an oblique testimonial for *In the Mood for Love*
     and telltale sign of the Wong Kar-wai "brand."

8   Rayns, *In the Mood for Love*, 69 (Rayns reports the claim without endors-
     ing it himself).

9   For a probing take on the lingering significance of MTV in early twenty-
     first-century Hollywood, see Ashby's introduction to *Popular Music and
     the New Auteur*.

10   The most comprehensive study of MTV as an artistic genre is Vernallis,
     Experiencing Music Video.

11   "Dreams" enjoyed multiple releases in the United Kingdom and the
     United States as both a single and a track on an album. For the latter,
     see the Cranberries, *Everybody Else Is Doing It, So Why Can't We?*, Island
     Records, 314-514 156-2 (1993) (US release).

12   Wong's cover was released a few months before the release of the film and
     is the only vocal track in Cantonese on the soundtrack. It subsequently
     became a vehicle for Faye Wong and the Cranberries in turn, as the latter
     enjoyed a brief but intense period of popularity in Hong Kong in the
     wake of the success of *Chungking Express*. See the poignant testimony in
     James Balmont, "How *Chungking Express* Brought Dream Pop to Hong
     Kong," *Little White Lies* (February 13, 2021).

13   On KTV aesthetic, see Kassabian, *Hearing Film*, 138–39; and especially
     Hu, "The KTV Aesthetic."

14   On the various releases of the soundtrack as a self-standing album, see
     chapter 3.

15   A necessarily brief list of "air stewardess" films would have to at least in-
     clude also *The Charming Girl* (1967), *Lovely Husbands* (1969), *The Adventur-
     ous Air Stewardess* (1974), and, post–*Chungking Express*, *The Stewardess* (2002).

16 See Jones, *Circuit Listening*, chapter 1.

17 On the not-so-subtle art of recycling the most outlandish names to sell property, see Jaworski and Yeung, "Life in the Garden of Eden."

18 Galasso wrote the incidental music for some of Robert Wilson's productions, for example.

19 Various, *Utopia Americana*, New Tone Records, NT 6707, CD (1992).

20 On *Chungking Express* as an allegorization of the "affective possibilities of mundane spaces" of Hong Kong, see Wendy Gan, "0,01 cm."

21 At the time of filming *Chungking Express*, Wong was still completing *Ashes of Time*, in which Lin plays a cross-dressing character.

22 On the synthesizer "as a marker of the Hong Kong cinema 'brand,'" see Springer, "Sounding Glocal," 39.

23 See chapter 3.

24 After the three-bar intro, omitted in the film, the first cello solo begins a somewhat anodyne pattern (the motives, E-E-D-D, E-E-C-C in dotted half notes), which it then repeats to land on what appears to be the target of this wavering motif, namely a twice struck D over a G minor chord approached via a turn. Given the tempo and the tension of the strings, the latter clouds the tone color and lends the music a sudden sense of urgency. As the solo reverts to G via a stepwise, rhythmically identical figure, the second solo cello joins the texture with an echo of the same stepwise figure a sixth above. Despite the relative simplicity of the line, the resulting six-note (3 + 3) ascent is highly dramatic and casts a spotlight on the high E from which the second solo will slowly descend form in homophony with the first solo.

25 Savinio, "La voce del violoncello," 532–33. Savinio continues: "More than the voice of the donkey, the parallel applies to the voice of that animal's progenitor, the onager [a species of the equine family prevalent in Central and East Asia]. And when that heartbreaking voice resonated, full of pathos and inhibited by desire and the nostalgia for dark memories and infinite longing, without being able to say what it wishes to say— when that voice suddenly stood out from the hum of the orchestra, it felt as if I'd heard, echoing, in the cacophony of the city, the miraculous voice of an onager" (533) [my translation from the Italian]. Alberto Savinio's real name was Andrea de Chirico, and he was the younger brother of the painter Giorgio de Chirico.

Abbas, Ackbar. *Hong Kong: Culture and the Politics of Disappearance*. Minneapolis: University of Minnesota Press, 1997.

Abbate, Carolyn. "Music: Drastic or Gnostic?" *Critical Inquiry* 30, no. 3 (2001): 505–36.

Abbate, Carolyn. "Wagner, Cinema, and Redemptive Glee." *Opera Quarterly* 21, no. 4 (2005): 597–611.

Allanbrook, Wye Jamison. *Rhythmic Gesture in Mozart: "Le Nozze di Figaro" and "Don Giovanni."* Chicago: University of Chicago Press, 1983.

Altglas, Véronique. "'Bricolage': Reclaiming a Conceptual Tool." *Culture and Religion* 15, no. 4 (2014): 474–93.

Appadurai, Arjun. "Playing with Modernity: The Decolonization of Indian Cricket." In *Consuming Modernity: Public Culture in a South Asian World*, edited by Carol A. Breckenridge, 23–48. Minneapolis: University of Minnesota Press, 1995.

Ashby, Arved, ed. *Popular Music and the New Auteur: Visionary Filmmakers after MTV*. New York: Oxford University Press, 2013.

Atkinson, Paul. "Making Opera Work: Bricolage and the Management of Dramaturgy." *Music and Arts in Action* 3, no. 1 (2010): 3–19.

Austin, J. L. *How to Do Things with Words*. Cambridge, MA: Harvard University Press, 1975 (1962).

Bartlett, Frederic C. *Remembering: A Study in Experimental and Social Psychology*. Cambridge: Cambridge University Press, 1932.

Bassetti, Sergio. *La musica secondo Kubrick*. Torino: Lindau, 2002.

Baumgartner, Michael. "Jean-Luc Godard's *Le Mépris*: Conventional Film Music in an Unconventional Guise." *The Soundtrack* 13, no. 1 (October 2021): 17–41.

Baumgartner, Michael. *Metafilm Music in Jean-Luc Godard's Cinema*. New York: Oxford University Press, 2022.

Belton, John. *Widescreen Cinema*. Cambridge, MA: Harvard University Press, 1992.

Bettinson, Gary. *The Sensuous Cinema of Wong Kar-wai: Film Poetics and the Aesthetics of Disturbance*. Hong Kong: Hong Kong University Press, 2015.

Biancorosso, Giorgio. "Melodrama, Anti-melodrama, and Performance: Rereading *Le mépris*." In *Il melodramma*, edited by Elena Dagrada, 263–322. Rome: Bulzoni, 2007.

Biancorosso, Giorgio. "Romance, Insularity, and Representation: Wong Kar-wai's *In the Mood for Love* and Hong Kong Cinema." *Shima: The International Journal of Research into Island Cultures* 1, no. 1 (2007): 88–95.

Biancorosso, Giorgio. "The Shark in the Music." *Music Analysis* 29, no. 1/2 (2010): 306–33.

Biancorosso, Giorgio. *Situated Listening: The Sound of Absorption in Classical Cinema*. New York: Oxford University Press, 2016.

Biancorosso, Giorgio. "Songs of Delusion: Popular Music and the Aesthetics of the Self in Wong Kar Wai's Cinema." In *Popular Music and the New Auteur: Visionary Filmmakers after MTV*, edited by Arved Ashby, 109–25. New York: Oxford University Press, 2013.

Bishop, Claire. "History Depletes Itself." *Artforum International* 54, no. 1 (September 2015): 324–29.

Bloom, Harold. *The Anxiety of Influence: A Theory of Poetry*. New York: Oxford University Press, 1973.

Bondanella, Peter. *The Cinema of Federico Fellini*. Princeton, NJ: Princeton University Press, 1992.

Bordwell, David. "Ashes to Ashes (*Redux*)." *Observations on Film Art*. December 18, 2008. http://www.davidbordwell.net/blog/2008/12/18/ashes-to-ashes-redux/.

Bordwell, David. *Planet Hong Kong: Popular Cinema and the Art of Entertainment*. 2nd ed. Madison, WI: Irvington Way Institute Press, 2011.

Brill, Mark. "Truffaut's Reuse of Jaubert's Film Scores." Paper read at the American Musicological Society Conference, Kansas City, November 4–7, 1999.

Bourriaud, Nicolas. *Postproduction. Culture as Screenplay: How Art Reprograms the World*. Translated by Jeanine Herman. London: Sternberg Press, 2002.

Brown, Royal S. *Overtones and Undertones: Reading Film Music*. Berkeley: University of California Press, 1994.

Buckley, William J. "Does Betrayal Music Transform Sexual Pessimism into Optimistic 'Love with a Laugh.'" *Camino Real* 3, no. 5 (2011): 59–75.

Burkholder, Peter J. "Borrowing." In *The New Grove Dictionary of Music and Musicians*, 2nd ed., edited by John Tyrrell, 6–8, 29. London: Grove, 2001.

Butler, David. *Jazz Noir: Listening to Music from the "Phantom Lady" to the "Last Seduction."* Westport, CT: Praeger, 2002.

Cage, John. *Silence: Lectures and Writings by John Cage*. Middletown, CT: Wesleyan University Press, 1973.

Calabretto, Roberto. *Pasolini e la musica*. Pordenone, Italy: Cinema Zero, 1999.

Carrouges, Michel. *André Breton and the Basic Concepts of Surrealism*. Translated by Maura Prendergast. Tuscaloosa: University of Alabama Press, 1974.

Cecchi, Alessandro. "Collaboration and/as Bricolage: Petri, Pirro, Volonté, and Morricone between Common Practice and Authentication in the Aftermath of 1968." In *Scoring Italian Cinema: Patterns of Collaboration*, edited by Giorgio Biancorosso and Roberto Calabretto. London: Routledge, forthcoming.

Chen, Timmy Chih-ting. "In the Mood for Music: Sonic Extraterritoriality and Musical Exchange in Hong Kong Cinema." PhD diss., University of Hong Kong, 2015.

Chen, Timmy Chih-ting. "Sonic Secrets as Counter-Surveillance in Wong Karwai's *In the Mood for Love*." In *Surveillance in Asian Cinema: Under Eastern Eyes*, edited by Karen Fang, 156–75. New York: Routledge, 2017.

Cheung, Esther M. K., Gina Marchetti, and Esther C. M. Yau, eds. *A Companion to Hong Kong Cinema*. Malden, MA: Wiley Blackwell, 2015.

Chiao-Yin (游巧瑩) Yu. "節奏性的影像變化—《花樣年華》中音樂與影像的互動關係" [The transformation of rhythmic visual images—The interactive relation of music and image in *In the Mood for Love*]. Master's thesis, National Taiwan University, 2005.

Chion, Michel. *Kubrick's Cinema Odyssey*. London: British Film Institute, 2001.

Chow, Rey. "Nostalgia of the New Wave: Romance, Domesticity, and the Longing for Oneness in *Happy Together*." In *Sentimental Fabulations, Contemporary Chinese Films: Attachment in the Age of Global Visibility*, 46–63. New York: Columbia University Press, 2007.

Chu, Stephen. *Hong Kong Cantopop: A Concise History*. Hong Kong: Hong Kong University Press, 2017.

Clark, Suzannah, and Elizabeth Eva Leach, eds. *Citation and Authority in Medieval and Renaissance Musical Culture*. Suffolk, UK: Boydell and Brewer, 2005.

Clarke, A. C. *2001: A Space Odyssey*. Fiftieth anniversary ed. London: Orbit, 2018.

Compagnon, Antoine. *La second maine: Ou, le travail de la citation*. Paris: Editions du Seuil, 1979.

Cook, Nicholas. *Analysing Musical Multimedia*. Oxford: Clarendon, 1998.

Cook, Nicholas. *Music, Imagination, and Culture*. Oxford: Oxford University Press, 1990.

Corbella, Maurizio, "Introduzione: La *compilation soundtrack* nel cinema sonoro Italiano come ipotesi di lavoro sulla storia della musica nel cinema Italiano." In *La "compilation soundtrack" nel cinema sonoro Italiano*, edited by M. Corbella, 7–27. Special issue, *Schermi* 4, no. 7 (June 2020).

Coulthard, Lisa. "Torture Tunes: Tarantino, Popular Music, and the New Hollywood Ultraviolence." *Music and the Moving Image* 2, no. 2 (Summer 2009): 1–6.

Danto, Arthur. *Andy Warhol*. New Haven, CT: Yale University Press, 2009.

Danto, Arthur. "The End of Art: A Philosophical Defense." *History and Theory* 37, no. 4 (December 1998): 127–43.

Danto, Arthur. "Moving Images." *Quarterly Review of Film Studies* 4, no. 1 (1979): 1–21.

Darnton, Robert. *The Great Cat Massacre and Other Episodes in French Cultural History*. New York: Basic Books, 1984.

Davies, Stephen. "Works of Music: Approaches to the Ontology of Music from Analytic Philosophy." *Music Research Annual* 1, no. 1 (2020): 1–29.

Davis, Darrel William. "Questioning Diaspora: Mobility, Mutation, and Historiography of the Shaw Brothers Film Studio." *Chinese Journal of Communication* 4, no. 1 (2011): 40–59.

De Certeau, Michel. *The Practice of Everyday Life*. Third ed., translated by Steven Rendall. Berkeley: University of California Press, 2011.

Decker, Todd. "The Filmmaker as DJ: Martin Scorsese's Compiled Score for *Casino* (1995)." *Journal of Musicology* 34, no. 2 (2017): 281–317.

Deleuze, Gilles, and Félix Guattari. *Anti-Oedipus: Capitalism and Schizophrenia*. With a preface by Michel Foucault. Translated by Robert Hurley, Mark Seem, and Helen R. Lane. London: Athlone, 1984.

Derrida, Jacques. "Sign, Structure and Play in the Discourse of the Human Sciences." In *A Postmodern Reader*, 2nd ed., edited by Linda Hutcheon and Natoli Joseph, 223–42. Albany: State University of New York Press, 1993.

De Rosa, Alessandro, ed. *Ennio Morricone, in His Own Words*. Translated by Maurizio Corbella. New York: Oxford University Press, 2019.

Dezeuze, Anna. "Assemblage, Bricolage, and the Practice of Everyday Life." *Art Journal* 67, no. 1 (Spring 2008): 31–37.

Dissayanake, Wimal. *Wong Kar-wai's "Ashes of Time."* Hong Kong: Hong Kong University Press, 2003.

Donnelly, Kevin. *Occult Aesthetics: Synchronization in Sound Film*. New York: Oxford University Press, 2015.

Eco, Umberto. "*Casablanca*: Cult Movies and Intertextual Collage." *Substance* 14, no. 2 (1985): 3–12.

Eliot, T. S. "Tradition and the Individual Talent." *Egoist* 6, no. 4 (September 1919): 54–55; *Egoist* 6, no. 5 (December 1919): 72–73.

Erdmann Hans, Giovanni Becce, and Ludwig Brav. *Allgemeines Handbuch der Film-Musik*. Berlin: Lichterfelde u.a Schlesinger'sche Buch-und Musikhandlung Lienau, 1927.

Fang, Karen. "'Pity about the Furniture': Violence, Wong Kar-wai Style." In *A Companion to Wong Kar-wai*, edited by Martha Nochimson, 272–94. London: Wiley, 2015.

Feld, Steven. "A Sweet Lullaby for World Music." *Public Culture* 12, no. 1 (2000): 145–71.

Field, Simon, and Tony Rayns, eds. *Branded to Thrill: The Delirious Cinema of Suzuki Seijun*. London: Institute of the Arts, 1995.

Fisher, John Andrew. "Rock 'n' Recording: The Ontological Complexity of Rock Music." In *Musical Worlds: New Directions in the Philosophy of Music*, edited by Philip Alperson, 109–23. University Park: Pennsylvania State University Press, 1993.

Flinn, Caryl. *The New German Cinema: Music, History, and the Matter of Style.* Berkeley: University of California Press, 2003.

Foster, Paul B. *Jin Yong's Martial Arts Fiction and the Kungfu Industrial Complex.* Lanham, MD: Rowman and Littlefield, 2022.

Foucault, Michel. "What Is an Author?" In *Language, Counter-Memory, Practice: Selected Essays and Interviews by Michel Foucault*, edited by Donald F. Bouchard and translated by Donald F. Bouchard and Sherry Simon, 124–27. Ithaca, NY: Cornell University Press, 1977.

Fu Poshek and David Desser, eds. *The Cinema of Hong Kong: History, Arts, Identity.* Cambridge: Cambridge University Press, 2002.

Gabriel, Markus. *Why the World Does Not Exist.* Translated by Gregory S. Moss. Cambridge, UK: Polity, 2015.

Gan, Wendy. "0,01 cm: Affectivity and Urban Space in Chunking Express." *Scope: An Online Journal of Film Studies.* https://www.nottingham.ac.uk/scope/documents/2003/november-2003/gan.pdf.

Garner, Ken, "You've Heard This One Before: Quentin Tarantino's Scoring Practices from *Kill Bill* to *Inglourious Basterds*." In *Popular Music and the New Auteur: Visionary Filmmakers after MTV*, edited by Arved Ashby, 157–79. New York: Oxford University Press, 2013.

Genette, Gérard. *Palimpsests: Literature in the Second Degree.* Translated by Channa Newman and Claude Doubinsky. Lincoln: University of Nebraska Press, 1997.

Godsall, Jonathan. "Pre-existing Music as Authorial Signature in the Fiction Films of Martin Scorsese." *Humanities Commons.* http://dx.doi.org/10.17613/6df8-rn54. Last accessed November 24, 2023.

Godsall, Jonathan. *Reeled In: Pre-existing Music in Narrative Film.* Abingdon, UK: Routledge, 2019.

Goodman, Nelson. *Languages of Art: An Approach to a Theory of Symbols.* Indianapolis, IN: Bobbs-Merrill Company, 1968.

Goodman, Nelson. *Ways of Worldmaking.* Indianapolis, IN: Hackett, 1978.

Gorbman, Claudia. "Auteur Music." In *Beyond the Soundtrack: Representing Music in Cinema*, edited by Daniel Goldmark, Lawrence Kramer, and Richard Leppert, 149–62. Berkeley: University of California Press, 2007.

Hamm, Christopher. *Paper Swordsmen: Jin Yong and the Modern Chinese Martial Arts Novel.* Honolulu: University of Hawai'i Press, 2004.

Hebdige, Dick. *Subculture: The Meaning of Style.* London: Routledge, 1979.

Hennessey, William. "Deconstructing Shanzhai—China's Copycat Counterculture: Catch Me If You Can." *Campbell Law Review* 34, no. 3 (2012): 609–60.

Hennion, Antoine. *The Passion for Music: A Sociology of Mediation*. Translated by Margaret Rigaud and Peter Collier. Burlington, VT: Ashgate, 2015.

Holbrook, Morris B. *Music, Movies, Meanings, and Markets: Cinemajazzamatazz*. New York: Routledge, 2011.

Howard, V. A. "On Musical Quotation." *Monist* 58, no. 2 (1974): 307–18.

Hu, Brian. "The KTV Aesthetic: Popular Music Culture and Contemporary Hong Kong Cinema." *Screen* 47, no. 4 (2006): 407–24.

Hu, Brian. *Worldly Desires: Cosmopolitanism and Cinema in Hong Kong and Taiwan*. Edinburgh: Edinburgh University Press, 2018.

Hubbert, Julie, ed. *Celluloid Symphonies: Texts and Contexts in Film Music History*. Berkeley: University of California Press, 2011.

Hubbert, Julie. "The Compilation Soundtrack from the 1960s to the Present." In *The Oxford Handbook of Film Music Studies*, edited by David Neumeyer, 291–318. New York: Oxford University Press, 2013.

Iampolski, Mikhail. *The Memory of Tyresias: Intertextuality and Film*. Translated by Harsha Ram. Berkeley: University of California Press, 1998.

Jameson, Fredric. *Postmodernism, or, The Cultural Logic of Late Capitalism*. Durham, NC: Duke University Press, 1990.

Jaworski, Adam, and Simone Yeung. "Life in the Garden of Eden: The Naming and Imagery of Residential Hong Kong." In *Linguistic Landscape in the City*, edited by Elana Shohamy, Eli Ben-Rafael, and Monica Barni, 153–81. Bristol, UK: Multilingual Matters, 2010.

Jenkins, Henry. *Textual Poachers: Television Fans and Participatory Culture*. New York: Routledge, 1992.

Jenkins, Keith A. *Charlotte Brontë's Atypical Typology*. New York: Peter Lang, 2010.

Johnson, Christopher. "Bricoleur and Bricolage: From Metaphor to Universal Concept." *Paragraph* 35, no. 3 (November 2012): 355–72.

Jones, Andrew. *Circuit Listening: Chinese Popular Music in the Global 1960s*. Minneapolis: University of Minnesota Press, 2020.

Jones, Andrew. *Yellow Music*. Durham, NC: Duke University Press, 2001.

Kassabian, Anahid. *Hearing Film: Tracking Identifications in Contemporary Hollywood Film*. London: Routledge, 2001.

Katz, Mark. *Groove Music: The Art and Culture of the Hip-Hop DJ*. New York: Oxford University Press, 2012.

Kelly, Julia. "The Anthropology of Assemblage." *Art Journal* 67, no. 1 (Spring 2008): 24–30.

Kerman, Joseph. *Contemplating Music: Challenges to Musicology*. Cambridge, MA: Harvard University Press, 1985.

de Kloet, Jeroen, Chow Yiu Fai, and Lena Scheen. *Boredom, Shanzhai, and Digitisation in the Time of Creative China*. Durham, NC: Duke University Press, 2019.

Knapp, Raymond. Reviews of *Motives for Allusion: Context and Content in Nineteenth-Century Music*, by Christopher Reynolds and *Quotation and*

Cultural Meaning in Twentieth-Century Music, by David Metzer. *Journal of the American Musicological Society* 58, no. 3 (2005): 736–48.

Kristeva, Julia. *Desire in Language: A Semiotic Approach to Literature and Art*. New York: Columbia University Press, 1980.

Laderman, David, and Lauren Westrup, eds. *Sampling Media*. New York: Oxford University Press, 2014.

Lau, Dorothy. *Chinese Stardom in Participatory Cyberculture*. Edinburgh: Edinburgh University Press, 2019.

Lee, Silver Wai-ming, and Micky Lee, eds. *Wong Kar-wai: Interviews*. Jackson: University Press of Mississippi, 2017.

Lessig, Lawrence. *Remix: Making Art and Commerce Thrive in the Hybrid Economy*. London: Penguin, 2008.

Levin, Thomas Y. "The Acoustic Dimension: Notes on Cinema Sound." *Screen* 25, no. 3 (1984): 55–68.

Levinson, Jerrold. "Film Music and Narrative Agency." In *Post-Theory: Reconstructing Film Studies*, edited by David Bordwell and Noel Carroll, 248–82. Madison: University of Wisconsin Press, 1996.

Lévi-Strauss, Claude. *The Raw and the Cooked*, vol. 1 of *Mythologiques*. Translated by Doreen and Jonathan Weightman. New York: Harper and Row, 1969.

Lévi-Strauss, Claude. *The Savage Mind*. Chicago: University of Chicago Press, 1966.

Livingston, Paisley. *Art and Intention: A Philosophical Study*. Oxford: Clarendon, 2005.

Ma, Jean. *Sounding the Modern Woman: The Songstress in Chinese Cinema*. Durham, NC: Duke University Press, 2015.

Manuel, Peter. "Music Cultures of Mechanical Reproduction." In *The Cambridge History of World Music*, edited by Philip Bohlman, 43–55. Cambridge: Cambridge University Press, 2013.

Markham, Annette N. "Bricolage." In *Keywords in Remix Studies*, edited by Owen Gallagher, Eduardo Navas, and xtine burrough, 43–55. New York: Routledge, 2018.

Martinez-Malo, Aldo. *Rita: La única*. Havana, Cuba: Editor Abril, 1988.

Mathews, Gordon. *Ghetto at the Center of the World: Chungking Mansions, Hong Kong*. Hong Kong: Hong Kong University Press, 2011.

McQuiston, Kate. *We'll Meet Again: Musical Design in the Films of Stanley Kubrick*. New York: Oxford University Press, 2013.

Mera, Miguel. "Inglo(u)rious Basterdization? Tarantino and the War Movie Mashup." In *The Oxford Handbook of Sound and Image in Digital Media*, edited by Carol Vernallis, Amy Herzog, and John Richardson, 437–61. New York: Oxford University Press, 2013.

Metzer, David. *Quotation and Cultural Meaning in Twentieth-Century Music*. Cambridge: Cambridge University Press, 2007.

Meyer, Birgit. *Mediation and the Genesis of Presence: Towards a Material Approach to Religion*. Utrecht: Universiteit Utrecht, Faculteit Geesteswetenschappen, 2012.

Moore, Robin D. *Nationalizing Blackness: Afrocubanismo and Artistic Revolution in Havana, 1920–1940*. Pittsburgh, PA: University of Pittsburgh Press, 1997.

Mulvey, Laura. "Le Mépris and Its Story of Cinema: A Fabric of Quotations." *L'Atalante* 18 (July–December 2014): 27–35.

Needham, Gary. "Sound and Music in Hong Kong Cinema." In *Sound and Music in Film and Visual Media: A Critical Overview*, edited by Graeme Harper, Ruth Doughty, and Jochen Eisentraut, 363–74. New York: Continuum, 2009.

Neumeyer, David. *Meaning and Interpretation of Music in Cinema*. Bloomington: Indiana University Press, 2015.

Panofsky, Erwin. "Style and Medium in the Motion Pictures." In *Three Essays on Style*, edited by Irving Lavin, 91–128. Cambridge, MA: MIT Press, 1995.

Pasolini, Pier Paolo. Liner notes to *Dimensioni Sonore I, Musiche per l'immagine—e l'immaginazione*. Composto e Diretto da Ennio Morricone, RCA SP 100 36 (1972).

Peng, Edward Enhua. "The Role of Allusion in Classical Chinese Poetry." PhD diss., University of California, Irvine, 1994.

Peng, Hsiao-yen, ed. *The Assassin: Hou Hsiao-hsien's World of Tang China*. Hong Kong: Hong Kong University Press, 2019.

Pollock, Sheldon. "The Cosmopolitan Vernacular." *Journal of Asian Studies* 57, no. 1 (1998): 6–37.

Powrie, Philip. "The Fabulous Destiny of the Accordion in French Cinema." In *Changing Tunes: The Use of Pre-existing Music in Film*, edited by Phil Powrie and Robynn Stilwell, 137–51. Burlington, VT: Ashgate, 2006.

Prieto, Eric. *Listening In: Music, Mind, and the Modernist Narrative*. Lincoln: University of Nebraska Press, 2002.

Rapee, Erno. *Encyclopaedia of Music for Pictures*. New York: Belwin, 1925.

Ratner, Leonard. *Classic Music: Expression, Form and Style*. New York: Schirmer, 1980.

Rayns, Tony. "In the Mood for Edinburgh." *Sight and Sound* 10, no. 8 (August 2000): 14–17.

Rayns, Tony. *In the Mood for Love*. London: BFI Publishing, 2015.

Recanati, François. "Open Quotation." *Mind* 110, no. 439 (2001): 637–87.

Reynolds, Christopher. *Motives for Allusion: Context and Content in Nineteenth-Century Music*. Cambridge, MA: Harvard University Press, 2003.

Reynolds, Simon. *Retromania: Pop Culture's Addiction to Its Own Past*. New York: Faber and Faber, 2011.

Rosen, Phil. *Change Mummified: Cinema, Historicity, Theory*. Minneapolis: University of Minnesota Press, 2001.

Rosenthal, Alan, ed. *Why Docudrama? Fact-Fiction on Film and TV*. Carbondale: Southern Illinois University Press, 1999.

Sala, Emilio. "Palimpsest, Mediation, *Déjà entendu*-Effect: The Musical Dramaturgy of Federico Fellini and Nino Rota's *La dolce vita*." In *Music, Author-*

ship, Narration, and Art Cinema in Europe: 1940s to 1980s, edited by Michael Baumgartner and Ewelina Boczkowska, 51–86. New York: Routledge, 2023.

Savinio, Alberto. "La voce del violoncello." In *La scatola sonora*, edited by Francesco Lombardi, 532–33. Milan, Italy: Il Saggiatore, 2017.

Sewell, Amanda. "A Typology of Sampling in Hip-hop." PhD diss., Indiana University, 2013.

Shumway, David R. "Rock 'n' Roll Soundtracks and the Production of Nostalgia." *Cinema Journal* 38, no. 2 (Winter 1999): 36–51.

Slobin, Mark, ed. *Global Soundtracks: Worlds of Film Music*. Middletown, CT: Wesleyan University Press, 2008.

Small, Christopher. *Musicking: The Meanings of Performing and Listening*. Middletown, CT: Wesleyan University Press, 1998.

Smith, Jeff. "O Brother, Where Chart Thou? Pop Music and the Coen Brothers." In *Popular Music and the New Auteur: Visionary Filmmakers after MTV*, edited by Arved Ashby, 129–56. New York: Oxford University Press, 2013.

Smith, Jeff. *The Sounds of Commerce*. New York: Columbia University Press, 1998.

Sontag, Susan. *Against Interpretation*. New York: Farrar, Straus and Giroux, 1966.

"The Soundtrack." Special issue of *Jazz and Cinema Journal* 6, no. 1/2 (2013).

Springer, Katherine. "Sounding Glocal: Synthesizer Scores in Hong Kong Action Cinema." In *American and Chinese Language Cinemas: Examining Cultural Flows*, edited by Lisa Funnell and Man Fung Yip, 38–52. New York: Routledge, 2014.

Stanfield, Peter. *Body and Soul: Jazz and Blues in American Film*. Bloomington: Indiana University Press, 2005.

Steintrager, James. "Sounding against the Grain: Music, Voice, and Noise in *The Assassin*." In *The Assassin: Hou Hsiao-hsien's World of Tang China*, edited by Peng Hsiao-yen, 133–44. Hong Kong: Hong Kong University Press, 2019.

Stilwell, Robynn. "Vinyl Communion: The Record as Ritual Object in Girls' Rites-of-Passage Films." In *Changing Tunes: The Use of Pre-existing Music in Film*, edited by Phil Powrie and Robynn Stilwell, 153–67. Burlington, VT: Ashgate, 2006.

Szeto, Kin Yan. *Martial Arts Cinema of the Chinese Diaspora: Ang Lee, John Woo and Jackie Chan in Hollywood*. Carbondale: Southern Illinois University Press, 2011.

Tagg, Philip. "Nature as a Mood Music Category." https://www.tagg.org/articles/nature.html. Last accessed March 22, 2024.

Taylor, Timothy D. *Music in the World*. Chicago: University of Chicago Press, 2017.

Teo, Stephen. *Wong Kar Wai*. London: BFI Publishing, 2005.

Teo, Stephen. "Wong Kar-wai's Genre Practice and Romantic Authorship: The Cases of *Ashes of Time Redux* and *The Grandmaster*." In *A Companion to Wong Kar-wai*, edited by Martha Nochimson, 521–39. London: Wiley, 2015.

Théberge, Paul. "'Ethnic Sounds': The Economy and Discourse of World Music Sampling." In *Music and Technoculture*, edited by René T. A. Lysloff and Leslie C. Gay Jr., 93–108. Middletown, CT: Wesleyan University Press, 2003.

Vernallis, Carol. *Experiencing Music Video*. New York: Columbia University Press, 2004.

Vernallis, Carol. Review of *Analysing Musical Multimedia*, by Nicholas Cook. *American Music* 19, no. 4 (Winter 2001): 480–85.

Walton, Kendall. *Mimesis as Make-Believe*. Cambridge, MA: Harvard University Press, 1990.

Wang, Yiman. "Remade in China: Cinema with 'Chinese Elements' in the *Dapian* Age." In *The Oxford Handbook of Chinese Cinemas*, edited by Carlos Rojas and Eileen Chow, 610–25. New York: Oxford University Press, 2013.

Watkins, Lee. "Minstrelsy and Mimesis in the South China Sea: Filipino Migrant Musicians, Chinese Hosts, and the Disciplining of Relations in Hong Kong." *Asian Music* 40, no. 2 (Summer–Fall 2009): 72–99.

Williams, Justin A. "Intertextuality, Sampling, and Copyright." In *The Cambridge Companion to Hip-Hop*, edited by Justin A. Williams, 206–20. Cambridge: Cambridge University Press, 2015.

Williams, Justin A. *Rhymin' and Stealin': Musical Borrowing in Hip-Hop*. Ann Arbor: University of Michigan Press, 2013.

Williams, Nicholas Morrow. *Imitations of the Self: Jiang Yan and Chinese Poetics*. Leiden, Netherlands: Brill, 2014.

Wilson, George. *Seeing Fictions in Film: The Epistemologies of Movies*. Oxford: Oxford University Press, 2011.

Wong, Ain-ling, ed. *The Cathay Story*. Hong Kong: Hong Kong Film Archive, 2009.

Wong Kar-wai and John Powers. *WKW: The Cinema of Wong Kar Wai*. New York: Rizzoli, 2016.

Yang, Hon-Lun. "Cosmopolitanism, Vernacular Cosmopolitanism, and Sound Alignments: Covers and Cantonese Cover Songs in 1960s Hong Kong." In *Sound Alignments: Popular Music in Asia's Cold Wars*, edited by Michael K. Bourdaghs, Paola Iovene, and Kaley Mason, 153–69. Durham, NC: Duke University Press, 2021.

Yau, Esther C. M. "Urban Nomads, Exilic Modernisms: The Cine-modernism of Patrick Tam." In *Hong Kong Screenscapes: From the New Wave to the Digital Frontier*, edited by Esther M. K. Cheung, Gina Marchetti, and Tan See-Kam, 75–92. Hong Kong: Hong Kong University Press, 2011.

Yau, Esther C. M. "Watchful Partners, Hidden Currents: Hong Kong Cinema Moving into the Mainland of China." In *A Companion to Hong Kong Cinema*, edited by Esther M. K. Cheung, Gina Marchetti, and Esther C. M. Yau, 17–50. London: Wiley, 2015.

Yeh, Emilie Yueh-yu, and Lake Wang Hu. "Transcultural Sounds: Music, Identity and the Cinema of Wong Kar-wai." In LEWI Working Paper Series no. 69. Hong Kong: David C. Lam Institute for East-West Studies, 2007. Also published in *Asian Cinema* 19, no. 1 (Spring–Summer 2009): 32–46.

金庸与《明报》[Jin Yong and Ming Pao Daily] / 张圭阳. 武汉市: 湖北长江出版集团: 湖北人民出版社, 2007.

金庸與報業 = Jin Yong (Louis Cha) and the Press / 張圭陽香港：明報, 2000.

Young, James O. *Cultural Appropriation and the Arts*. Chichester, UK: Wiley-Blackwell, 2010.

Zappa, Frank. *The Real Frank Zappa Book*. New York: Touchstone, 1989.

Page numbers in *italics* refer to illustrations.

on soundscapes in Hong Kong, 194n21; story and character linked to music in films of, 88–89; uncanny in films of, 22–24
world music, film music as, 123–26
Wu Tong, 74
wuxia pian (China), martial arts films and, 127, 130

"Yesterday" (song), 68
Yojimbo (film), 135, 156, 203n27
Yoshimitsu, Morita, 140
"You Can't Always Get What You Want" (song), 41–42
YouTube, 64
"You've Got to Hide Your Love Away" (song), 68

Yo-Yo Ma, 66, 133, 135, 156
Yumeji (film), 71–72, 95–100, 186, 206n7
"Yumeji's Theme" (Umebayashi): as aural fabric, 200n19; as block, 96–97; Galasso's "Angkor Wat Finale" and, 101, 180, 184–86; global popularity of, 71; in *In the Mood for Love*, 71–72, 86, 94–102, 200n16, 206n7; in *My Blueberry Nights*, 101–2; in *Yumeji*, 97–98, 101

Zappa, Frank, 39, 90
Zatōichi (film series), 126–27, 136–37
Zhang Che, 137
Zhang Yimou, 138, 156
Zhang Zhiyi, 81, 116
Zimmer, Hans, 134

www.ingramcontent.com/pod-product-compliance
Lightning Source LLC
Chambersburg PA
CBHW020858270326
41928CB00006B/757